MW01156196

100 CLASSIC HIKES
MONTANA

100 CLASSIC HIKES

MONTANA

DOUGLAS LORAIN

Glacier National Park | Western Mountain Ranges | Beartooth Range | Madison and Gallatin Ranges | Bob Marshall Wilderness | Eastern Prairies and Badlands

MOUNTAINEERS BOOKS

MOUNTAINEERS BOOKS is the publishing division of The Mountaineers, an organization founded in 1906 and dedicated to the exploration, preservation, and enjoyment of outdoor and wilderness areas.

1001 SW Klickitat Way, Suite 201 • Seattle, WA 98134
800.553.4453 • www.mountaineersbooks.org

Copyright © 2018 by Douglas Lorain
All rights reserved. No part of this book may be reproduced or utilized in any form, or by any electronic, mechanical, or other means, without the prior written permission of the publisher.

Printed in China
Distributed in the United Kingdom by Cordee, www.cordee.co.uk
First edition, 2018

Copyeditor: Sarah Gorecki, Outdoor Prose
Series design: Kate Basart
Layout: Peggy Egerdahl
Cartographer: Lohnes+Wright
Cover photograph: *Black Mountain from basin east of Pine Creek Lake*
Frontispiece: *Lake Janet, Glacier National Park*
All photographs by the author unless otherwise noted.

The background maps for this book were produced using the online map viewer CalTopo. For more information, visit caltopo.com.

Library of Congress Cataloging-in-Publication Data
Names: Lorain, Douglas, 1962- author.
Title: 100 classic hikes Montana : Glacier National Park, Western Mountain
   ranges, Beartooth range, Madison and Gallatin ranges, Bob Marshall
   wilderness, Eastern prairies and badlands / Douglas Lorain.
Description: Seattle, WA : Mountaineers Books, [2018] | Includes index.
Identifiers: LCCN 2017045816 (print) | LCCN 2017053861 (ebook) | ISBN
   9781594859120 (ebook) | ISBN 9781594859113 (pbk)
Subjects: LCSH: Hiking--Montana--Guidebooks. | Trails--Montana--Guidebooks. |
   Backpacking--Montana--Guidebooks. | Montana--Guidebooks.
Classification: LCC GV199.42.M9 (ebook) | LCC GV199.42.M9 L67 2018 (print) |
   DDC 796.5109786--dc23
LC record available at https://lccn.loc.gov/2017045816

Mountaineers Books titles may be purchased for corporate, educational, or other promotional sales, and our authors are available for a wide range of events. For information on special discounts or booking an author, contact our customer service at 800-553-4453 or mbooks@mountaineersbooks.org.

ISBN (paperback): 978-1-59485-911-3
ISBN (ebook): 978-1-59485-912-0

Contents

Northwest Montana

West-Central Montana

Southwest Montana

Glacier National Park

The Bob Marshall Wilderness Complex

Central Montana's "Island" Ranges

South-Central Montana

Eastern Montana

Hikes at a Glance

NO.	NAME	DIFFICULTY	SEASON	HIGHLIGHTS
SHORT DAY HIKES				
1	Northwest Peak Scenic Area	Moderate-Strenuous	Mid-July-early Oct	Mountain views, lake
2	Mount Henry	Strenuous	July-mid-Oct	Lake, lookout, views
7	Baldy Mountain and Lake	Moderate-Strenuous	July-Oct	Great views, scenic lake
17	Bear Creek Overlook	Moderate	Mid-June-Oct	Stunning viewpoint
19	Fuse Lake	Moderate	July-Oct	Scenic lake and meadow
26	Harrison Lake	Moderate-Strenuous	Mid-June-Oct	Mountain lake, solitude
35	Gneiss Lake	Moderate-Strenuous	July-mid-Oct	Views, scenic alpine lake, meadows
38	Chief Mountain	Moderate-Strenuous	Mid-July-mid-Oct	Unique mountain scenery, views
42	Hidden Lake	Moderate	Mid-July-mid-Oct	Outstanding mountain scenery, wildlife
59	Willow Creek Falls	Moderate	June-early Nov	Tall waterfall, alpine pass
65	Trout Creek Canyon	Easy-Moderate	May-Oct	Stunning cliffs and canyon scenery
68	Collar Peak Loop	Moderate-Strenuous	Mid-May-early Nov	Views, solitude
70	Sacagawea Peak	Strenuous	July-Oct	Great views, mountain goats
88	Line Creek Plateau	Easy-Moderate	Late July-Sept	Enormous tundra plateau, endless views
90	Mickey Butte	Moderate-Strenuous	March-Nov	Views, solitude, wildlife
91	Frenchman Creek Breaks	Moderate	All year	Grasslands, coulees, wildlife
92	Bitter Creek	Easy-Moderate	All year	Vast grasslands, solitude
93	Sand Arroyo Badlands Loop	Moderate	All year	Dramatic badlands, solitude
95	Big Pryor Mountain	Moderate	June-early Nov	Views, wildflowers, ice cave
97	Tongue River Breaks	Easy-Moderate	March-Nov	Wildflowers, rock formations, badlands
100	Chalk Buttes	Moderate-Strenuous	April-Nov	Scenic white cliffs, wildflowers

Opposite: Mount Helen and fall color in Bighorn Basin (Hike 48)

NO.	NAME	DIFFICULTY	SEASON	HIGHLIGHTS
HALF-DAY HIKES				
6	Terrace Lake	Moderate	Mid-July–Oct	Very scenic lake, solitude
13	Cliff Lake	Easy	Mid-July–Oct	Lush vegetation, scenic lake
33	Lewis and Clark Caverns	Easy	May 1–Sept 30	Spectacular cave formations
43	Avalanche Lake	Easy–Moderate	Late May–Nov	Lush forest and canyon, mountain lake
55	Buffalo Lakes	Easy–Moderate	Mid-May–Nov	Scenic lakes, wildlife
96	Bighorn Canyon	Moderate	All year	Deep and colorful canyon
98	Terry Badlands Natural Bridges	Moderate	All year	Natural bridges, badlands
99	Makoshika State Park	Easy–Moderate	All year	Spectacular and colorful badlands
LONG DAY HIKES				
3	Little Spar Lake	Strenuous	Mid-July–Oct	Scenic mountain lake, deep canyon
9	Stahl Peak Loop	Strenuous	Mid-July–mid-Oct	Lookout, views
10	Krinklehorn Peak Loop	Strenuous	Mid-July–mid-Oct	Views, small lake, dramatic peak
11	Nasukoin Mountain	Very Strenuous	Late July–early Oct	Views, solitude
14	Heart Lake	Moderate	Late June–Oct	Large mountain lake, great ridgetop viewpoints
15	Kid and Mud Lakes	Strenuous	Mid-July–Oct	Wildflowers, views, lakes
16	Cha-paa-qn Peak	Strenuous	Late June–Oct	Extensive views
18	Canyon Lake	Strenuous	Late June–Oct	Spectacular mountain lake, waterfall
20	Piquett Mountain	Strenuous	July–mid-Oct	Great views, scenic lakes
21	Dempsey Basin	Strenuous	Late June–mid-Oct	Scenic mountain lakes
24	Rock Island Lakes	Strenuous	Late June–mid-Oct	Very scenic mountain lakes, exploring options, solitude
28	Gorge Lakes	Strenuous	July–mid-Oct	Gorgeous mountain lakes
29	Eighteenmile Peak Loop	Very Strenuous	Mid-June–Oct	Spectacular lake, stunning viewpoint, wildlife
31	Lima Peaks Loop	Strenuous	Mid-June–Oct	Views, mountain scenery, wildflowers
32	Table Mountain	Very Strenuous	Late June–Oct	Views, mountain scenery
34	Lost Cabin Lake	Strenuous	July–mid-Oct	Very scenic mountain lake
40	Grinnell Glacier	Strenuous	Mid-July–mid-Oct	Outstanding mountain scenery, wildlife, glacier

NO.	NAME	DIFFICULTY	SEASON	HIGHLIGHTS
LONG DAY HIKES (CONT.)				
41	Highline Trail	Moderate-Strenuous	Late July-mid-Oct	Amazing views, mountain scenery, wildlife
45	Piegan Pass	Strenuous	Late July-early Oct	Mountain scenery, views
46	Otokomi Lake	Strenuous	July-mid-Oct	Impressive mountain lake, waterfalls
47	Triple Divide Pass	Strenuous	Mid-July-mid-Oct	Outstanding mountain scenery
49	Firebrand Pass	Strenuous	Late June-Oct	Great mountain scenery, solitude
50	Jewel Basin	Strenuous	Late June-Oct	Fine views, numerous mountain lakes
52	Rumble Creek Lakes	Very Strenuous	Mid-July-early Oct	Dramatic mountain lakes, views
54	Crescent Mountain Lakes	Strenuous	July-mid-Oct	Scenic mountain lakes, solitude
57	Volcano Reef Loop	Strenuous	Late May-Oct	Dramatic cliffs, mountain scenery, wildlife
61	Anaconda Hill	Strenuous	June-Oct	Views, sprawling ridgetop meadows
62	Sweetgrass Hills: Mount Brown	Strenuous	Mid-May-mid-Nov	Outstanding views, wildflowers
63	North Fork Highwood Creek Loop	Strenuous	Late May-early Nov	Views, wildflowers
64	Missouri River Canyon	Strenuous	April-Nov	Canyon scenery, wildflowers
67	Big Baldy Mountain	Moderate-Strenuous	July-Oct	Wildflowers, ridgetop views, scenic mountain lake
71	Sunlight Lake	Strenuous	Mid-July-Oct	Stunning mountain lake, views
75	Tumbledown Basin	Strenuous	Mid-July-mid-Oct	Excellent mountain scenery, solitude, wildflowers
77	Sheep Lake	Strenuous	Mid-July-Oct	Scenic mountain lake, wildflowers
78	Emerald and Heather Lakes	Strenuous	Mid-July-Oct	Scenic mountain lakes, waterfall, wildflowers
81	Elephanthead Mountain	Very Strenuous	Mid-July-mid-Oct	Wildflowers, unique mountain views
82	Pine Creek Lake	Strenuous	Mid-July-mid-Oct	Spectacular lake, waterfalls
89	Bull Creek	Moderate-Strenuous	All year	Solitude, sandstone cliffs
94	Weatherman Draw	Moderate-Strenuous	All year	Sandstone formations, pictographs

NO.	NAME	DIFFICULTY	SEASON	HIGHLIGHTS
SHORT BACKPACKS				
4	Granite Lake	Strenuous	Mid-July–Oct	Scenic mountain lake, waterfall
5	Wanless Lake	Strenuous	Mid-July–mid-Oct	Dramatic mountain lake, views
8	Ten Lakes Scenic Area Loop	Strenuous	Mid-July–mid-Oct	Mountain scenery, wildflowers, lakes
12	Turquoise Lake	Strenuous	Mid-July–early Oct	Spectacular mountain lake, views
22	Goat Flat and Upper Seymour Lake	Strenuous	Mid-July–mid-Oct	Huge alpine meadow, mountain lake, wildlife
23	Lake of the Isle	Strenuous	Mid-July–Oct	Scenic mountain lake, solitude
25	Pioneer Lake	Strenuous	July–mid-Oct	Scenic mountain lakes, solitude
27	Crescent Lake	Strenuous	July–mid-Oct	Gorgeous mountain lakes, fishing
48	Oldman and No Name Lakes Loop	Strenuous	Late July–mid Oct	Outstanding mountain scenery, wildlife, lakes
51	Sunburst Lake	Strenuous	July–mid-Oct	Spectacular mountain lake, wilderness stream
53	Koessler Lake	Strenuous	July–Oct	Spectacular mountain lakes, views
56	Walling Reef	Very Strenuous	June–late Oct	Stunning cliffs and lake, wildflowers, solitude
66	Mount Baldy Basin Loop	Very Strenuous	Mid-July–mid-Oct	Scenic mountain lakes, high ridgeline views
72	Blue and Twin Lakes	Moderate	July–Oct	Several scenic mountain lakes, deep canyon, views
74	No Man Lake	Very Strenuous	Mid-July–mid-Oct	Scenic mountain lake, views
83	Silver Lake	Strenuous	July–mid-Oct	Very scenic mountain lake
84	Bridge Lake	Very Strenuous	July–mid-Oct	Scenic mountain lake, solitude
86	Lake Mary	Strenuous	Mid-July–mid-Oct	Scenic mountain lake, wildlife, waterfalls

NO.	NAME	DIFFICULTY	SEASON	HIGHLIGHTS
LONG BACKPACKS				
30	Italian Peaks Loop	Strenuous	Mid-June–Oct	Great mountain scenery, wildlife, solitude
36	Snowcrest Loop	Strenuous	Mid-June–Oct	Superb alpine ridge walk, solitude
37	Boulder Pass	Strenuous	Late July–early Oct	Dramatic mountain scenery, lakes, wildlife
39	Northern Loop	Very Strenuous	Late July–early Oct	Spectacular mountain scenery, views, lakes, waterfalls
44	Gunsight Pass Traverse	Strenuous	Late July–early Oct	Great mountain scenery, wildlife
58	North Wall Loop	Strenuous	July–Oct	Solitude, dramatic limestone walls, lakes, wildlife
60	Scapegoat Mountain	Strenuous	July–Oct	Towering limestone walls, views
69	Big Snowy Crest	Very Strenuous	Mid-June–Oct	Ice caves, views, alpine plateau
73	Spanish Peaks Loop	Strenuous	July–mid-Oct	Outstanding mountain scenery, lakes, waterfall
76	Hilgard Basin	Strenuous	July–mid-Oct	Outstanding mountain scenery, scenic lakes
79	Gallatin Divide Loop	Very Strenuous	Mid-July–mid-Oct	Extended alpine ridge walk, views
80	Sky Rim Loop	Very Strenuous	Mid-July–mid-Oct	Rugged alpine ridge, views, wildlife
85	Lake Plateau	Strenuous	Mid-July–early Oct	Base camp exploring to dozens of high mountain lakes
87	Black Canyon Lake and Sundance Pass	Strenuous	Mid-July–early Oct	Outstanding mountain scenery, moose, views

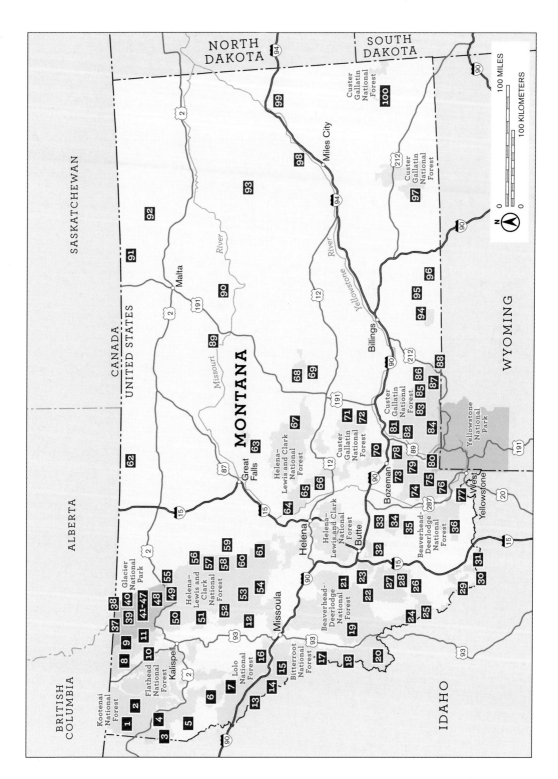

SASKATCHEWAN

NORTH DAKOTA

SOUTH DAKOTA

100 MILES

100 KILOMETERS

Custer Gallatin National Forest **100**

94

99

90

Miles City

98

212

Custer Gallatin National Forest **97**

93

92

River

91

Malta

90

191

River

Yellowstone

96

95

94

Billings

90

212

88

87

86

85

83

84

CANADA
UNITED STATES

2

191

Missouri

89

MONTANA

12

Custer Gallatin National Forest

71

72

81

82

Custer Gallatin National Forest

68

69

67

63

70

78

89

80

79

Yellowstone National Park

191

62

87

Great Falls

Helena–Lewis and Clark National Forest

12

191

Bozeman

73

75

76

West Yellowstone

77

20

WYOMING

15

65

66

74

287

36

15

Helena

64

Helena–Lewis and Clark National Forest

Butte

33

34

35

Beaverhead-Deerlodge National Forest

31

30

ALBERTA

15

32

15

29

93

Glacier National Park

37–**38**

40

39

55

49

56

57

58

59

60

61

Helena–Lewis and Clark National Forest

27

28

26

24

25

11

41–**47**

48

50

51

53

54

12

21

23

22

90

Beaverdodge National Forest

Missoula

93

52

Lolo National Forest

16

19

8

9

10

Flathead National Forest

Kalispell

2

15

17

18

20

1

2

Kootenai National Forest

6

7

Bitterroot National Forest

93

93

13

14

IDAHO

3

4

5

90

BRITISH COLUMBIA

Introduction

If you mention Montana to an avid hiker living almost anywhere else in the United States, the reaction is usually a big smile, a wistful sigh, long stories about a much-treasured vacation to this glorious state, and a comment like "Now *that's* God's country." Those of us fortunate enough to live here completely understand this reaction because we can personally attest that it's all absolutely true. The state *is* glorious, vacations here *are* unbeatable, and, if a certain amount of pride is acceptable on these pages, this truly *is* God's country. With thousands of sparkling lakes, incredibly abundant wildlife, towering glacier-clad mountains, deep and colorful canyons, and vast stretches of prairies and badlands, Montana offers the hiker a cornucopia of outdoor riches and a lifetime's worth of trails.

Carefully selected from many hundreds of hikes in the Treasure State, the trips in this book are 100 of the best walks in Montana. Every part of the state is represented, so no matter where you live or where you're visiting, a choice of great hikes is nearby. The hikes also include a mix of difficulty levels, from easy strolls suitable for everyone to extended backpacking trips on which experienced hikers can fully escape the rat race.

Personal preferences were necessarily a factor in selecting these hikes, but understanding the criteria used will give you a better idea of what kind of trips you can expect to find in this book. Although no single attribute was required for every hike, the most important criterion was outstanding scenery. Water features, such as clear streams, waterfalls, and mountain lakes, were also significant attractions. Similarly, wildlife sightings enhance any outdoor experience, as do wildflowers, fall colors, old-growth forests, and interesting geologic features. Although the quality of fishing played no part in the selection criteria, when good fishing is available, I make sure to mention it.

My goal was to include only the best of my countless trips around this state. Somewhat surprisingly, most of these hikes have never been covered in any previous statewide guidebook. Thus, even veteran Montana adventurers will find dozens of trails that they have never hiked and, perhaps, never even knew existed. Apart from subjective judgments, the following *objective* criteria apply to all hikes in this book:

- The trailhead is accessible in a typical passenger car, although that car will sometimes need better than average ground clearance. Your car may get a little banged up, but under normal driving conditions and in the season recommended, a four-wheel-drive vehicle should not be required to reach the starting point.
- The hike follows an established trail or, in a few cases, a logical cross-country route that any reasonably experienced hiker can travel.
- The hike is natural in character. Features such as fire lookouts, historic mines, and old homesteads are acceptable (even welcome), but the bulk of a hike's attributes must be the work of nature rather than human beings.

The best and most intimate way to experience Montana is at a hiker's self-propelled pace. To answer the question of *why* go hiking, simply glance at the photographs and hike overviews to be inspired about what you will experience. Questions about *where* and *when* to go are answered in the individual hike descriptions. That leaves the question of *how* to do these hikes. Some tips will help you spend more happy hours exploring the spectacular trails of Montana.

GETTING STARTED

If you are new to Montana's trails, a good place to start is with a local hiking or outdoor club. These groups have a full schedule of hikes suitable for all ability levels. This allows you to save money by carpooling with others, gives you the chance to meet like-minded people, and lets you learn from local experts. The Recommended Resources section lists most of the larger hiking, outdoor, and conservation organizations in Montana.

Mountain goat in Glacier National Park

WHAT TO TAKE

A comprehensive discussion of hiking gear is beyond the scope of this book, but years of experience have shown that no hiker should leave the trailhead without carrying the **Ten Essentials**, developed by The Mountaineers. In an emergency, these may save your life.

1. Navigation: map (preferably topographic) and compass or GPS device
2. Headlamp: a flashlight will also work; bring extra batteries
3. Sun protection: sunglasses, sun-protective clothing, and sunscreen (SPF 30 or more), especially needed in the open prairies and high mountains
4. First-aid supplies: and the skills to use them
5. Knife: also a repair kit and multitool, including whatever tools you need for your equipment
6. Fire: firestarter and matches in a waterproof container
7. Shelter: a tent on an overnight trip; on day hikes, bring an emergency shelter, such as a trash bag, bivy sack, or reflective emergency blanket
8. Extra food: enough so you return with a little left over
9. Extra water: and a means to purify water on longer trips
10. Extra clothes: be prepared in case the weather turns colder or you end up spending a night outside unexpectedly

When it comes to equipment, day hikes don't require much gear. All you need are a few basics thrown into a small pack and you're ready to go. If you want to be more comfortable, your first purchase should be a pair of lightweight hiking shoes. These will give you better traction and keep your feet dry and free of blisters.

If you plan on backpacking, the least expensive alternative is to borrow gear from friends or purchase used equipment at army surplus or similar stores. From there, the possibilities range all the way up to a dizzying array of high-tech (and costly) clothing and hiking boots, lightweight tents, wonderfully warm sleeping bags,

Lake Ha Hand (Hike 76)

and all kinds of nifty and imaginative accessories. The best approach is to keep it simple and low-cost, at least until you determine whether backpacking is something you want to pursue regularly.

PERMITS AND FEES

In many parts of the country hiking has become an increasingly regulated activity with a variety of permits required to park at trailheads, stay overnight in wilderness areas, or even to enter public lands at all. So far, most of Montana has escaped this trend. Unlike many states, the national forests in Montana do not charge a fee for parking at trailheads. The same is usually true for Bureau of Land Management lands, city parks, and national wildlife refuges in the state.

The state of Montana requires that anyone using state lands for noncommercial purposes, such as hiking, obtain a special use permit. As of 2017, the permits, which cost $10 for individuals or $5 for children (under 18) or seniors (over 59), are available from any Montana Fish, Wildlife & Parks agent or online. They are valid for one license year from March 1 to the end of February.

Most Montana state parks require a day-use permit (prices vary). Residents of the state can avoid this by paying a fee when they obtain their car license plates. This allows unlimited access to all state parks. As of 2017 the annual charge was $6, which only covers *entry* into the parks, not additional charges for car camping, boat launches, or guided tours.

Glacier and Yellowstone National Parks charge entrance fees to all visitors and also charge for backpacking permits and the right to reserve a permit in advance. For details, see the information on permits in the introductory material for hikes in these parks.

How to Use This Book

The hikes are grouped by region from west to east and north to south. An overview of each region's outstanding features and unique characteristics are described in the section introductions. The **Hikes at a Glance** chart at the front of this book will help you choose hikes by their duration, difficulty, season, and highlights. Every hike begins with an information summary of the most important facts about that outing.

Distance is given for each hike's round-trip. For hikes that exceed 20 miles or that include any significant cross-country travel, distances are generally rounded to the nearest mile.

The *Difficulty* rating is a subjective assessment of how strenuous the hike is in comparison to other trips. This takes into account distance, elevation gain, and times when a hike is unusually steep, covers exceptionally rough terrain, or requires cross-country travel.

Hiking time indicates if the trip is best done as a day hike, overnight hike, or extended backpacking trip.

Elevation gain includes *all* of a hike's ups and downs in a cumulative total roundtrip elevation gain.

Legend

------	Featured trail	🅣	Trailhead	**8**	Hike number
········	Featured cross-country route	Ⓣ	Alternate trailhead	~	River or creek
- - - -	Optional trail	🅟	Parking	─╫─	Falls
········	Optional cross-county route	■	Point of interest	◯	Water
········	Other trail	▲	Peak		Park or forest boundary
··········	Other cross-country route	⋀	Campground		Wilderness boundary
		⛰	Backcountry campsite		State or county boundary
——	Highway	⊼	Picnic area		National boundary
——	Paved road	) (	Pass	-·-·-	Powerline
=====	Gravel road	⊷	Gate		
::::::::::	Dirt/primitive road	)(	Bridge	🧭 N	True north (magnetic north varies)
15 215	Interstate highway	→←	Tunnel		
6 89 191	US highway	🔥	Lookout		
9 24 128	State route	⚲	Spring		
24 200	Forest route				
24	County road				

Late evening clouds in a canyon north of Greathouse Peak (Hike 69)

The *Season* entry lists when a trip is usually snow-free enough for hiking (which varies considerably from year to year), while the following entry indicates when the trail is at its *Best time*—when the flowers peak, the huckleberries are ripe, the mosquitoes have died down, etc.

The *Contact* is the land management agency that administers the area where the hike is located. Their full contact information is listed in the Recommended Resources in the back of the book.

This book includes a contour map for each hike, but if you want a topographic map that covers more area, the best available *Map(s)* are listed in the information summary.

GPS coordinates are shown for the hike's trailhead in degrees and decimal minutes. They use the WGS 84 datum and will vary slightly depending on your device, the current weather conditions, the local geology, and other factors.

Following the information summary are *Getting there* directions to the trailhead, an overview of the hike's highlights, and a detailed trail description.

TRAIL ETIQUETTE

As more people hit the trails, we must all work harder to follow some simple, commonsense rules of wilderness etiquette. For the most part, these involve simple common courtesy and trying to make yourself unobtrusive.

Crowds are incompatible with wilderness, so keep your group as small as possible. In many designated wilderness areas, the maximum allowable party size ranges from twenty down to as few as six people, but even smaller groups are preferable.

One of the attractions of wilderness travel is the chance to enjoy natural peace and quiet. Do not yell back and forth, play a radio in camp, or produce any of the noise pollution that many of your fellow hikers are trying to escape.

Respect other trail users you encounter. When you meet horse parties, step off on the downhill side of the trail to allow them to pass. Talk in a soft, friendly manner so the horses don't get spooked by this strange creature with an odd-colored hump on its back. Theoretically, hikers have the right-of-way over mountain bikes, but it's usually easier to simply step aside and let these folks pedal past. As for motorcycles and all-terrain vehicles (ATVs), you will hear them approaching for miles (it's impossible for a machine to be unobtrusive), so just step off the trail until they have passed.

Leave No Trace

Hikers today are strongly encouraged to minimize their impact on the land. For decades the standard advice was "Take only photographs and leave only footprints," but in fragile areas even footprints can be damaging, so be careful about *them* as well. Fortunately, most hikers try their best to follow Leave No Trace principles.

Fall color of huckleberry bushes, Mission Range

The idea is to leave the wilderness just as you found it (or, preferably, even better). Never litter and always pick up trash left by others. Never pick wildflowers, chop limbs off trees, feed wildlife, trample plants, or cut switchbacks. Generally, do not build fires—rely instead on lightweight backpacking stoves. Camp only in established sites (preferably on durable surfaces), well away from fragile meadows and lakeshores. Use backcountry toilets when available, or bury human waste 6 to 8 inches deep and at least 200 feet from water sources and trails. Do not wash *anything*—dishes, clothes, or yourself—in natural water sources, even with biodegradable soap. Carry water at least 200 feet away and wash there.

Your responsibility to the land does not end with the Leave No Trace principles. Hikers must also be concerned about large-scale conservation issues. Part of the admission price for enjoying these hikes is your responsibility to get involved with grassroots organizations that work to protect the land. If you don't know where to start, contact the Montana Wilderness Association or any of the other conservation groups listed in the Recommended Resources section. They'll be happy to help you get involved.

SAFETY

If they are careful and properly equipped, hikers are statistically in greater danger driving to the trailhead than they are once they get out of the car. Nonetheless, there are some important safety concerns for trail users.

You should generally not hike alone unless you are an experienced wilderness traveler. Always let someone know of your itinerary and when you expect to return, so they can raise the alarm should you not arrive home as planned.

At the trailhead, place all valuables out of sight and lock your car. Don't be deceived into believing, however, that this will stop a determined thief. The best plan is to drive a beat-up car and leave nothing worth stealing in it. If all hikers did this, the thieves would soon give up.

Hypothermia is probably the biggest danger to hikers. Generally, this potentially deadly

Bull moose, Beartooth Mountains

condition occurs when you lose too much body heat due to being wet and cold for too long. Always carry clothing that will keep you warm, dry, and protected from the wind.

Never drink untreated water. Nasty little microorganisms may reside there and they have the ability to make you sick enough to swear off hiking for the rest of your life (take this giardia victim's word for it).

And on the subject of water, the other hydro hazard with which hikers must contend is stream crossings. Most trails in Montana were originally designed for equestrians. Often little regard was given to the difficulties that hikers face in crossing larger streams. In late spring and early summer rivers and creeks run high with snowmelt, which makes fording them cold and potentially dangerous. If a ford looks too dangerous when you get there, *do not risk it*! Turn around and head back the way you came. The best way to make a ford is to wear lightweight wading shoes,

for traction, and use trekking poles, for extra support. Also, keep in mind that where the trail crosses a stream is not necessarily the best place to make a ford. Spend some time searching for the shallowest and best location.

Lightning is a potential hazard, especially in the high mountains on summer afternoons. If you see thunderheads building, get off the open ridges and head as quickly as possible for lower and preferably forested terrain.

Animal Concerns

One of the joys of Montana is that the state has more large wildlife than any state except Alaska. Moose, elk, mountain goats, bighorn sheep, pronghorns, grizzly bears, black bears, mountain lions, and wolves are all fairly common and the potential of seeing them is a real attraction for hikers. Some animals, however, can pose dangers to hikers, so a few cautions are in order. Bears are a special case, so advice on how to deal with them is covered in a separate section below.

Rattlesnakes are a potential hazard, especially in the prairies of eastern Montana and in a few of the drier canyons of western and central Montana. Watch your step and check the area carefully before reaching in between rocks or sitting down.

Mountain lions are fairly common throughout the state but they are generally shy around people and it is a rare treat to see one. Should a lion stand its ground or growl at you, gather up your children and pets and stand tall with your arms above you to look as large as possible. Toss sticks or rocks at the animal and it will almost always run away. In the extremely unlikely event that a mountain lion attacks, fight back.

Elk and moose can be dangerous, especially during the fall mating season (the "rut"). At that time the hormone-driven males may charge hikers and even attack cars. Moose have forced more than a few hikers to climb a tree where they may be stranded for hours while the agitated bull struts menacingly around the base of the tree. Give these animals a wide berth and have an escape route in mind in the event of an unpleasant encounter.

In recent decades wolves have moved back into Montana from Canada and spread from reintroduction sites in Yellowstone National Park and central Idaho. There are now wolf packs in most of the major mountain ranges of Montana. Although wolves pose a potential danger to livestock, hikers should have no fear of these animals. There has never been a recorded wolf attack on a person in Montana history.

The biggest wildlife problems come from the insect world, most notably ticks and mosquitoes. Ticks in Montana are known to carry the potentially deadly Rocky Mountain spotted fever, so they should be considered more than just an annoyance. A good repellent, a long-sleeved shirt, and long pants are the best preventive measures.

Be Bear Aware

Probably the most famous wild animals in Montana are its bears. Statistically, attacks are very rare, but almost every year one or two people are

Black bear, Bob Marshall Wilderness

injured or killed by bears in Montana, so hikers need to take reasonable precautions.

Since there are important differences in how you deal with a black versus a grizzly bear, you need to know how to identify the two species. Black bears are smaller, with adults weighing between 150 and 300 pounds, while adult grizzlies tip the scales at between 300 and (very rarely) 1000 pounds. But when you're face-to-face with a bear, both species look plenty big, so size is not a reliable indicator. Color isn't helpful either because both species range from very light brown to almost jet black. A better way to tell the bears apart is by their physical characteristics. Black bears have a fairly narrow face, relatively tall ears, and a rear end that sticks up slightly higher than their shoulders. Grizzly bears have a wide, dished-in face, short and rounded ears, a rear end that slopes downward, and a prominent shoulder hump.

Black bears are generally shy around people, but they can become dangerous, especially once they grow accustomed to human food. Grizzlies are more unpredictable and tend to be more aggressive than black bears.

Although black bears inhabit all of the forested regions of Montana, grizzly bears have a more limited range. They are most common in the mountains north of Yellowstone and in northern Montana in Glacier National Park and the Bob Marshall Wilderness Complex. Smaller populations are in northwestern Montana's Cabinet Mountains, Mission Range, and the Yaak area. However, grizzly bear numbers, especially around Yellowstone National Park, are increasing and their range is expanding. Every hike in this book that passes through known grizzly bear territory is designated with a bear symbol beside the trip title.

The best strategy is to avoid encountering bears in the first place. Never approach *any* bear, especially females with cubs. Never approach or camp near an animal carcass. Bears, especially grizzlies, will feed upon and aggressively defend carcasses against intruders. Never camp in an area with obvious signs

Grizzly bear, Glacier National Park

of recent bear activity—diggings, tracks, torn-up stumps, or scat.

In grizzly bear country, make noise while you hike. When a bear is surprised they are much more likely to attack. In grizzly country, travel in a group and stay on established trails. Bears almost never attack groups of more than three people and attacks often occur when people are traveling cross-country. Never hike at night, when bears are most active, and avoid traveling late in the evening and early in the morning.

Leave all smelly foods (tuna, heavily cured jerky, or the like) at home. Bears have a terrific sense of smell and will investigate anything that seems even remotely interesting. Cook and store all food (and other odorous items) a minimum of 100 yards from your sleeping area. Use either a bear-resistant canister or hang your food at least 10 feet off the ground and 4 feet away from a tree trunk. In grizzly country, make those numbers 12 feet from the ground and 5 feet from the tree trunk.

Dogs and bears do not get along, so it is usually unwise to bring your pet when hiking in grizzly bear country. Dogs are not allowed in the backcountry of Glacier or Yellowstone National Parks.

If you encounter a bear, here are some tips for what to do:

- In grizzly country, carry bear spray, stored outside your pack and available for immediate use. If you see a grizzly, pull out the spray, release the safety, and carry the bottle in your hand. Should the bear charge, spray a Z pattern toward the animal's face starting when it is about 30 feet away. If you have the time to pull out the spray, have practiced how to use it, can stay calm in a very stressful situation, and there is not a cross wind or (much worse) it's not blowing in your face, then bear spray is marvelously effective. But that's a lot of "ifs," so never think of bear spray as a substitute for the other advice listed here.
- If you encounter a black bear, back away and make noise. The bear will almost always leave once it knows a human is nearby.
- If you see a grizzly bear, make a wide detour around the area on the downwind side. If that's not possible, turning around is probably your safest option. If you encounter a grizzly bear with cubs, abandon the hike and return the way you came.
- If the bear sees you but makes no aggressive moves (such as huffing or clacking its teeth), stand your ground.
- In the rare instance that a bear approaches or charges you, the experts say to remain calm and **do not run**. You cannot outrun a bear and running will only encourage them to chase you. Talk in a soothing voice, back away slowly, and never look the bear directly in the eye. Most charges are "bluff charges" where the bear will turn away shortly before it reaches you.
- If a black bear attacks you, use bear spray and fight back with anything you have (your walking stick, a rock, your fists, etc.). Black bears will often give up and go away.
- If a grizzly bear attacks you, use bear spray and then play dead. Drop to the ground, lying flat on your stomach, with your hands clasped behind your neck. Leave your pack on for added protection. Do not provide any resistance—you can't win and the movement will only encourage the bear to continue mauling you. Wait for the bear to leave before tending to injuries or making any other movement.
- The only instances where experts advise fighting back against a grizzly bear is when a bear attacks after stalking you as prey or goes into a tent and drags a person out. Fortunately, such events are extremely rare, but in such circumstances, the person will almost certainly be killed, so you may as well fight back, since you have nothing to lose.

All of that said; *do not* be so afraid of bears that it ruins your trip. Remember that bear attacks are very rare and certainly not a sufficient reason to avoid enjoying the spectacular backcountry of Montana.

A Note about Safety: Safety is an important concern in all outdoor activities. No guidebook can alert you to every hazard or anticipate the limitations of every reader. Therefore, the descriptions of roads, trails, routes, and natural features in this book are not representations that a particular place or excursion will be safe for your party. When you follow any of the routes described in this book, you assume responsibility for your own safety. Under normal conditions, such excursions require the usual attention to traffic, road and trail conditions, weather, terrain, the capabilities of your party, and other factors. Keeping informed on current conditions and exercising common sense are the keys to a safe, enjoyable outing.

—Mountaineers Books

Lake Levale (Hike 58)

TIPS FOR HIKING IN MONTANA

This book is not a "how to" guide for hikers and backpackers. It is assumed that readers already know about equipment, conditioning, how to select a campsite, first aid, and all the other aspects of this sport. It *is* appropriate, however, to discuss some tips and ideas that are specific to Montana.

The winter's snowpack has a significant impact not only on when a trail opens, but also on peak wildflower times, the height of streams you'll have to ford, and the availability of seasonal water sources. Snowpack information is available on the Natural Resources Conservation Service website (see Recommended Resources section at the end of the book). If the snowpack is significantly above or below average, then adjust a trip's seasonal recommendation accordingly.

Trail maintenance in Montana is often infrequent. Some trails are cleared only once every few years and many get no maintenance at all. You should expect to encounter downed logs or other obstacles and many unsigned trail junctions.

When driving on rural roads, beware of free-ranging livestock, which often loiter in the middle of the road. Calves are particularly notorious for unexpectedly darting in front of cars. Wildlife may also be present, so drive carefully and be alert.

Hunting is a long-standing Montana tradition. The overwhelming majority of hunters are responsible citizens who respect other users. Still, with all those guns in the woods hikers should take reasonable precautions. General rifle season for deer and elk, which draw the most hunters, begins in the last weekend of October and runs through the end of November (although in some areas the season starts as early as September). The seasons for other animals (bighorn sheep, mountain goats, pronghorns, moose, turkeys, upland game birds, and black bears) are usually in the fall, but it varies from place to place and from year to year. Check the latest hunting regulations for the area you plan to visit, which are available at most ranger stations and sporting goods stores. Anyone hiking during hunting season should wear a bright red or orange vest, pack, or other conspicuous article of clothing.

In the mountains of southern Montana, trails regularly reach 10,000 feet and higher. Until you get acclimated, you may experience symptoms of altitude sickness such as shortness of breath, lack of appetite, and headaches. At a minimum, these symptoms will slow your progress and make you uncomfortable. For some people, however, the symptoms can become severe and it will be necessary to retreat to lower elevations and possibly cancel your trip. Try to take a few day hikes in the area before tackling a longer trip into the high mountains.

In the last few decades, forest fires have become a fact of life in the northern Rocky Mountains. Most summers experience at least some large fires, often producing significant amounts of smoke over the state. Check media reports, weather forecasts, and fire and air quality websites to determine if your planned trip will be significantly impacted by fire activity. Always have a backup plan to avoid a wasted trip. The 2017 fire season was particularly bad. Many parts of northwest and west-central Montana, as well as Glacier National Park, were hard hit. The west side of Hike 44, for example, over Glacier National Park's Gunsight Pass was badly burned and the Sperry Chalet lost in the fire. It is therefore especially important that hikers check with land managers about the current status of trails in these areas.

Finally, a melancholy note about a natural phenomenon that is currently sweeping across Montana's forests. Mountain pine beetles are chewing their way across the Treasure State and are killing hundreds of millions of trees. In some areas, most of the mature trees are dead, leaving the hillsides covered with a patchwork of brown, black, and green. These cyclical bug infestations have occurred for millennia, however, so we have reason to hope that the forests will eventually return to their former health.

Opposite, top: Swallowtail butterfly, Cabinet Mountains

Opposite, bottom: Fall color with Daughter of the Sun Mountain

Northwest Montana

Welcome to the wettest, greenest, and iciest corner of Montana. Pacific storms dump lots of precipitation in northwest Montana, resulting in the state's densest forests and relatively low timberlines as trees struggle to survive under all that snow. Most hiking in this region involves long approaches through shady forest, beside rushing streams, leading to a spectacular mountain lake or viewpoint. For added interest, it is the rare stream that does *not* have a waterfall or two to enjoy along the way. All the winter snow compacts into glaciers, which have carved these mountains into exceptionally jagged peaks and ridges and left behind countless cirque lakes awaiting your discovery.

Given the climate, visitors should be prepared for rain or snow in any season, although during the summer the skies are *usually* clear and the hiking is both green and grand. Wildlife is abundant and that includes just enough grizzly bears to make things interesting. Numerous outstanding scenic mountain ranges touch the northwest Montana sky. The best known are the Cabinet Mountains and Mission Range, but several others are also worth exploring and all offer tremendous scenery.

So bring your raingear (just in case), bear spray, fishing gear, and your camera, and enjoy what this lush and magnificent land has to offer.

1 *Northwest Peak Scenic Area*

Distance: 4.6 miles roundtrip
Difficulty: moderate to strenuous
Hiking time: day hike
Elevation gain: 1650 feet
Season: mid-July through early October
Best time: late July, late September

Contact: Kootenai NF, Three Rivers Ranger District
Map: USGS Northwest Peak
GPS coordinates: N48° 58.098', W115° 55.728'

Getting there: From US 2 about 28 miles west of Libby, turn north on Yaak River Road (State Route 508). Drive 27 miles, then turn left on Pete Creek Road (Forest Road 338). After 6.8 miles, go right at a fork, and reach the end of pavement 4.9 miles later. You stay on the main road at a few minor intersections as the route becomes increasingly rough and rocky. At 20 miles from the Yaak River Road, the Northwest Peak Trailhead is on the left.

For Hawkins Lake, continue on FR 338 for 1.5 miles to a fork. Cars without good ground clearance should park here. Go straight (uphill) on a very rough road and drive 0.7 mile to another fork where a small sign points right to Upper Hawkins Lake. Bear left and proceed 80 yards to the road-end Hawkins Lake Trailhead.

The Northwest Peak Scenic Area is in such an isolated corner of Montana, the trails are never crowded despite offering superb views, fishable lakes, and excellent scenery. If you're willing to make the drive, exploring this area is highly rewarding. There are numerous worthwhile destinations (Hawkins Lake, Upper Hawkins Lake, and any walk along the high ridgelines are particularly recommended) but the view from atop Northwest Peak itself is not to be missed.

Note: Many trails are shown incorrectly on the USGS map for this area.

The Northwest Peak trail ascends through a spruce-fir forest, climbing a pair of switchbacks to the top of a wide and rounded ridge, which you then follow to the west. Although the Forest Service map shows a trail branching off this ridge toward an unnamed lake to the southwest, there is no indication of any trail on the ground. The main trail to Northwest Peak remains obvious and in good condition as it ascends, steeply at times, through increasingly open forests. As you gain altitude, the tree cover is dominated by wispy alpine larches. Like arboreal alchemists, in late September these trees turn their light green needles into gold, offering visual riches for the lucky hiker.

Most of the last 0.7 mile is over rocky areas and through alpine meadows dotted with larch trees. The views grow more expansive with each upward step, and while the tread is often indistinct, frequent cairns keep you on course.

Water droplets on a glacier lily

At Northwest Peak's rocky summit are some extremely large cairns and a wooden lookout building (no longer in use). This is the highest point for many miles, so the views are superb,

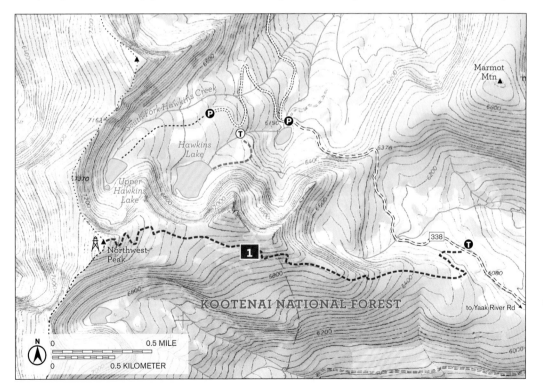

Old lookout building atop Northwest Peak

encompassing a huge expanse of wild country in two states and one Canadian province. The distant snowy peaks to the northwest are part of British Columbia's magnificent Bugaboo Range. You can explore either north or south on the rocky ridgeline, but without making a long car shuttle, you'll eventually have to turn around and return the way you came.

Extend your hike: Good-sized Hawkins Lake is at the end of an easy 0.35-mile trail northeast of Northwest Peak and offers fine scenery, a good campsite, and fishing for small cutthroat trout.

2 *Mount Henry*

Distance: 7 miles roundtrip
Difficulty: strenuous
Hiking time: day hike or overnight
Elevation gain: 1900 feet
Season: July to mid-October
Best time: mid-July

Contact: Kootenai NF, Three Rivers Ranger District
Map: USGS Mount Henry
GPS coordinates: N48° 54.534', W115° 30.378'

Getting there: From US 2 about 28 miles west of Libby, turn north on Yaak River Road (State Route 508). Drive a little over 47 miles, or 16.6 miles past the community of Yaak, then turn right on gravel Solo Joe Road (Forest Road 6035). Proceed 2.9 miles to a fork, bear left on FR 6034, and drive 4.3 miles to the road-end trailhead.

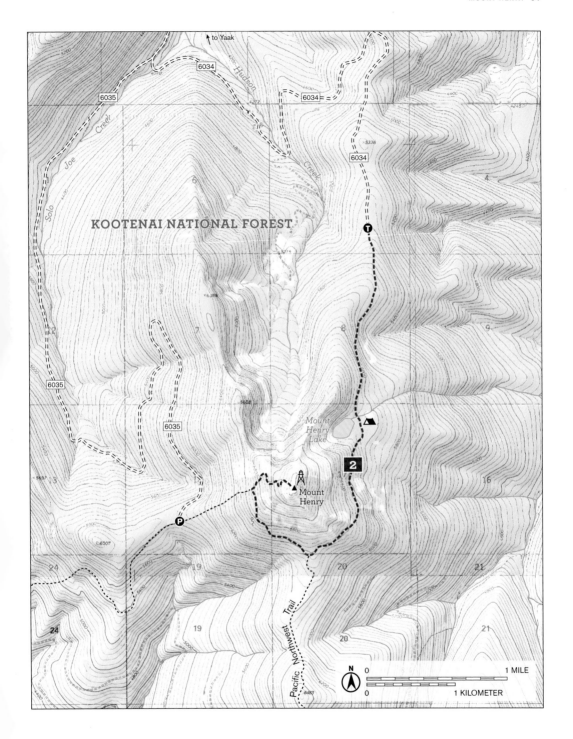

to Yaak

6034

6035

Hudson Creek

6034

6034

KOOTENAI NATIONAL FOREST

Solo Joe Creek

6035

6035

Mount Henry Lake

2

Mount Henry

P

Pacific Northwest Trail

N

0   1 MILE

0   1 KILOMETER

Looking north across fog-shrouded Yaak Valley from atop Mount Henry

Mount Henry is an out-of-the-way summit that doesn't attract a lot of visitors. But this fun and scenic hike deserves your attention. The trail passes by fields of huckleberries, wildflower-covered hillsides, and a delightful and scenic little lake that makes an ideal family backpacking destination. At the summit is a historic fire lookout that commands a particularly outstanding view.

The signed and easy-to-follow trail heads uphill through mid-elevation forests of Engelmann spruce, western larch, and Douglas fir. By the lush standards of northwest Montana, the groundcover is relatively sparse with a mix of grouse whortleberry, huckleberry, beargrass, and a few wildflowers.

The steadily ascending route stays to the left of a rounded ridgeline, then levels out shortly before coming to a very comfortable campsite beside Mount Henry Lake at 1.4 miles. This scenic lake sits directly under the talus slopes of Mount Henry and offers better than average swimming. Originally fishless, in 2013 this lake was stocked with redband trout, a rare Montana native found only in the far northwest corner of the state.

To reach Mount Henry, take the trail that veers left away from the lake and makes a mostly level arc around the rocky and partly forested southeast slopes of Mount Henry. At 2.4 miles is an unsigned junction with a faint trail going downhill to the left.

Continue straight and gradually ascend the mostly open slope, which is covered with wildflowers such as beargrass, aster, harebells, lousewort, yarrow, arnica, fernleaf, and wild carrot. Pass a small spring, then steeply climb beside a rockslide amid stunted high-elevation conifers to a junction at 3.1 miles. Go straight and complete your ascent in six steep and rocky switchbacks to the top of Mount Henry.

The historic lookout building still stands at the summit, although it's seen better days. Climbing the short staircase and walking on the rotting deck is neither safe nor recommended. The views, however, are unimpaired by time and include a plethora of peaks and valleys in two countries.

3 *Little Spar Lake*

Distance: 9.4 miles roundtrip
Difficulty: strenuous
Hiking time: day hike or overnight
Elevation gain: 2050 feet
Season: mid-July through October
Best time: late July

Contact: Kootenai NF, Three Rivers
Ranger District
Maps: USGS Scotchman Peak, Sawtooth
Mountain
GPS coordinates: N48° 14.580',
W115° 57.510'

Getting there: From US 2 about 2 miles east of Troy or 0.4 mile west of the junction with State Route 56, turn south onto Lake Creek Road. Drive 5.3 miles, go left at a fork with Keeler-Rattle Road, and proceed 0.9 mile to a fork just after a bridge. Go right, staying on the paved road, and drive 2.8 miles to where the road, now Forest Road 384, turns to gravel. The road reverts back to pavement after 5.2 miles and brings you to a junction 0.4 mile later. Go left and drive 1.2 miles to where the paved road turns left into Spar Lake Campground. Keep straight on a narrow gravel road and drive 2.2 miles to a bridge over a dry flood channel. You may prefer to park here and walk the final 0.1 mile to the road-end trailhead since the last bit goes through a flood-damaged area and requires a shallow ford of Spar Creek.

This beautiful hike leads to gorgeous Little Spar Lake, which is tucked beneath rocky cliffs and tall peaks in the remote northern part of the Cabinet Mountains. Along the way the trail passes through old-growth forests, lush meadows, and a dramatic cliff-walled canyon. All of this scenic terrain is part of the Scotchman Peaks Roadless Area, a large and spectacular region that is proposed for wilderness designation.

Little Spar Lake

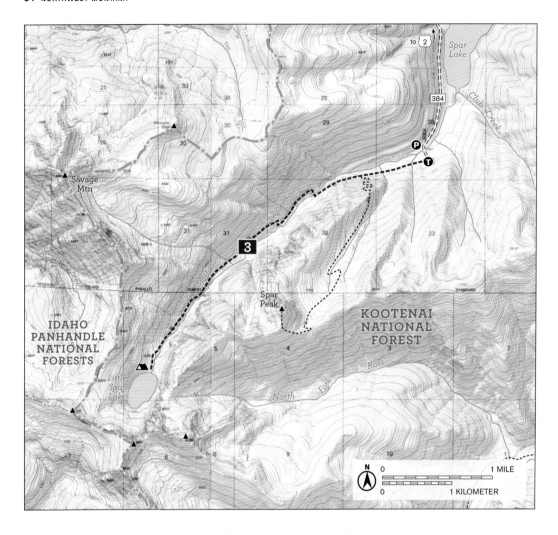

The gently ascending trail follows a long-abandoned jeep road for 0.8 mile through dense forests of Engelmann spruces, western hemlocks, grand firs, Pacific yews, and other conifers. Thimbleberries, elderberries, devils clubs, lady ferns, Douglas maples, slide alders, various grasses, and a wide variety of other moisture-loving plants crowd the forest floor. Spar Creek can be heard splashing through the forest on your right.

Just before the end of the old road, the brushy Spar Peak Trail takes off to the left. You go straight, and 80 yards later veer left onto Little Spar Lake Trail.

The path is fairly rugged with rocks and tangles of overhanging brush, which in this wet environment grows too quickly for trail crews to keep in check. Dense thickets of shrubbery up to 15 feet tall create a green tunnel that surrounds the path. At 1.5 miles you drop to a crossing of Spar Creek, where the tread disappears amid a jumble of flood debris. The trail resumes on the other side of the creek about 40 yards upstream.

You now ascend through a dense old-growth forest of western hemlocks. This strikingly beautiful evergreen, with its drooping limbs and small needles, has only a limited range in Montana, but those found here are some of the most impressive in the state. Some are 5 feet in diameter and over 150 feet tall. There is much less brush under the shady canopy of these trees, which is a blessing as you climb intermittently steep sections of trail.

Openings in the forest become increasingly common, giving you the opportunity to check out the scenery. And it's fine scenery indeed, because the canyon of Spar Creek is exceptionally deep and features steep cliffs. The sunlight of these forest openings provides good growing conditions for huckleberries, which ripen in late July. The

trail's last 1.5 miles are mostly on open, brushy slopes beneath the dark cliffs of Spar Peak.

Little Spar Lake offers a scene that will delight any mountain-loving hiker. The tall, snowy cliffs of an unnamed mountain provide a dramatic backdrop while mountain goats gambol around on the cliffs providing additional entertainment. The lake has plenty of cutthroat trout, but they tend to be pretty small. Camping and swimming also look inviting, but snow remains unusually late in this basin, so be prepared for a cold shock if you enter the water.

4 *Granite Lake*

Distance: 12.2 miles roundtrip
Difficulty: strenuous
Hiking time: overnight
Elevation gain: 1850 feet
Season: mid-July through October
Best time: late July through August

Contact: Kootenai NF, Libby Ranger District
Map: USFS Cabinet Mountains Wilderness
GPS coordinates: N48° 17.730', W115° 37.488'

Getting there: From Libby, drive 0.5 mile southeast on US 2, then veer right (uphill) onto paved Shaughnessy Road. Go 0.7 mile to a four-way junction, turn left on Snowshoe Road, and 0.5 mile later turn right on Granite Lake Road. Follow this paved road for 0.8 mile, keep left at a junction, and proceed 4 miles to where the paved road abruptly becomes narrow gravel-and-dirt Forest Road 618. This road requires careful driving and decent ground clearance. After 3.1 miles the public road ends at a large gravel parking area on the left.

Possibly the most dramatically scenic lake in the Cabinet Mountains, Granite Lake is fed by a 1000-foot-high waterfall that carries the meltwater from Blackwell Glacier, the only remaining alpine glacier in the range. The lake sits beneath the dark ramparts of A Peak and is surrounded by strikingly beautiful forests and meadows. And the hike into this paradise is almost equally lovely, passing through impressive old-growth cedar groves, climbing through wildlife-rich meadows, and taking you past a lovely little waterfall. Be warned, however, that the hike requires a fair amount of sweat and that the upper third of the trail is so brushy you may walk for miles without seeing your feet.

Take the unsigned but obvious route that goes west up the heavily forested canyon of Granite Creek. The wide path initially follows a jeep road that is still used by ATV riders accessing a mine not far upstream. The forest cover, mostly western hemlocks, grand firs, and western red cedars, blocks any views. Still, the cascading creek offers joyful company and the hiking is relatively easy. In addition, thimbleberries are common and their tart, raspberry-like fruit offers a delicious diversion in early August. At 0.3 mile is a trail register, after which the route narrows to become a true trail. As this path ascends the canyon, there are many steep little ups and downs, so the total elevation gain adds up to much more than the map suggests.

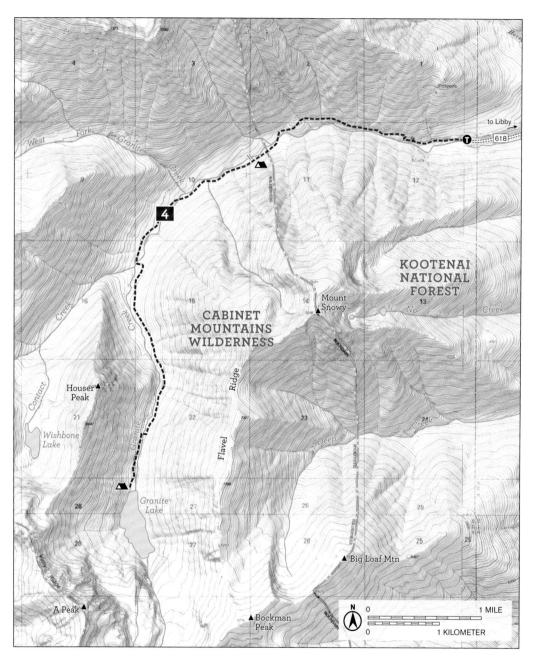

You cross the creek on a large log at 2.1 miles and shortly thereafter enter the Cabinet Mountains Wilderness amidst a grove of stately, old-growth western red cedars. Just 0.2 mile later is a spacious campsite next to an exceptionally pretty 10-foot-tall waterfall on Granite Creek. A deep plunge pool at its base makes a terrific (but chilly) swimming hole.

The canyon now curves to the south, gradually climbing through ancient forests of cedar,

Falls on Granite Creek

hemlock, and a few Douglas fir. You cross the creek on a log at around 3 miles, then cross again about 0.6 mile later either by a ford or a jumble of logs a little upstream. From here the ascent becomes more noticeable, leading to a brushy avalanche chute that tends to accumulate lots of downed trees and debris after a hard winter. Beyond this point, much of the next mile is on exceptionally brushy slopes where the overhanging greenery is so thick it is impossible to see the tread. The brush fiendishly hides lots of rocks and roots that create a significant tripping hazard. Montana was once known as the Stub Toe State (no kidding) and you may conclude

it was a hiker on this trail who came up with the nickname.

You cross Granite Creek a final time at 5.6 miles, this time via a calf-deep ford, then wade through more brush for 0.5 mile to a small campsite near the outlet of Granite Lake.

Rising fully 4000 feet from the southwest shore, craggy A Peak forms a spectacular backdrop to this extremely scenic lake. On the southeast side of A Peak an amazingly long and steep waterslide-type waterfall (one of the tallest in the American Rockies) tumbles down from unseen Blackwell Glacier. It's a wonderful scene and well worth the long hike required to enjoy it.

5 *Wanless Lake*

Distance: 18.2 miles roundtrip
Difficulty: strenuous
Hiking time: overnight
Elevation gain: 4800 feet
Season: mid-July through mid-October
Best time: late July through mid-August

Contact: Kootenai NF, Cabinet Ranger District
Map: USFS Cabinet Mountains Wilderness
GPS coordinates: N47° 58.238',
W115° 38.578'

Getting there: From Thompson Falls, go 22.5 miles northwest on State Route 200 to a junction near milepost 18.5 directly across from the turnoff to Noxon Rapids Dam. Turn right (east) on rough gravel Forest Road 1022, following signs to McKay Creek, and drive 4.1 miles to the road-end trailhead.

It takes plenty of sweat to reach Wanless Lake in the Cabinet Mountains Wilderness, but those who have made the effort are nearly unanimous in saying that this is one of the finest backpacking trips in Montana. This large and deep mountain lake fills an exceptionally scenic basin beneath the towering cliffs of Engle Peak. The outlet features a pretty little waterfall and there are very good campsites with fine views. And the hike in, while challenging, includes miles of juicy huckleberries, climbs to an excellent viewpoint, and passes several very scenic smaller lakes before reaching the main attraction. Begin with full water bottles, because after an early creek crossing, there is usually no water until you reach Upper Lake at 6.3 miles, a stretch that includes a long, tiring climb.

Wanless Lake Trail #924 starts next to a large signboard at the northeast end of the road's turn-around loop and goes gradually up the heavily forested canyon of North Fork McKay Creek. A relatively wide swath has been cut through the forest to accommodate the trail, which takes you 0.3 mile to a bridged crossing of North Fork McKay Creek, your last reliable water for 6 miles. After the crossing you briefly follow the creek upstream then make the first of what will turn out to be numerous long switchbacks. The ascent is well graded but it takes hours, so get an early start to tackle this section in the cool and shade of the morning.

Huckleberry bushes crowd the forest floor, offering tasty treats from late July through mid-August. Keep an eye out for bears, however, as they appreciate the berries too. After several long switchbacks, make a half turn to the left and climb into a higher-elevation environment of sparse forest dominated by mountain hemlocks and subalpine firs. Five short switchbacks and then a winding uphill traverse lead you through

Wanless Lake

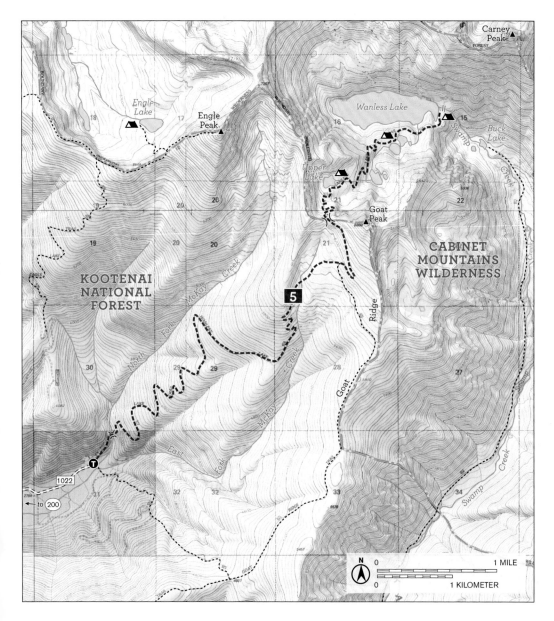

an attractive mountain basin with open forests, plenty of wildflowers, and views of peaks both near and far. In the middle of this pretty basin you pass an easily missed junction where you continue straight on the main trail and then make one final switchback up a talus slope to the wilderness boundary at a 6400-foot pass. The pass features excellent views, especially

looking northeast down to Upper Lake, the highest of four small lakes tucked into forested basins above Wanless Lake. The tall mountain to the northwest is Engle Peak.

Some twenty well-graded and mostly short switchbacks take you down to Upper Lake, which has fine scenery and a couple of excellent campsites. Unfortunately, this lake is plagued by mosquitoes through most of July and early August.

The downhill continues beyond Upper Lake as you cross the small outlet creek several times on a switchbacking course through an old burn where you'll have terrific views down to huge Wanless Lake. You approach but never quite reach a second lake, then make six gently graded switchbacks in unburned forest to some very good campsites near a pair of beautiful but marshy lakes. Livestock are not allowed beyond this point.

The trail now goes east, descending through forest to the campsites at the east end of Wanless Lake. This mile-long lake offers mediocre fishing, good swimming, and absolutely gorgeous scenery with the towering cliffs of Engle Peak rising to the west, while Flat Top Mountain dominates the north. Be sure to check out Swamp Creek, which pours over a pretty little waterfall right at the outlet of Wanless Lake. Expect plenty of mosquitoes from mid-July to mid-August.

6 *Terrace Lake*

Distance: 2.7 miles roundtrip
Difficulty: moderate
Hiking time: half-day hike or overnight
Elevation gain: 1100 feet
Season: mid-July through October
Best time: August and mid-October

Contact: Lolo NF, Plains/Thompson Falls Ranger District
Maps: USGS Fishtrap Lake, Vermilion Peak
GPS coordinates: N47° 46.248', W115° 14.416'

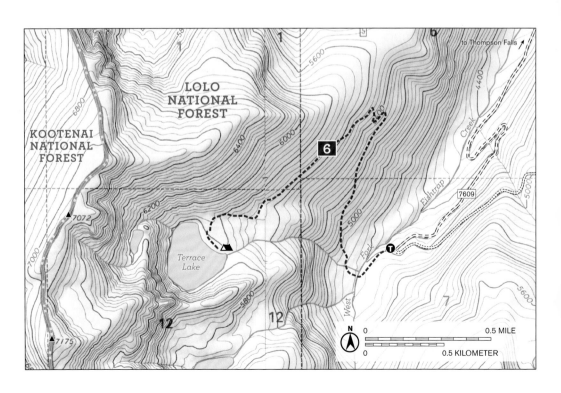

Fall color along Terrace Lake Trail

Getting there: From Thompson Falls, go 4 miles east on State Route 200 then turn north (left) on Thompson River Road. After 15.4 miles you turn left on Forest Road 516, following signs to Fishtrap Lake; drive 10.3 miles, then veer left on FR 7609 and proceed 3.2 miles to a fork. Bear left and continue 3.3 miles to the signed trailhead at a road switchback.

This relatively new trail isn't on the Forest Service or USGS maps, so it's unknown to most hikers. But it's there nonetheless, and is even officially signed and maintained. Best of all, this short trail offers relatively easy access to an exceptionally scenic, fish-filled lake that makes an ideal day hike or family backpacking destination.

The path goes steeply uphill through a relatively dense forest of Douglas firs and western larches before dropping briefly to an unbridged but easy crossing of West Fork Fishtrap Creek. From here you climb to a hop-over crossing of the Terrace Lake outlet creek then settle in for a 900-foot ascent on a forested hillside. The dense undergrowth is dominated by beargrass and abundant huckleberries (beware of bears). A long traverse to the north-northeast is followed by three well-engineered switchbacks, which keep the grade from being too steep. While you climb, listen for the loud staccato calls of pileated woodpeckers and look for small forest openings that provide partial views of rugged Mount Headley to the south-southwest.

A final extended traverse followed by a brief descent leads to Terrace Lake. Dramatic craggy cliffs rise to unnamed peaks to the west of this deep lake, making for outstanding scenery. An obvious use path goes left taking you to campsites and easier access to the water.

7 *Baldy Mountain and Lake*

Distance: 6.4 miles roundtrip
Difficulty: strenuous (moderate to summit)
Hiking time: day hike or overnight
Elevation gain: 2450 feet
Season: July through October
Best time: July through October

Contact: Lolo NF, Plains/Thompson Falls Ranger District
Maps: USGS Baldy Lake, Coney Peak
GPS coordinates: N47° 37.656', W114° 50.778'

Getting there: From Plains, go north on Clayton Street, which becomes Upper Lynch Creek Road and eventually FR 1025. At 9 miles veer left onto Corona Road and drive this dusty gravel road for 4.3 miles to a junction. Go right on FR 886, following a simple brown hiker's sign, and proceed on this narrow and somewhat rocky dirt and gravel road for 2.4 miles to a fork. Veer right and just 0.1 mile later pass the lower trailhead for Baldy Mountain.

To reach the upper trailhead, continue on FR 886, which gets narrower and quite brushy, for 1.5 miles to the road-end turnaround.

Baldy Mountain is a hulking peak at the southern end of the Cabinet Mountains that looms majestically over the meadows near the town of Plains. A well-engineered trail climbs to the top of this landmark where there are grand vistas over numerous valleys, forested ridges, and distant mountains. The trail then continues down the back side of the mountain to an exceptionally

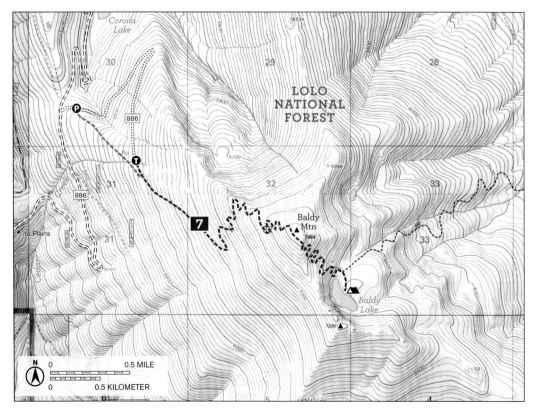

Hiker relaxing at Baldy Lake

scenic lake in a dramatic cirque basin. Here you can camp, fish, or swim in a marvelous setting; it's a wonder so few hikers make this trip.

From the upper trailhead, go southeast, following an abandoned road across a heavily forested hillside. The groundcover includes grouse whortleberry and some huckleberry, but is dominated by a thick growth of beargrass. The old road ends after 0.1 mile at the top of an old clear-cut where you meet the route from the lower trailhead.

Go straight and begin a steady uphill on a well-maintained tread. As you gain elevation, frequent forest openings offer pleasant views of the lowlands around Plains and the rounded mountains to the west.

At 0.8 mile, reach the edge of a large rockslide and make the first of fifteen switchbacks that take you up the west side of Baldy Mountain. The terrain becomes rockier as you approach the summit, opening up far-ranging vistas of the Cabinet Mountains to the north-northwest. At the top, a stone foundation is all that remains of the lookout that once stood here, but the views remain, with particularly good ones to the southeast of the jagged Mission Range.

For Baldy Lake, keep straight on the trail that goes past the old lookout foundation and descends the rocky and partly forested southeast side of Baldy Mountain. Twenty-five short switchbacks drop 700 feet to the deep, kidney-shaped lake. There are very good campsites nearby as well as excellent fishing for large cutthroat trout. But the scenery is what really steals the show, as the lake is backed by dark 500-foot cliffs on its south and west shores.

8 Ten Lakes Scenic Area Loop

Distance: 10.5-mile loop
Difficulty: strenuous
Hiking time: day hike or overnight
Elevation gain: 2450 feet
Season: mid-July through mid-October
Best time: late July and August or late September

Contact: Kootenai NF, Eureka Ranger Station
Map: USGS Ksanka Peak
GPS coordinates: N48° 56.628', W114° 54.054'

Getting there: From Eureka, drive almost 9 miles south on US 93, then turn left on Grave Creek Road, following signs to Ten Lakes. Take this paved county road, which becomes Forest Road 114, for 10.3 miles to a junction with FR 7021. Go straight, reach the end of pavement just 0.2 mile later, and drive 17.6 miles to a major fork. Go right on FR 7085 and drive 0.8 mile to a junction with the access road to Little Therriault Lake Campground. Keep right and continue a final bumpy 0.6 mile to the road-end trailhead.

The Whitefish Range is a narrow line of mountains stretching down from Canada just east of Eureka. In many ways they have more in common with our northern neighbors than they do with the United States, including healthy populations of that country's wilderness-loving wildlife: grizzly bears, wolverines, lynx, and gray wolves. This loop is the best of an excellent

Wolverine Cabin

network of trails that visits several very scenic lakes, some unusually lovely mountain meadows, fine ridgetop viewpoints, and miles of beautiful high-elevation forests.

For a clockwise tour, take the Bluebird Trail, which starts from the west side of the parking area. This path follows an old road through a decades-old clear-cut, which is now regrowing with 30-foot-tall subalpine firs and Engelmann spruces. The old road ends in 0.2 mile, after which you follow a well-traveled trail through forest. The brush is fairly thick, but the trail is regularly maintained, so the brush is kept well back from the tread.

You steadily gain elevation as the brush gives way to small meadows and lush wildflower gardens hidden beneath the trees. Look for the colorful blossoms of paintbrush, fernleaf, arnica, false hellebore, beargrass, aster, and Sitka valerian. At about 0.8 mile you make two quick switchbacks then climb at a somewhat steeper grade making two crossings of small creeks. Near 1.9 miles you reach shallow Paradise Lake where a signed spur trail crosses the outlet to a camping area.

The main trail skirts the southwest shore of Paradise Lake and then climbs a slope covered with a wide variety of wildflowers. At 2.2 miles you meet the Highline Trail in a meadow below a looming rock face. Go right and contour for 0.1 mile to another junction.

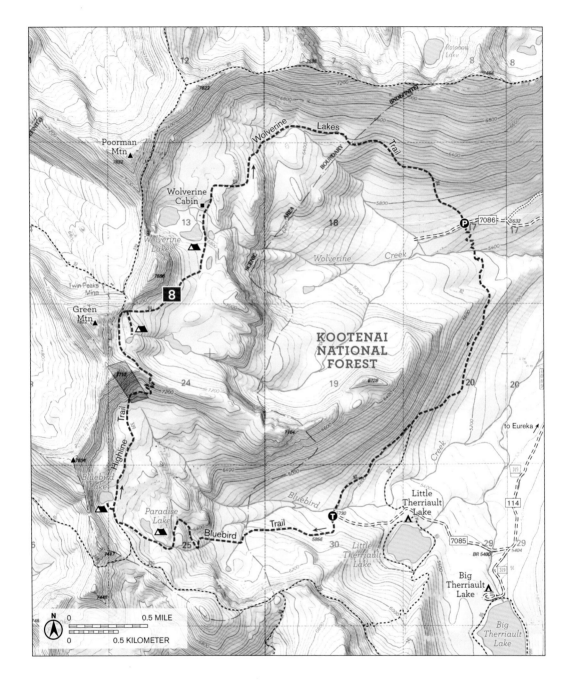

The loop trail goes straight, but first turn left on the 125-yard spur trail to supremely scenic Bluebird Lake. Surrounded by flowery meadows and set beneath a cliff with many jagged pinnacles, this fish-filled gem is a must-see. There are good camps for those who want to spend a night at this wilderness paradise.

Back on the loop trail, you go gently up and down through open forests and occasional meadows beneath a line of rugged cliffs on your left. Keep an eye out for bighorn sheep, which inhabit these cliffs. At 2.9 miles you begin a well-graded 400-foot switchbacking climb to the top of a spur ridge where there are fine views framed by wispy alpine larch trees.

The sometimes-rocky trail now descends a bit before contouring across a lovely subalpine bench below Green Mountain to a junction. Turn right (downhill) on Wolverine Lakes Trail and soon pass a faint spur trail that goes right to a shallow pond with a small campsite and excellent views of Green Mountain. This pond is especially appealing in late September when the alpine larch trees are in their full autumn splendor.

The loop trail descends back into forested terrain, passes a marshy little lake, and soon reaches larger Wolverine Lake. This beautiful mountain lake offers good campsites and fine views of rugged Poorman Mountain to the northwest. The lake also has plenty of cutthroat trout to entice the angler. Just below the lake is Wolverine Cabin, a comfortable log structure that is open to backpackers on a first-come, first-served basis.

The trail crosses the splashing outlet creek of Wolverine Lake, and then spends the next couple of miles going mostly downhill in forest to a remote trailhead on Forest Road 7086.

Cross the road and pick up an obvious but brushy trail that continues downhill for 0.4 mile to an easy crossing of Wolverine Creek. From here the trail goes up and down in viewless forest for 0.4 mile to meet a long-abandoned road that is now so overgrown it is hard to discern that it was once a vehicle route. Your course goes gently downhill on this old road for about 0.5 mile, then turns right and begins climbing. At 9.9 miles you turn right at a signed junction and climb for 0.6 mile to a rock-hop crossing of Bluebird Creek and the trailhead.

9 *Stahl Peak Loop*

Distance: 9-mile loop
Difficulty: strenuous
Hiking time: day hike
Elevation gain: 3000 feet
Season: mid-July through mid-October
Best time: late July

Contact: Kootenai NF,
Eureka Ranger Station
Map: USGS Stahl Peak
GPS coordinates: N48° 55.782',
W114° 49.110'

Getting there: From Eureka, drive almost 9 miles south on US 93, then turn left on Grave Creek Road, following signs to Ten Lakes. Take this paved county road, which becomes Forest Road 114, for 10.3 miles to a junction with gravel FR 7021. Turn left, following signs to Clarence Creek, drive 0.7 mile, then go right on FR 7022 and drive 2.9 bumpy miles to the road-end trailhead.

The tall, spiked pyramid of Stahl Peak is a striking landmark in the Whitefish Range and from the top there are wonderful views extending 50 or more miles in all directions. The wooden lookout building at the top still stands and is both quaint and photogenic. The cliff-edged mountain makes a wonderful hiking goal and an alternate return route along a scenic ridge allows for a pleasant loop with lots of huckleberries and possible wildlife sightings.

Warning: The first 2.5 miles of this loop go through very dense brush. Millions of spider webs hang across the trail creating a virtual wall of tiny threads. I mean, whoever invented the term "world wide web" had probably recently hiked this trail. Bring a walking stick to wave in

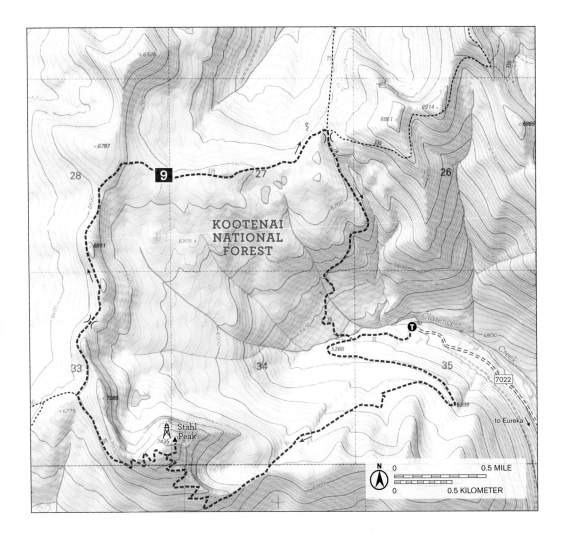

front of you or, better, an oblivious hiking partner to take the lead.

The trail is marked with a large yellow sign telling cross-country skiers that this is the end of their groomed trail. The summer hiker's route is in good shape as it follows a long-closed road that is now largely overgrown with grasses, wildflowers, and 10-foot-tall alders. You gain elevation at a steady but moderate grade for a little over 0.3 mile to a fork and the start of the recommended loop.

Bear left and continue your steady uphill, enjoying improving views of Stahl Peak, a sharp pinnacle rising into the Montana sky. The route soon makes a sweeping switchback to the left, followed by a long uphill traverse and then another switchback that takes you almost directly toward Stahl Peak. About 0.25 mile later a sign directs you into a sharp left turn onto a foot trail.

This path makes one switchback, then climbs a forested slope with lots of brush and millions of spider webs. Views are restricted by trees but the forest provides welcome shade. At 2.6 miles you switch to the south side of the ridge, which has less brush.

Cliffs and a small lake on the north side of Stahl Peak

The trail now begins a series of eight relatively long, well-graded switchbacks up a mostly forested slope. *Tip:* At the second switchback, a 25-yard bushwhack out to the ridge crest provides breathtaking views of the sheer cliffs below the summit of Stahl Peak.

At 3.7 miles is a junction. The loop trail goes left (downhill), but first turn right and climb 0.2 mile to the summit of Stahl Peak. The wooden cupola-style lookout remains in good shape and is unlocked so hikers can poke around inside. But what really sets this location apart is the setting. Amazing, dun-colored, 1000-foot cliffs drop off the north and east sides of the peak, making for a dizzying view. At the base of the northern cliffs is a small unnamed lake. Needless to say, the distant views of the rugged peaks and valleys of the Whitefish Range are spectacular.

Once you've had enough of the view (which could take a while) go back down the summit spur trail and resume the clockwise loop hike. This rocky path switchbacks steeply down a partly forested slope to a notch in the cliff where you can look directly down to the unnamed little lake. From there descend a wildflower-studded slope to a junction.

Go right and cut across a steep, lushly vegetated slope where you'll have excellent views to the northwest down to Big Therriault Lake and across to the peaks beyond. After about 0.4 mile you'll reach a saddle; then you'll go up and down along the scenic ridge, eventually curving to the right to follow a side ridge in that direction. Near 6.5 miles you pass a cluster of small lakes on your right. Although the lakes remain out of sight you'll know they are there by the noticeable increase in the number of mosquitoes.

At 7.3 miles is a four-way junction. Turn right, following signs to Clarence Creek Road, go through a narrow saddle, and then begin an extended downhill. At about 1.4 miles from the junction you make a rock-hop crossing of Clarence Creek just before closing the loop at the junction 0.3 mile above the trailhead.

10 *Krinklehorn Peak Loop*

Distance: 10.7-mile loop
Difficulty: strenuous
Hiking time: day hike or overnight
Elevation gain: 3400 feet
Season: mid-July through mid-October
Best time: late July

Contact: Kootenai NF,
Eureka Ranger Station
Maps: USGS Mount Marston,
Mount Thompson Seton
GPS coordinates: N48° 47.357',
W114° 47.175'

Getting there: From Eureka, drive 13 miles south on US 93, and then turn east onto Deep Creek Road. After 1.1 miles, turn left on gravel Jeager Road (Forest Road 368) and proceed 5.4 miles to the trailhead parking lot just before a bridge and a gate.

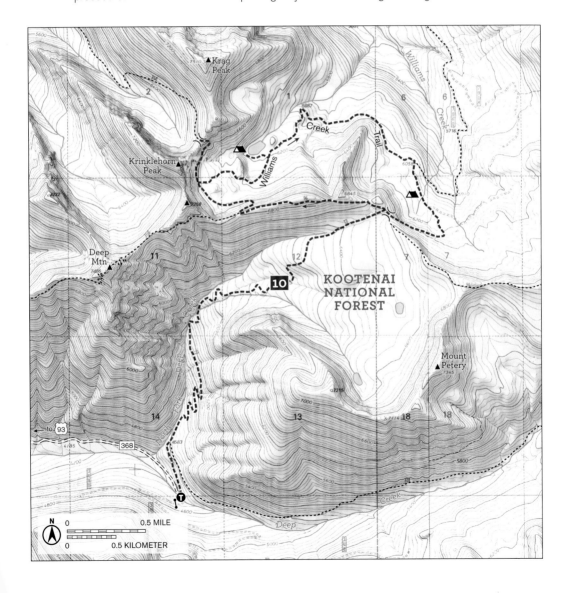

Krinklehorn Peak from a small meadow to the east

which includes a visit to an unnamed lake that offers great views up to Krinklehorn's Matterhorn-like summit.

The trail heads uphill, following a closed road to a junction and switchback at 0.3 mile. The old road goes right, but you turn left onto a narrower hiker's route and ascend along splashing North Fork Deep Creek. Scattered switchbacks keep the grade moderate as you make a long and tiring climb on a hillside covered with mixed conifers. The path is lined with thimbleberries at lower elevations and huckleberries higher up, offering tasty diversions in late summer. You reach the top of the ridge near 2.8 miles at a junction and the start of the loop.

Go left and climb to a spot where you can finally see the dramatic cliff-edged tower of spectacular Krinklehorn Peak. Soon thereafter you turn sharply right at a junction near 3.6 miles and descend one switchback to a junction in the meadows and talus fields at the base of the soaring cliffs on the east side of Krinklehorn Peak.

The loop goes right on Williams Creek Trail, but first you'll want to take a side trip; go straight and climb open slopes for 0.4 mile to a saddle featuring stupendous views of a long line of tall cliffs on the north side of Krinklehorn Peak.

Back on the loop trail, head downhill past some miniature meadows with exceptional views up to Krinklehorn Peak's impressive tower. After losing 450 feet in 0.5 mile, you reach a flat area where you should look closely for an unsigned social trail to the left. This path crosses soggy areas for 0.2 mile to a secluded campsite at the west end of a lovely turquoise-colored lake. From the east end of this pool are photogenic views up to the pinnacle of Krinklehorn Peak.

From the lake junction the main trail descends to a sharp right turn and then goes gently up and down for 0.8 mile to a signed junction. Turn right (slightly uphill) and climb to an easy crossing of a small creek and a campsite just beyond. About 0.1 mile later the trail curves to the right and then climbs a heavily forested hillside to a ridgetop junction. Go straight and 10 yards later return to the junction at the close of the loop.

Only savvy locals seem to know about Krinklehorn Peak's dramatic spire and tall cliffs and fewer still hike the fun loop that explores this impressive mountain. Thus, solitude is usually a bonus on this scenic hike,

11 Nasukoin Mountain

Distance: 10.2 miles roundtrip
Difficulty: very strenuous
Hiking time: day hike
Elevation gain: 3300 feet
Season: late July through early October
Best time: late July, late September

Contact: Flathead NF, Glacier View Ranger District
Map: USGS Red Meadow Lake
GPS coordinates: N48° 45.700', W114° 35.518'

Getting there: From Columbia Falls, go 23 miles north on State Route 486 to a junction with Camas Creek Road into Glacier National Park. Go left, still on SR 486, and drive 18.6 miles (5.5 miles past Polebridge), then turn left onto Red Meadow Creek Road (Forest Road 115). Drive this narrow and pothole-filled gravel road for 9.7 miles to the unsigned Chain Lakes Trailhead (which is 0.5 mile after a bridge over Red Meadow Creek and just a few yards after a bridge over an unnamed side creek).

For Nasukoin Mountain, continue 2.8 miles on FR 115, then turn sharply right onto FR 589. Slowly drive this rough road for 1.6 miles to the road-end trailhead.

Nasukoin Mountain is the highest point in the Whitefish Range, and reaching its summit requires a long and challenging hike with lots of up and down. But the rewards are great, with superb views from two high peaks and a very scenic ramble along a larch-studded subalpine ridge. If you want an easier outing, the nearby Chain Lakes offer a scenic setting beneath the craggy ramparts of Lake Mountain.

Go east on the Link Lake Trail, which loops to the right to briefly parallel the access road before switchbacking several times up a hillside. As you climb, there are frequent views to the southwest of rugged Whitefish Mountain. At 0.8 mile the route to island-studded Link Lake splits to the right, a pleasant and easy side trip.

You bear left (uphill) and climb fourteen well-graded switchbacks to the top of a little knob. The path then ascends four much longer switchbacks on a slope covered with beargrass and perky subalpine firs. At the top is an excellent ridgetop viewpoint where you can look up to Lake Mountain, down to the east to a narrow unnamed lake, and north to the hulking mass of Nasukoin Mountain.

Nasukoin Mountain from the ridge to the south

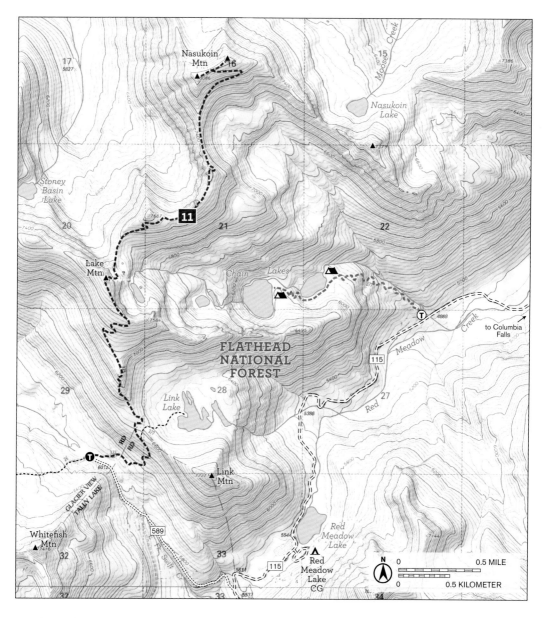

The trail now makes a short, steep climb to the top of Lake Mountain, near 2.3 miles, from which there are superb views of the Chain Lakes and the distant Kintla Peaks and Livingston Range in Glacier National Park. Lake Mountain makes a fine destination if you're not up for the more demanding trip to Nasukoin Mountain.

About 50 yards along Lake Mountain's summit ridge, a cairn marks where the trail goes right and rapidly descends fifteen short switchbacks. At the bottom of this 450-foot descent the trail follows a delightfully scenic ridge to the north. This ridge, which is sprinkled with lovely alpine larch trees, offers excellent views of distant peaks and close-up looks at Lake and Nasukoin Mountains.

After a couple of downhill switchbacks, the final assault up Nasukoin Mountain begins with a long traverse up the mountain's colorful southeast face. The trail then turns and traces a ridge to the dual-summited top. The western summit is slightly taller, but the eastern high point features a tall pole and some ancient metal bed springs where you can sit to eat lunch. From either location the views seem to extend forever.

Extend your hike: For a shorter and easier hike, the very scenic Chain Lakes sit at the end of a steep 1.3-mile route. The second of the two lakes is more scenic but requires a bit more work to reach. Both lakes sit under rugged crags and have decent campsites.

12 *Turquoise Lake*

Distance: 12.2 miles roundtrip
Difficulty: strenuous
Hiking time: overnight
Elevation gain: 2650 feet
Season: mid-July through early October
Best time: late July through September

Contact: Flathead NF, Swan Lake Ranger District
Map: Cairn Cartographics, Mission Range
GPS coordinates: N47° 22.896', W113° 47.628'

Getting there: From Seeley Lake, go 23 miles north on State Route 83 to a junction near milepost 37.1. Turn west on gravel Forest Road 561, following signs to Kraft Creek, and drive 11.6 miles to the road-end trailhead.

Turquoise Lake is one of the most delightful hikes in Montana. Although you'll do a fair amount of climbing, the path is well graded and feels easier than the elevation gain would suggest. And the scenery is enchanting, with fine vistas, striking rock formations, wildflower-covered slopes, and even a few smaller lakes before you get to the main attraction. The destination itself couldn't be more beautiful with the rugged, glacier-clad summits of Daughter of the Sun Mountain, Mount Shoemaker, and the Glacier Peaks rising in the background and a shoreline that is picturesquely sprinkled with rocks, trees, and driftwood.

The wide and heavily used trail goes gradually uphill in a forest of western larches, subalpine firs, and Engelmann spruces with a few low-growing western yews in wetter places. The waters of Glacier Creek loudly cascade along on your left. After passing a low waterfall, you cross Crazy Horse Creek at 0.3 mile on a narrow log bridge, enter the Mission Mountains Wilderness, and

Glacier Peak from the overlook above Turquoise Lake

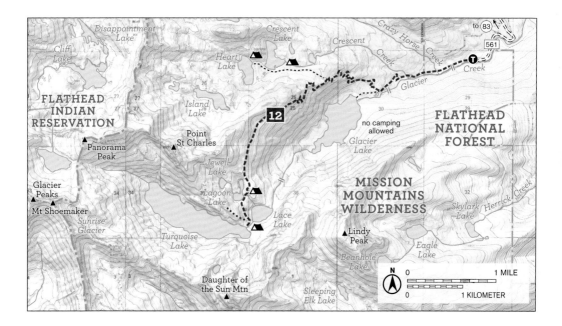

then cross Crescent Creek at 0.6 mile. From here you make one uphill switchback, then continue gently climbing past a low, sliding waterfall to a fork at 1.2 miles. The very popular route to Glacier Lake goes left and in 0.2 mile reaches that large and attractive lake. Due to overuse, camping is prohibited within 0.25 mile of Glacier Lake.

For Turquoise Lake, go right and climb a less-used trail on a series of eight relatively gentle switchbacks. At the fifth switchback a 15-yard side trail goes straight to an excellent rocky viewpoint above Glacier Lake.

At the top of this climb is a junction with the trail to Crescent and Heart Lakes. To reach Turquoise Lake, go straight and make eight irregularly spaced uphill switchbacks. The trail then begins an extended and unusually attractive traverse in open forest and across rocky slopes with excellent views of Glacier Lake, a line of rugged peaks to the south, and a long waterfall cascading out of the basin holding Turquoise Lake. Abundant huckleberries provide tasty treats in midsummer and good fall color in early October.

At about 5.2 miles you pass below a large area of sloping, glacier-polished rock and then descend to beautiful Lagoon Lake. This scenic pool is backed by colorful rock buttresses and has one fair campsite.

At a confusing spot a little below Lagoon Lake the trail makes a jog to the right and then takes a circuitous up-and-down course as it passes above Lace Lake before arriving at the eastern shore of Turquoise Lake. This huge subalpine gem is extremely scenic: Mount Shoemaker and the Glacier Peaks are draped by the white mass of Sunrise Glacier, forming a very photogenic backdrop. With a little searching, you'll find a few scattered campsites hidden in nooks around the rocky shoreline. Don't be surprised if mountain goats visit your camp in the evening or chew on your sweaty boots and pack straps during the night.

Tip: Be sure to make the easy, off-trail scramble up to a rocky overlook about 300 feet above the northeast shore of Turquoise Lake. Here you'll have a superb vista overlooking the entire basin and surrounding mountains.

Opposite, top: Buck white-tailed deer, Bitterroot Mountains

Opposite, bottom: Beargrass, Great Burn Roadless Area

West-Central Montana

Centered on the outdoor-oriented city of Missoula, west-central Montana, with its deep canyons and lofty summits, is a hiker's dream. Mountain ranges stack up like cordwood here, starting with the jagged Bitterroot Range straddling the Idaho border, then moving east to the more subdued Sapphire Mountains, the impressive Rattlesnake Range at Missoula's back door, and the often-overlooked Flint Creek Range to the east. To the south, the region is bordered by the towering peaks of the Anaconda-Pintler Wilderness along the Continental Divide. Several smaller lines of peaks tuck themselves into the narrow spaces between these major ranges. Trails radiate through these mountains and they are among the most popular in Montana. Almost any kind of hiking experience you could want—streamside forest walks, strolls to mountain lakes, alpine rambles to high viewpoints, remote wilderness backpacking adventures, and even grand walks literally within the city limits—are on the menu here, and most are reasonable day hikes from Missoula. Locals use the trails a lot, but few people from outside the region travel these paths, heading instead to more famous hiking areas like Glacier National Park or the Beartooth Range.

Although this area is not as soggy as northwest Montana, your trip here could turn wet, so be prepared for the weather. But also be prepared for outstanding scenery, plenty of wildlife, and some of Montana's best fishing, because west-central Montana reveals all of these treasures in magnificent variety and abundance.

13 *Cliff Lake*

Distance: 2.2 miles roundtrip
Difficulty: easy
Hiking time: half-day hike or overnight
Elevation gain: 550 feet
Season: mid-July through October

Best time: late July
Contact: Lolo NF, Superior Ranger District
Map: USGS Torino Peak
GPS coordinates: N47° 08.892',
W115° 10.404'

Getting there: Take Dry Creek Road, exit 43 off Interstate 90 a little west of Superior, go 0.8 mile south on a paved county road, then turn right onto Forest Road 342. After 9.8 miles go left, now on FR 7843, a narrow and winding dirt-and-gravel road that is bumpy but okay for most passenger cars. Drive 4.1 miles to the road's end at the outlet to Diamond Lake.

It is hard to imagine an easier hike to a more dramatic but generally uncrowded mountain lake than Cliff Lake in the northern Bitterroot Mountains. This part of the Bitterroot Range lacks the deep, cliff-lined canyons and tall granite peaks that characterize the more famous southern Bitterroots, but makes up for it with exceptionally lush vegetation and some of the finest fishing

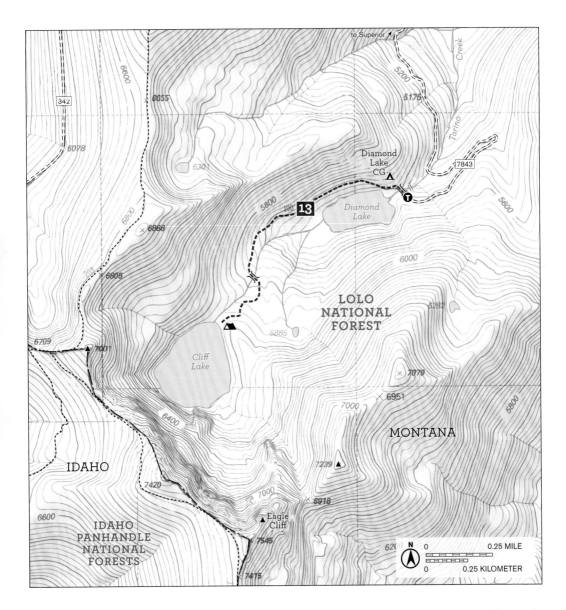

lakes in Montana. And as Cliff Lake proves, there are places hidden in these forest-cloaked hills with dramatic, craggy peaks forming classic backdrops to beautiful mountain lakes.

The trail immediately crosses a bridge over Torino Creek and reaches a restroom building. Below the bridge the creek spills over a broad, rocky ledge to form a beautiful waterfall. An unmarked social trail begins behind the developed campsite just past the restroom and leads steeply down to an excellent photo spot for these falls.

The wide and easy-to-follow main trail climbs a bit before contouring across the hillside above forest-rimmed Diamond Lake. Long, sloping meadows rise above you as Eagle Cliff forms a dramatic backdrop to the southwest. Dense spruce and fir forest shades the trail, while a lush understory of mixed shrubs provides a

Waterfall on Torino Creek below Diamond Lake

wonderland of greenery. Look for elderberry, slide alder, thimbleberry, and lady fern, among other water-loving plants. Late July-blooming wildflowers abound, including such varieties as monkshood, mountain spiraea, cow parsnip, false hellebore, bluebells, horsemint, Sitka valerian, and coneflower. All of these grow in such quantities they hide every square inch of the ground beneath. Several trickling creeks cross the trail giving further evidence of the wetness of this terrain.

Beyond Diamond Lake the trail curves south, reenters forest, and crosses Torino Creek on a wooden bridge at 0.8 mile. From here you wind uphill beside the cascading creek, often taking wooden boardwalks over particularly muddy spots. At 1.1 miles the trail levels off just before reaching Cliff Lake. The dark, snow-streaked ramparts of Eagle Cliff provide a stupendous backdrop for this scenic lake, which also offers good swimming and fishing for cutthroat trout. There are a couple of inviting campsites nearby if you want to turn this into an easy overnighter. Mosquitoes can be a problem until about mid-August.

14 *Heart Lake*

Distance: 6.2 miles roundtrip
Difficulty: moderate
Hiking time: day hike or overnight
Elevation gain: 1100 feet
Season: late June through October

Best time: July
Contact: Lolo NF, Superior Ranger District
Map: USGS Straight Peak
GPS coordinates: N46° 59.019', W114° 58.694'

Getting there: Leave Interstate 90 at Superior exit 47, take River Street to the south side of the freeway, and then go left on Diamond Match Road. After 6.3 miles the pavement ends where the road becomes Forest Road 250. Drive another 15.4 miles to the Heart Lake Trailhead on the left.

Heart Lake is the largest and arguably the most scenic lake in the northern Bitterroot Mountains. The lake is popular with both day hikers and backpackers, so don't expect solitude. If you're willing to expend a bit more energy, however, you can escape the lakeshore crowds by

extending your hike to beautiful Pearl Lake and a pair of ridgetop overlooks from which you'll enjoy outstanding views down to Heart Lake.

The trail begins in a dense forest of Engelmann spruces, Douglas firs, and western red cedars with a heavy undergrowth of thimbleberry,

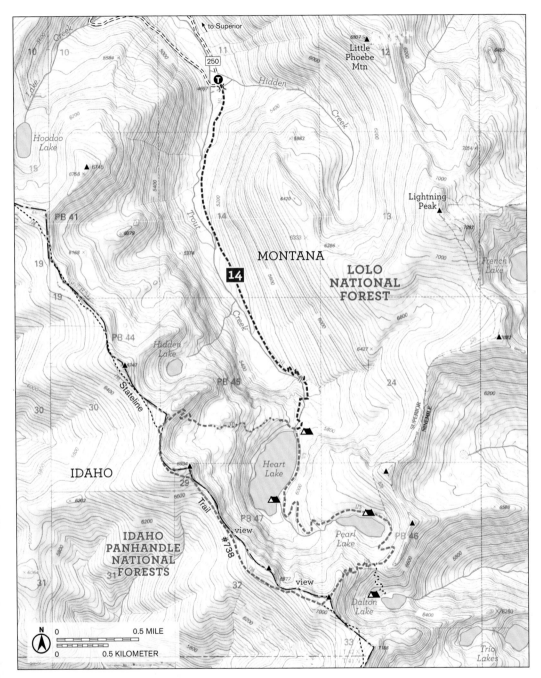

elderberry, huckleberry, and lady fern mixed with a wide variety of grasses and wildflowers. At just under 0.2 mile you cross a creek on a wooden bridge, after which the grade remains fairly gentle as you ascend the deep canyon of Trout Creek. Plank bridges take you over particularly soggy places but you should still expect some mud in early summer.

The pass above Pearl Lake is well worth the climb.

As you approach an unseen waterfall, six switchbacks take you up to a rock-hop crossing of Trout Creek just before you reach Heart Lake at 3.1 miles. Here there are numerous popular campsites and tremendous scenery with views toward an unnamed cliff rising above the lake's southwest shore. If you have the energy, hike further for even more views and campsites.

Extend your hike: To reach the amazing viewpoints atop those cliffs, cross Heart Lake's outlet, take the trail around the east side of the lake, and then climb to the open basin holding Pearl Lake. This sparkling gem is nearly as scenic as Heart Lake, but is much less visited.

The trail loops around the north side of Pearl Lake and then climbs a pair of switchbacks to an unsigned junction in an open saddle above secluded Dalton Lake. To reach the ridgetop viewpoints, turn right and steeply ascend an open wildflower-covered slope. After gaining 500 feet, you reach the ridge forming the Montana/Idaho border and a signed junction. From a clifftop overlook just to the right of this junction there is a supremely photogenic view of Heart Lake and its surrounding basin.

For a second grand overlook, take Trail #738 to the northwest and make a gradual downhill traverse around the Idaho side of a cliff-edged butte. After about 0.5 mile you'll come to an excellent viewpoint above Heart Lake. From here you can also see Pearl Lake and enjoy a fine view down the canyon of Trout Creek.

The Forest Service map shows an enticing loop possibility using a trail that drops to the right off Trail #738 about 0.4 mile beyond this second viewpoint. This obscure path, however, tends to disappear, leaving you with a frustrating bushwhack to reach the lake. It's better to turn around and return the way you came.

15 *Kid and Mud Lakes*

Distance: 10.6 miles roundtrip
Difficulty: strenuous
Hiking time: day hike or overnight
Elevation gain: 2050 feet
Season: mid-July through October
Best time: late July to early August and
mid to late September

Contact: Lolo NF, Ninemile Ranger District
Map: USGS Schley Mountain
GPS coordinates: N46° 47.484',
W114° 47.304'

Getting there: Take Fish Creek Road exit 66 off Interstate 90 west of Alberton and follow
the road on the south side of the freeway. After 0.8 mile bear right at a fork, now on Lower
Fish Creek Road, and proceed 0.7 mile to a junction where the pavement ends. Turn left
on Fish Creek Road (Forest Road 343), drive 7.6 miles, and then bear left at a fork and
proceed 6.5 miles to another junction. Turn right on FR 7734 (Surveyor Creek Road) and
drive this narrow and bumpy gravel road for 11.7 miles to a saddle and the well-developed
Schley Mountain Trailhead. Start your hike here if your car does not have good ground
clearance, adding 5.2 roundtrip miles to your hike. Those who don't shirk from a bit of
vehicular abuse can continue another 2.9 miles on a very bumpy, brushy, and rocky road to
its end at the Upper Schley Trailhead.

The drought-ridden summer of 1910 was plagued with many small forest fires throughout the northern Rockies. Then when a front came through packing hurricane force winds, these small fires suddenly coalesced into one enormous blaze in what has been called

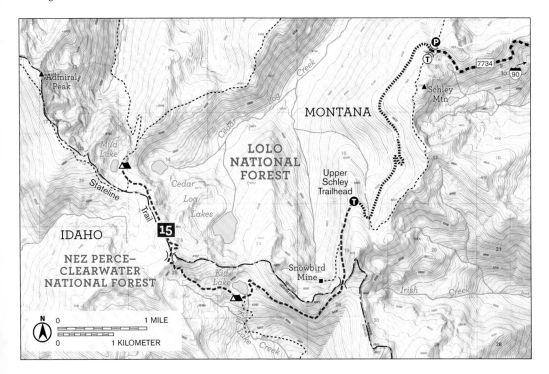

the Big Blowup. In just 36 horrific hours, the so-called Great Fire of 1910 burned an almost unimaginable 3 million acres (nearly the size of Connecticut) across a swath of northeast Washington, northern Idaho, and northwest Montana. The blaze killed at least 85 people, most of them hopelessly overmatched firefighters. It was the largest forest fire in US history and one of the largest in the recorded history of the world.

Today the legacy of this event can still be seen in the Great Burn Roadless Area along the Montana-Idaho border. This spectacular 250,000-acre region still has a few picturesque snags, but mostly what you'll see is mile after mile of relatively open terrain where the forests have never fully recovered in the century since the fire. The result is a dramatic landscape with great views, jagged peaks, sparkling lakes, unusually abundant wildflowers, and an alpine-like feel even though elevations are relatively low. This hike explores only a small corner of this area, but provides an excellent sampling of the beauty of this realm and a taste of why conservationists have been working for over three decades to ensure that this slice of once-charred heaven receives the wilderness protection it deserves.

Tiny pond above Mud Lake

If you started from the easier-on-your-car Schley Mountain Trailhead, you can either walk the road to the upper trailhead, or take the ruggedly scenic trail over Schley Mountain. This path climbs over the shoulder of the peak and then descends to meet the road at a switchback about 0.3 mile from the upper trailhead.

From the upper trailhead, the route starts behind a green gate and follows an old road through a relatively young forest of spruces, hemlocks, and firs. Along the way there are partially obstructed views to the north of orange-tinged Admiral Peak. After 0.3 mile, veer left at a junction and climb gradually for 0.5 mile to a 6548-foot pass on the Montana-Idaho border. From here you'll soak in terrific views of Kelly Creek canyon with rugged Williams and Rhodes Peaks in the background.

The rather rocky trail goes mostly downhill across a partly forested hillside, then descends a pair of switchbacks to reach Kid Lake at 2.3 miles. This lovely lake is backed by the rounded, multi-colored hump of a nameless butte to the northwest. In the latter half of July there are often thousands of beargrass blooming around the lake. A good campsite is located across the lake's outlet.

Go straight at a trail junction here and wind uphill through enchanting wildflower-covered meadows and over open hillsides. The well-maintained trail then makes a steep and rocky ascent to another crossing of the Idaho-Montana divide. From here enjoy excellent views northwest to Admiral Peak and Mud Lake.

The trail now descends the Montana side of the divide along a relatively gradual downhill through mostly forested terrain. At about 5 miles you pass an easy-to-miss junction with the continuation of the Stateline Trail, which goes sharply left. Keep straight and in a little under 0.3 mile come to the large and very beautiful meadows around scenic and misnamed Mud Lake. Pink elephanthead and yellow paintbrush bloom in profusion in these meadows, while white beargrass fills the transition zone between meadow and forest. There is a spacious campsite on the southeast side of the lake but backpackers should be prepared for mosquitoes through early August.

Tip: For a terrific side trip, follow the State-line Trail north along the ridge toward Admiral Peak. You can turn around after about 0.6 mile when you come to a nice viewpoint or go all the way to Admiral Peak, depending on your energy level.

16 *Cha-paa-qn Peak*

Distance: 7 miles roundtrip
Difficulty: strenuous
Hiking time: day hike
Elevation gain: 1850 feet
Season: late June through October

Best time: late June through October
Contact: Lolo NF, Ninemile Ranger District
Map: USGS Hewolf Mountain
GPS coordinates: N47° 08.214', W114° 18.606'

Getting there: From Missoula, go 19 miles west on Interstate 90 to Ninemile Road exit 82. Go north 1.5 miles, then veer right onto Remount Road, following signs to HISTORIC RANGER STATION. Proceed 2.7 miles to a four-way junction beside the Ninemile Ranger Station and go straight, still on Remount Road, which is now a good gravel thoroughfare that soon becomes Forest Road 476-1. After 1.6 miles, go right at a fork, then right again 1.4 miles later, now following signs for Edith Peak Road. This narrow road gets steep and rocky, but a high-clearance vehicle is not required. At 7.2 miles from the last junction you reach Reservation Divide and the signed trailhead on the left.

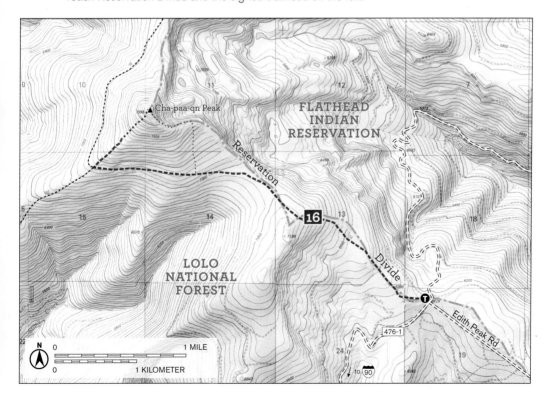

Looking west from atop Cha-paa-qn Peak

Missoula residents will recognize, although probably not be able to pronounce, Cha-paa-qn (formerly "Squaw") Peak as the tall pyramidal mountain to the west-northwest. Surprisingly few of those folks, however, actually visit this local landmark. But it's a fun hike and although the peak looks rather intimidating, the trail starts at high elevation, so most of the work is done before you even get out of the car. Although the hike's final 0.3 mile involves a steep scramble over a large boulder field, the route isn't dangerous as long as you check the stability of boulders as you go.

The trail goes west-northwest, never straying far from the top of the wide divide, which is covered with a high-elevation forest of spire-shaped subalpine firs. The well-maintained route ascends gradually through viewless forest for 0.9 mile—then the grade picks up as you gain almost 500 feet in the next 0.4 mile. After this steep section, the trail levels off and you cross a forested plateau where blue grouse and red squirrels often loudly announce their displeasure at your passing.

After crossing three seasonal trickles on plank bridges, you enter an open forest with plenty of midsummer wildflowers and partially obstructed views of the mountains and valley to the south. You then cross a series of open slopes with picturesque snags, talus fields, and lots of beargrass. These slopes provide better views to the south as well as glimpses of your destination, Cha-paa-qn Peak, still high above the trail on your right.

The easy hiking ends after 2.9 miles at a four-way junction. Turn right and climb an increasingly steep and rocky route that soon takes you above most of the trees to talus slopes with superb 180-degree vistas to the south toward the Bitterroot Mountains and the jumbled peaks in central Idaho.

To add another 180 degrees to the view, you must scramble to the top of Cha-paa-qn Peak, making your way up 0.3 mile of steep but non-technical talus and boulder fields dotted with occasional whitebark pines. Be sure to look back frequently, so you can recognize landmarks on the way back down. Also make sure to check the stability of boulders before putting your full weight on a possibly shifting rock.

From the top there are eye-popping views southeast to the Missoula area, northeast to the snowy Mission Range, and north to distant

Flathead Lake. Someone has built a low rock shelter at the summit with a colorful prayer flag, which adds to wonderful photo opportunities.

On the way back, you can either return the way you came, or for experienced scramblers only, pick your way down the steep eastern ridge of the peak to a relatively flat grassy area with excellent views back up to the rocky summit. From there walk downhill through sloping beargrass meadows and over talus fields to the trail you came in on.

17 *Bear Creek Overlook*

Distance: 5 miles roundtrip
Difficulty: moderate
Hiking time: day hike
Elevation gain: 1180 feet
Season: mid-June through October
Best time: late June through July

Contact: Bitterroot NF, Stevensville Ranger District
Map: USFS Selway-Bitterroot Wilderness: North
GPS coordinates: N46° 23.737', W114° 16.010'

Getting there: From Victor, on US 93 about 34 miles south of Missoula, go west on Fifth Street (one block south of the traffic light at Main Street) and drive 1.1 miles to a T intersection. Turn left on Pleasant View Drive and, shortly thereafter, veer right at a fork. The pavement ends in another 4.3 miles, after which you continue 2.2 miles and go left on Forest Road 1325, following signs to Bear Creek Overlook. Climb this narrow and sometimes rough road for 3.3 miles to an unsigned fork, go right, and proceed 0.4 mile to a wide pullout on the right on a minor ridgetop.

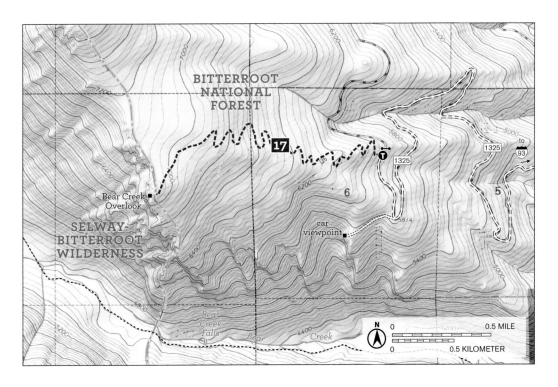

Sky Pilot from the Bear Creek Overlook

With a well-graded trail that travels just 2.5 miles to one of the best viewpoints in the Bitterroot Mountains, a hiker would have to look long and hard to find a trip with as much bang for the buck as Bear Creek Overlook. The mystery is why this overlook trail is so often overlooked. Since relatively few people take this route, there is a good chance you'll have the cliff-top grandstand, one of my favorite lunch spots in Montana, entirely to yourself.

An old trail climbs directly up the hill, but the better-graded new trail angles left and ascends gradually amid an open forest of lodgepole pines, Engelmann spruces, and Douglas firs. The forest floor supports a wealth of small shrubs and wildflowers, especially lousewort, fernleaf, grouse whortleberry, lupine, huckleberry, and beargrass. The trail climbs twenty-two mostly long switchbacks, recrossing the steeper old trail numerous times along the way. The ascent is pleasant and attractive, but mostly viewless. Things get much more interesting in the last 100 yards as you walk over rocky and increasingly open terrain to the incredibly dramatic cliff-edged viewpoint.

Wilderness vistas rarely get much better than this. Lichen-covered cliffs hundreds of feet tall drop off at your feet to the whitewater of Bear Creek Falls some 2400 feet below. Farther upstream, Bear Creek splits into three large sub-drainages, each carving its own dramatic canyon into the surrounding mountains. And those mountains are, perhaps, even more impressive than the canyons, as tall peaks fill the skyline, with the most prominent being craggy Totem Peak to the southwest and pyramid-shaped Sky Pilot to the northwest. Pull out your lunch and schedule at least an hour or two for enjoying this view.

18 *Canyon Lake*

Distance: 8.8 miles roundtrip
Difficulty: strenuous
Hiking time: day hike or overnight
Elevation gain: 2600 feet
Season: late June through October
Best time: late June through July

Contact: Bitterroot NF, Stevensville Ranger District
Map: USFS Selway Bitterroot Wilderness: North
GPS coordinates: N46° 15.155', W114° 14.851'

Getting there: From downtown Hamilton, go west on Main Street (SR 531) and follow this road through town and over a bridge across the Bitterroot River. At 1.8 miles go straight at a junction, now on Canyon Creek Road, drive 1 mile, and then turn left on Blodgett Camp Road. Go 1.4 miles, turn left on Canyon Creek Road North (Forest Road 735), and continue 2.9 miles on this rough and bumpy route to the road-end turnaround.

Although there are many strong contenders, Canyon Lake is perhaps the most beautiful body of water in the Bitterroot Mountains. The trail is a joy, with fine views of a 400-foot-tall sliding waterfall along the way, and the destination is an extremely photogenic mountain lake. A portion of the trail is quite steep, so you'll burn plenty of calories on the way in and abuse your knees on the way out, but such concerns disappear when you're sitting on the lakeshore enjoying scenery this great.

The trail goes west, following the north bank of unseen, but easily heard, Canyon Creek. After just 20 yards the Blodgett Canyon Overlook Trail bears right, but you keep straight and hike through lush streamside forests. Amid the Douglas firs, ponderosa pines, and tangled water-loving shrubs are lots of thimbleberry plants with their large, soft leaves and tart raspberry-like berries that ripen in late summer.

At about 0.8 mile, eight short switchbacks take you up an open slope with pungent deerbrush, small trees, and many silvery snags left over from an old forest fire. After this you reenter unburned forest and resume the pleasant ramble above Canyon Creek.

At 1.6 miles you pass beneath the towering cliffs of Romney Ridge on your right and enter

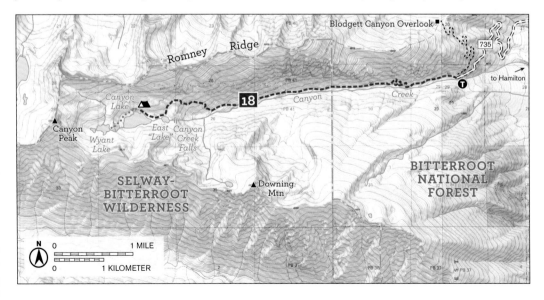

Canyon Peak over Canyon Lake

the Selway-Bitterroot Wilderness. Eventually you pull away from the creek and climb very steeply up a rocky and degraded trail. Partway up this tiring ascent you break out of the forest and cross sloping, ice-polished granite, which affords fine views to the southwest of several tall granite peaks and long Canyon Creek Falls.

At the top of this steep section, the trail descends almost 200 feet to a small meadow that holds a marshy pond called East "Lake" before reaching Canyon Lake at 4.4 miles. As with most lakes in the Bitterroots, this natural pool is made deeper by a rock irrigation dam. This intrusion, however, does little to detract from the superb scenery highlighted by the towering pinnacle of 9153-foot Canyon Peak rising over the lake's western shore. There are several popular camp-sites near the outlet and along the north shore.

Extend your hike: Explorers can follow a sketchy social trail around the north side of Canyon Lake. This path eventually devolves into a scramble route that goes up a steep boulder field to dramatic Wyant Lake. The neck-craning view of Canyon Peak and a portion of Romney Ridge backing this cold mountain lake (forget swimming) amply rewards your efforts to get here.

19 *Fuse Lake*

Distance: 5 miles roundtrip
Difficulty: moderate
Hiking time: day hike or overnight
Elevation gain: 900 feet
Season: July through October
Best time: mid-July to late September

Contact: Beaverhead-Deerlodge NF, Pintler Ranger District
Maps: USGS Mount Emerine, Stony Creek
GPS coordinates: N46° 13.568', W113° 43.769'

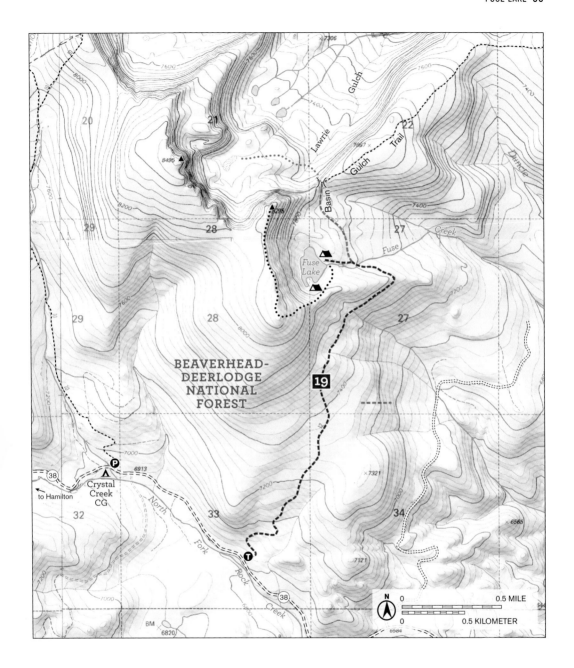

Getting there: From Hamilton, go 1.5 miles south on US 93, turn east on State Route 38, and drive 27 miles to Skalkaho Pass. Continue another 2.7 miles to a junction just past milepost 29, turn left onto a narrow gravel road with a sign for Trail #12, and go 0.1 mile to the trailhead parking lot.

Lawrie Gulch Meadow

The Sapphire Mountains, which rise from the east side of the Bitterroot Valley, generally lack the dramatic crags and ice-carved canyons that characterize the Bitterroot Mountains to the west. But the rolling Sapphires have many delights of their own, including attractive forests, plenty of wildlife, acres of wildflowers, and even a few hidden lakes set beneath craggy cliffs and peaks. This hike takes you to one of the best of those hidden lakes. Not only does Fuse Lake offer solitude and fine scenery, nearby is a wonderful off-trail exploration to a pretty meadow that is set beneath a dramatic line of rocky cliffs.

The trail gradually gains elevation as it follows an old gravel road up three sweeping switchbacks for 0.7 mile to the road's end at a small, recovering clear-cut. From here a rocky but well-defined path continues uphill at a moderate grade. The uphill eases off at about 1.5 miles when you begin contouring through attractive woods with lots of beargrass and grouse whortleberry covering the forest floor. You pass three talus fields where you may see or hear pikas, then reach a junction with Basin Gulch Trail at 2.3 miles.

For Fuse Lake go left and climb 0.2 mile past a tiny pond to the lake. This very scenic lake fills a compact bowl beneath an unnamed rocky ridge and offers better than average backcountry swimming and campsites. This lake contains arctic grayling, of particular interest to anglers.

Extend your hike: Since Fuse Lake is a fairly short hike, you may have energy left over for some exploring. The best option is a relatively easy off-trail route to the meadow at the head of Lawrie Gulch.

To reach it, backtrack 0.2 mile to the Basin Gulch Trail, turn north, and follow this indistinct route for 0.4 mile to a woodsy ridgetop saddle. Leave the trail here and drop down the north side of the ridge, following a very steep but well-defined elk trail that skirts a large rockslide. After losing about 200 feet of elevation, the elk trail peters out at the bottom of Lawrie Gulch. From here you turn left (west-northwest) and ascend through open forest for about 0.5 mile to a grassy meadow with a shallow seasonal pond. This unnamed meadow, which is home to a small herd of elk, sits below an extremely rugged line of cliffs with large talus fields at their base. It's a very scenic and photogenic location where solitude is virtually guaranteed.

20 *Piquett Mountain*

Distance: 10.2 miles roundtrip
Difficulty: strenuous
Hiking time: day hike or overnight
Elevation gain: 3800 feet
Season: July to mid-October
Best time: July

Contact: Bitterroot NF, West Fork
Ranger District
Maps: USGS Paintod Rocks Lake,
Piquett Mountain
GPS coordinates: N45° 43.142',
W114° 15.319'

Getting there: From US 93 about 4 miles south of Darby, turn right (south) onto West Side Road (State Route 473). Drive 22 miles to a junction atop Painted Rocks Dam, keep straight for another 0.2 mile, then turn left onto gravel Forest Road 1130, following signs to Little Boulder. Drive 1.1 miles to a T intersection and the trailhead directly in front of you.

Piquett Mountain is the tallest peak in a sprawling roadless area east of Painted Rocks Reservoir. Although not well known, the trail to the former lookout site is a rewarding and delightful hike despite demanding a fair amount of sweat to complete. The expansive summit views encompass wide swaths of two states and several towering mountain ranges. If you prefer relaxing beside scenic mountain lakes, a relatively easy side trip takes you to two beautiful high-elevation pools on the east side of the peak.

The brushy trail goes gradually uphill beside Little Boulder Creek in a relatively dense Douglas fir forest. At about 0.4 mile you cross the creek on narrow logs, then recross the stream at 1 mile, always maintaining a steady but never-too-steep uphill grade. Much of this area has been scarred by forest fires, and from early to midsummer beargrass, birchleaf spiraea, and fireweed bloom

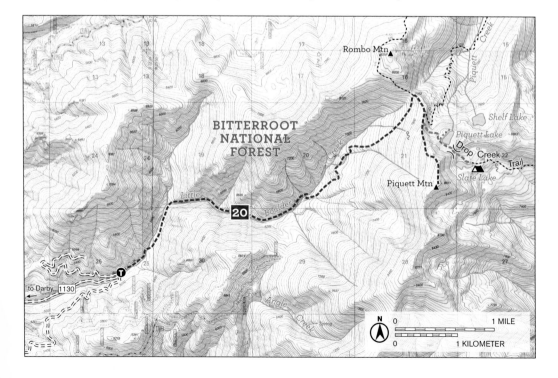

View to the north from atop Piquett Mountain

in abundant numbers in this blackened and sunny environment.

Hop over the creek a third time near 2.7 miles, cross a tributary creek 0.5 mile later, and then climb the now-rocky trail as it steeply ascends through a large burn area. At 4.2 miles is a signed ridgetop junction. Turn right (south) and follow the ridge toward Piquett Mountain. Ignore an unsigned trail that angles left about 0.15 mile later, then steeply climb to a signed junction at 4.5 miles.

To reach Piquett Mountain, climb a steep and rocky ridge that heads directly toward the summit. After 0.5 mile and a couple of switchbacks you'll reach the former lookout site on the treeless top of the peak. The superb views from this 8831-foot grandstand include Trapper Peak and the snowy Bitterroot Mountains dominating the skyline to the north, the rounded Sapphire Range to the northeast, and Painted Rocks Reservoir and the mountains of central Idaho to the west.

Extend your hike: To see Piquett and Slate Lakes, from the junction below Piquett Mountain, go left on Drop Creek Trail, which traverses a rocky hillside on the northeast side of the mountain. A short climb amid scraggly alpine larches takes you to the narrow basin holding beautiful Piquett Lake. There are no good campsites here but the fishing for cutthroat trout is usually very good and you'll want to explore to the oblong-shaped lake's northeast end to enjoy the excellent views up to snow-streaked Piquett Mountain.

To visit even prettier—but fishless—Slate Lake, take the trail skirting the southwest shore of Piquett Lake and climb briefly over a rocky saddle. The path then descends 150 feet to Slate Lake. The camping prospects are much better here than at Piquett Lake and the scenery is better as well, with wonderful views across the water to the talus fields and snowbanks of Piquett Mountain.

21 *Dempsey Basin*

Distance: 10.6 miles roundtrip
Difficulty: strenuous
Hiking time: day hike or overnight
Elevation gain: 2450 feet
Season: late June to mid-October
Best time: July

Contact: Beaverhead-Deerlodge NF,
Pintler Ranger District
Maps: USGS Mount Powell, Pozega Lakes
GPS coordinates: N46° 19.012',
W112° 55.435'

Getting there: Take Racetrack exit 195 off Interstate 90 south of Deer Lodge, go west, and then straight through a four-way junction. After 1 mile turn left at a T intersection onto Yellowstone Trail Road, drive 0.8 mile, and then turn right at an unsigned junction onto a paved road that soon changes to good gravel. Proceed 3.5 miles, then turn right at the second of two four-way junctions onto Upper Racetrack Road. Go 3.1 miles, bear left onto Perkins Road, and just 0.1 mile later turn right (uphill) on Forest Road 8507, following signs to Dempsey Creek. Stay on this narrow and rocky road, which eventually becomes FR 670, for 7.6 miles to the trailhead and horse loading ramp.

The Flint Creek Range is a cluster of tall peaks, forested uplands, and lake-filled basins which, except during hunting season, sees only light recreational use. But those who ignore this mountain range are making a mistake, because the upper basin of Dempsey Creek hides several scenic lakes surrounded by peaks up to 10,000 feet high. The access trail follows an old road but only a few motorized users come here, so it remains a pleasant hike, especially on weekdays.

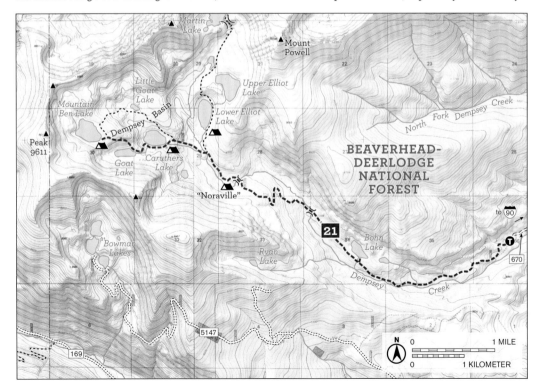

Peak 9611 over Mountain Ben Lake

Mountain Ben Lake, the area's highest and most scenic, is the destination of this adventure.

Walk up the continuation of the road, now just a rocky and eroded ATV route, through a fairly open lodgepole pine forest. At 2.1 miles a short spur road goes right to Bohn Lake, which is really a controlled reservoir, but still scenic and worth a look. Another 0.8 mile takes you to a wooden boardwalk over Dempsey Creek.

After this crossing, the road ascends a winding switchback. Then, at 3.7 miles, look for a marked trail that goes right to a second bridge over the creek. About 0.2 mile later you pass a developed hunter's campsite signed as NORAVILLE.

At 4.1 miles is an important junction. The Martin Lake Trail goes right (a good side trip), but you turn left on Mountain Ben Trail and almost immediately ford Dempsey Creek. The rocky trail then passes a beautiful meadow with excellent views of the high peaks in the Flint Creek Range before making a short but steep climb to large Caruthers Lake. The beauty of this lake is lessened by the large dam holding back its waters, but it's still very scenic and offers fishing and a good campsite.

To reach the area's prettiest lakes, cross the dam at Caruthers Lake, then pick your way along the southern shoreline for 0.2 mile to the inlet creek. Cross this creek and then pick up a well-defined trail that travels upstream to Goat Lake. This lake also has a dam, but offers excellent swimming and superb scenery.

From Goat Lake the rocky trail climbs steeply to Mountain Ben Lake. Beautiful Peak 9611 rises majestically above the lake's western shore and there is a scenic and comfortable campsite. Alpine larches rim the shore and put on a fine display in the fall, but the lake is stunning at any time of the year.

22 *Goat Flat and Upper Seymour Lake*

Distance: 5 miles roundtrip to Goat Flat; 11 miles roundtrip to Upper Seymour Lake
Difficulty: strenuous
Hiking time: day hike or overnight
Elevation gain: 1250 feet to Goat Flat; 2600 feet to Upper Seymour Lake
Season: mid-July to mid-October

Best time: late July to mid-August, late September
Contact: Beaverhead-Deerlodge NF, Pintler and Wise River Ranger Districts
Map: Cairn Cartographics Anaconda-Pintler Wilderness
GPS coordinates: N46° 04.470', W113° 16.116'

Getting there: From Anaconda, go 11 miles west on State Route 1, then turn south near milepost 21.3 onto gravel Storm Lake Road (Forest Road 675). Drive 0.4 mile, go left at a fork, and proceed 2.7 miles to a second fork. Keep left again, staying on FR 675, and drive 3.6 miles to a point where the road crosses a bridge over Storm Lake Creek. There is parking here, and if your vehicle doesn't have good ground clearance, you should walk the last 1.3 miles to Storm Lake. Once you reach the lake, cross the dam blocking the outlet to a small parking area and trailhead.

Goat Flat is one of the great wilderness treasures in the Treasure State. This enormous alpine meadow offers endless views, acres of delicate wildflowers in midsummer, and thousands of colorful yellow alpine larch trees in early fall. Wildlife is common, especially bighorn sheep, and the exploring opportunities are limitless. If you're backpacking, the best option is nearby Upper Seymour Lake, a large and exceptionally scenic lake at the base of massive Kurt Peak.

Kurt Peak over Upper Seymour Lake

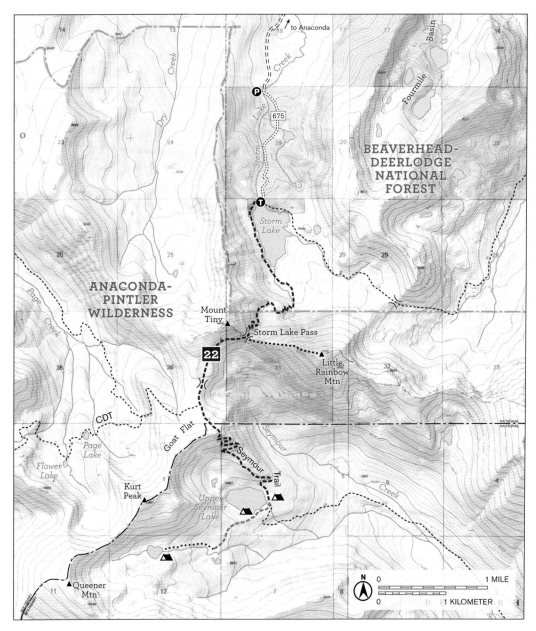

Large Storm Lake is backed by the bulky mass of Little Rainbow Mountain to the south and misnamed Mount Tiny to the southwest. You'll have fine views of both, as well as a distinctive haystack-shaped mountain to the east-southeast, as you hike the first 0.5 mile along the western shore of the lake. Once past the lake, the trail climbs briefly, crosses the inlet creek, and reaches a wilderness registration box. More climbing ensues as you ascend at a moderate grade through a high-elevation forest of lodgepole pines, Engelmann spruces, and alpine larches. As you switchback up a hillside, the tree cover is soon dominated by alpine larches, one of Montana's most beautiful trees, especially in late September and early October when they turn a lovely golden color. A dozen well-graded switchbacks take you up to an unofficial junction at Storm Lake Pass. The trail to the left is the climber's route up Little Rainbow Mountain, a steep but not technically difficult side trip.

Go right and make a gentle uphill traverse beneath tall cliffs for 0.4 mile to the edge of Goat Flat at 2.5 miles. A wide range of wildflowers carpet this mile-wide, gently rolling paradise, and alpine larches turn the place yellow in the fall. Together they make this one of the most colorful and delightful hiking destinations in Montana. In addition, the views of distant valleys and mountains as well as several nearby pyramid-shaped peaks are superb. Although it is named for mountain goats, bighorn sheep are more commonly seen, feeding on the area's nutritious grasses.

The faint trail (look for posts) descends to a saddle at the low point of Goat Flat, then climbs to a signed junction. Go left on Seymour Trail #131 and ascend the southeast side of Goat Flat over tundra and past wind-stunted alpine larches. The tread is nearly nonexistent, but posts and cairns mark the way, and if you stay fairly close to the drop-off on your left you can't get lost. After climbing for 0.3 mile you reach a drop-off at the southeast corner of Goat Flat. From here you can see the shimmering expanse of Upper Seymour Lake and enjoy fine views down the valley of Seymour Creek.

The trail now descends eleven gently graded switchbacks, losing 1100 feet before reaching forest-rimmed Upper Seymour Lake. The view

A male spruce grouse in the Bitterroot Mountains

across the calm waters of this lake to imposing Kurt Peak is awesome. There are fine campsites here offering the opportunity to enjoy a superb night in the wilderness, perhaps fishing for some of the lake's rainbow trout.

Extend your hike: For an additional fun exploration, follow the trail along the east shore of Upper Seymour Lake for 0.1 mile to the outlet creek. Turn right at a poorly marked junction, cross the outlet, and pick up an obvious trail that passes some superb campsites along the lake's southeast shore. The trail then pulls away from the water and climbs gently through forest for 0.8 mile to where the tread disappears just above a marshy little meadow on your left. From here simply wander cross-country uphill through open forest, generally staying to the right of a pretty little creek. After about 0.6 mile you'll come to a basin with a supremely scenic but unnamed lake. In late September the alpine larches around this lake put on a spectacular show, with Queener Mountain and Kurt Peak providing dramatic backdrops. Fires are prohibited within 0.25 mile of this lake.

23 *Lake of the Isle*

Distance: 9.2 miles roundtrip
Difficulty: strenuous
Hiking time: day hike or overnight
Elevation gain: 1800 feet
Season: mid-July to October
Best time: late July to mid-August, late
September

Contact: Beaverhead-Deerlodge NF,
Pintler Ranger District
Map: Cairn Cartographics Anaconda-
Pintler Wilderness
GPS coordinates: N46° 07.837',
W113° 12.805'

Getting there: From Anaconda, drive 9 miles west on State Route 1 to milepost 19.2, then turn left, following signs to Spring Hill Picnic Area. After less than 0.1 mile, turn left onto a gravel road that eventually becomes rather rough Forest Road 171. After 2 miles, pass the historic Twin Lakes Creek Flume and reach a junction. Go left and carefully drive 2.1 miles, following signs to Trails 44 and 113 at a couple of minor intersections, to the road-end trailhead.

Tucked away in a remote subalpine basin, Lake of the Isle is a strikingly beautiful destination well suited to either a rugged day hike or a fun overnight outing. The lake is also a good base camp for exploring to a higher off-trail lake or climbing nearby Mount Evans.

Climb along a continuation of the rocky road, traveling through an old clear-cut, now

Mount Evans towers over an unnamed lake above Lake of the Isle.

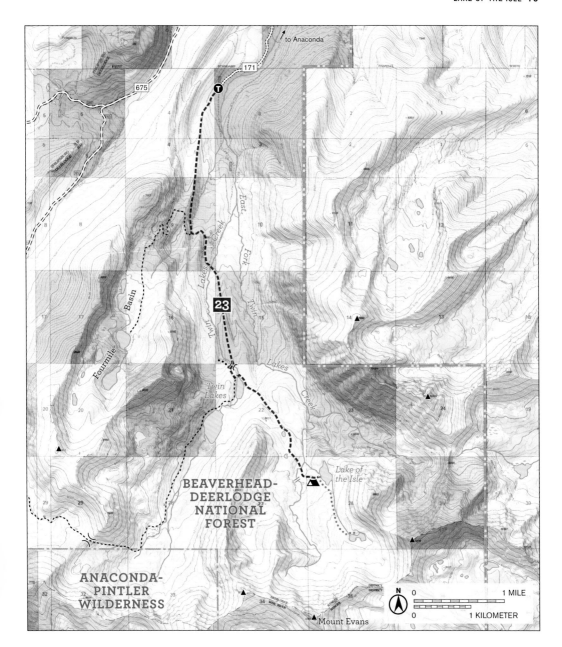

repopulating with young lodgepole pines. After 0.25 mile, reach the end of the road and fork left on a new trail that gradually gains elevation in the old logging scar. At 1.3 miles is a signed junction with the Fourmile Basin Trail, which goes right.

Keep left, and continue gradually climbing for 1.5 miles to where you finally leave the old clear-cut and enter forest. You then cross Twin Lakes Creek on a bridge and soon thereafter see the remains of the old trail coming in from the right. Keep left and 0.2 mile later look for a tree blaze marking an unsigned trail that goes left.

Take this unsigned trail and almost immediately make an easy but potentially wet crossing of Twin Lakes Creek. The route then follows the eastern shore of Lower Twin Lake, going about halfway around that pretty lake before climbing away from the water.

The rocky and intermittently steep route now ascends through viewless forest to a small, marshy lake with nice views of reddish-colored Mount Evans to the south. The trail then goes mostly downhill for 0.4 mile to a fork just before a meadow holding East Fork Twin Lakes Creek. Take the right fork and walk around and then through a boggy area to a crossing of the amazingly clear creek.

The distinct tread reappears after the creek crossing and goes steeply uphill past a small waterfall to a lush and scenic meadow. A final 200-foot climb takes you to the subalpine splendor of Lake of the Isle. Tall ridges and peaks rise dramatically above this forest-rimmed pool and there are excellent campsites for the overnight hiker. With relatively little effort, the trout are both large and fun to catch.

Extend your hike: From the southern tip of the lake, explorers can travel cross-country up the splashing inlet creek for 0.8 mile to a beautiful upper lake directly beneath colorful Mount Evans. This lake is surrounded by alpine larches that turn golden yellow in late September.

Opposite, top: Locoweed, Lima Peaks

Opposite, bottom: Along the trail to Upper Minor Lake

Southwest Montana

A black bear in the Beaverhead Mountains

Although less popular than Montana's more famous hiking areas, you could make a strong case that the state's finest trails are tucked away in its southwest corner. The peaks are almost as tall and rugged as in better-known destinations, but here they are more open in character with high valleys and huge alpine expanses offering seemingly endless views. The wildlife is abundant, the wildflower displays are superb, the weather is usually better, and the trails are never crowded. In fact, on most hikes it is unusual to see more than one or two other people in a full day of hiking.

This part of Montana is characterized by sagebrush-covered, high-elevation basins surrounded by tall and generally lightly forested mountain ranges. The most prominent ranges are the dramatic Beaverhead Mountains along the Idaho border, the craggy and lake-dotted Pioneer Mountains, the meadow-covered Gravelly and Snowcrest Ranges, and the tall Tobacco Root Mountains featuring everything from lakes to sky-scraping peaks. Situated in the rain shadow of several lofty Idaho mountain ranges, southwest Montana gets less snow than other parts of the state, so the hiking season starts weeks earlier than similar high-elevation areas.

Thunderstorms are fairly common on summer afternoons, so watch the skies carefully. There are also a few grizzly bears, especially in the Gravelly and Centennial Ranges, where you should carry bear spray. Finally, the road access is often pretty lousy, so bring a rugged car with good ground clearance. Still, you won't be sorry about hiking in this little-visited paradise. In fact, the scenery and solitude will soon have you coming back for more.

24 *Rock Island Lakes*

Distance: 6.7 miles roundtrip
Difficulty: strenuous
Hiking time: day hike or overnight
Elevation gain: 1600 feet
Season: late June through mid-October
Best time: September

Contact: Beaverhead-Deerlodge NF, Wisdom Ranger District
Maps: USGS Homer Youngs Peak, Miner Lake
GPS coordinates: N45° 17.655', W113° 37.284'

Getting there: From the resort community of Jackson, drive 0.5 mile south on State Route 278, then turn right on gravel Miner Lake Road (Forest Road 182). Go 13.5 miles to a well-signed trailhead at the far end of Miner Lake Campground. If you don't have a rugged car with good ground clearance, park here. If you can, drive very rough and rocky FR 182 for 2.9 miles to the road-end trailhead.

The Rock Island Lakes offer a subdued but attractive setting beneath the slopes of Homer Youngs Peak. The lakes are particularly appealing to adventurous hikers because they serve as the portal for some superb exploring to a host of wildly scenic lakes deep among the crags of the Beaverhead Mountains.

Warning: The Beaverhead Mountains suffer from plagues of mosquitoes in early summer, so plan to visit in late summer or fall.

Pick up the continuation of the abandoned jeep track and go gradually uphill through a mostly lodgepole pine forest. At 0.2 mile there is a junction with the Continental Divide Trail

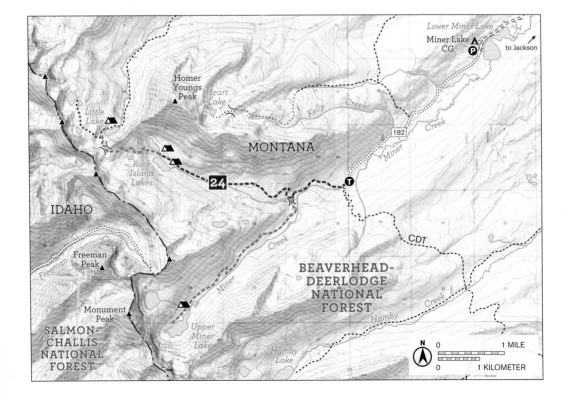

A reflective lake above Rock Island Lakes

(CDT). Keep straight, still on what's left of the jeep track, and steadily climb a forested hillside broken up by one sloping meadow. Pass through a wooden fence, and at just under 1 mile, reach an obvious junction beside a bridge.

The trail to the left crosses the bridge then in 2 easy miles takes you to exceptionally scenic Upper Miner Lake, a superb side trip. To reach the Rock Island Lakes, however, you veer right at the junction and follow a trail that switchbacks once and crosses the bed of the old road. You soon return to the rocky jeep track, which steeply climbs as it plays hide and seek with a cascading creek on your left. Things level out where you pass a small, lush meadow with good views of Homer Youngs Peak. From here it's a gentle streamside ascent to the first Rock Island Lake at 3.2 miles. This long, oval-shaped pool has good campsites and pleasant views of some rounded peaks to the south and west. The trail veers to the right at the first lake and climbs a bit to the meadow-rimmed and slightly more scenic upper lake.

Extend your hike: For the most dramatic scenery, continue on the CDT as it crosses the strip of land between the two Rock Island Lakes and climbs three moderately graded switchbacks to a gorgeous unnamed lake with a pretty little island and stunning views of a tall snow-streaked peak to the southwest. This lake gets far fewer visitors than the Rock Island Lakes, so solitude is a bonus.

If you're still bursting with energy, continue on the CDT as it climbs steeply to a high pass. From there you'll have a great view of the rugged peaks of the Beaverhead Mountains stretching to the north. Experienced hikers can scramble to a pair of off-trail lakes in the high basins west and northwest of Little Lake. The scenery and solitude are off the charts.

25 *Pioneer Lake*

Distance: 11 miles roundtrip
Difficulty: strenuous
Hiking time: overnight
Elevation gain: 1900 feet
Season: July through mid-October
Best time: July through September

Contact: Beaverhead-Deerlodge NF, Wisdom Ranger District
Map: USGS Goldstone Pass
GPS coordinates: N45° 12.413', W113° 31.207'

Getting there: From the resort community of Jackson, drive 0.8 mile south on State Route 278, then turn right on gravel Skinner Meadows Road. Follow this route, which eventually becomes Forest Road 381, for 11.3 miles to South Van Houten Campground. Continue another 2.9 miles to the turnoff for FR 7328, which goes right. A sign here

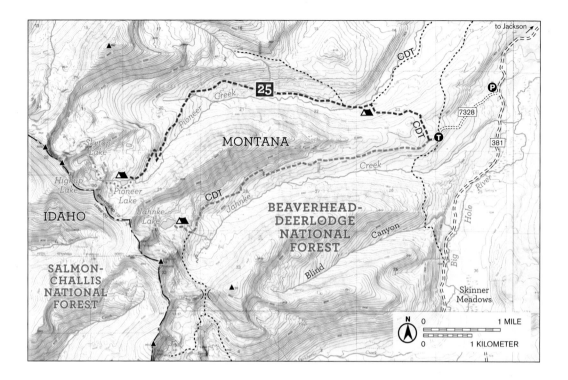

correctly warns PRIMITIVE ROAD. Unless you are an experienced driver and your vehicle has very good ground clearance, park here. Those whose vehicles can make it should drive FR 7328 another 1.2 miles to the road's end.

Pioneer Lake is a superb short backpacking trip to a small but gorgeous lake set beneath the remote crags of the little-visited Beaverhead Mountains. Although worth the effort all by itself, the lake also offers excellent opportunities for side trips.

The trail gradually ascends a long-abandoned road through open forest for 0.25 mile to a junction with the Continental Divide Trail (CDT). If you are looking for a shorter hike, you could go straight here and wander over grassy areas and through open forests for almost 4 miles to a junction where you go right and climb for another 0.3 mile to lovely Jahnke Lake.

For the star attraction, however, turn sharply right on the northbound CDT as it goes over a low, rounded ridge, and then slowly descends to an unsigned junction above Pioneer Creek at 1.2 miles. The CDT goes sharply right, but you veer left and follow a wide track upstream for 0.1 mile to a mediocre campsite and a creek crossing; logs are usually available to allow for dry feet.

Just 0.1 mile after the crossing, bear left at a fork onto an unsigned but distinct trail. For the next 1.5 miles, follow this gentle path along meandering Pioneer Creek, passing a series of little meadows where moose are sometimes present. The tread briefly disappears in a few grassy places but it's always easy to relocate on the other side. Eventually the trail climbs more noticeably as it pulls away from the stream.

In a lush little meadow near 3.9 miles, hop over an unnamed creek, and then climb at a fairly steep grade. After a pair of switchbacks, the last 0.5 mile is fairly gentle as you cross a hillside with increasingly frequent breaks in the tree cover offering views of a tall and rugged ridge to the south.

Clouds above Pioneer Lake

Small Pioneer Lake makes its appearance at 5.5 miles. This forest- and rock-rimmed lake offers fine scenery with several beautiful but unnamed peaks and ridges rimming its basin. The lake also has a small population of good-sized cutthroat trout and a couple of lightly used campsites, one near the outlet and another along the south shore.

Extend your hike: From Pioneer Lake, consider making an off-trail side trip to the two higher and even more scenic lakes in this basin. To reach the first, Highup Lake, follow Pioneer Lake's trickling inlet creek up a steep and rocky slope to the west-northwest. This gorgeous lake is situated right below a row of unnamed cliffs that top out near 10,000 feet.

Even more dramatically scenic is oblong-shaped Skytop Lake, situated in a miniature basin north-northwest of Highup Lake. It can be reached with an easy climb over open and rocky ground. The lake provides stupendous views of a 10,000-foot peak and has a permanent snowfield at its western end. Golden trout live in this cold lake, for those interested in trying to catch these beautiful fish.

26 *Harrison Lake*

Distance: 8.2 miles roundtrip
Difficulty: moderate to strenuous
Hiking time: day hike or overnight
Elevation gain: 1550 feet
Season: mid-June through October
Best time: late June through July

Contact: Beaverhead-Deerlodge NF, Dillon Ranger District
Map: USGS Tash Peak
GPS coordinates: N45° 17.346', W113° 10.704'

Getting there: From Big Hole Pass on State Route 278 about halfway between Dillon and Wisdom, turn south on the access road to a paved parking area. After 50 yards, turn right on Forest Road 7350 where a sign says HARRISON LAKE TRAIL 6. Drive this narrow dirt-and-gravel road for 1.1 miles, keep left at a fork, and then continue 4.6 miles through a gate to the road-end trailhead.

Harrison Lake is an exceptionally pretty pool set beneath the talus slopes of Harrison Peak in the Big Hole Divide. When I first spotted this place on the map, my inquiries to local hiking experts came up empty, since, without exception, not a soul had ever been there. (A few couldn't even locate the Big Hole Divide, so perhaps I should take them off my list of "experts.") The point is that if you're seeking a swimmable mountain lake with fine scenery and plenty of solitude, Harrison Lake may be the perfect destination.

The trail takes a wooden stair-step hiker's access over a fence and then descends briefly to a hop-over crossing of Wakefield Creek. For the next mile, head south with only minor ups and downs through a mostly Douglas fir forest. In late June, wildflowers are everywhere with vetch, yarrow, pussytoes, blue-eyed Mary, monument plant, penstemon, goldenrod, and a particular abundance of arnica with its cheery yellow blossoms.

Eventually the trail curves to the west heading up the canyon of Harrison Creek. Cross this rushing little stream on a rotting log bridge at 1.5 miles, then steadily ascend through forests of lodgepole pines and Engelmann spruces on the south side of the stream. Jump across the creek three times in the next 0.7 mile before ascending into increasingly open forests and small meadows along a tributary creek.

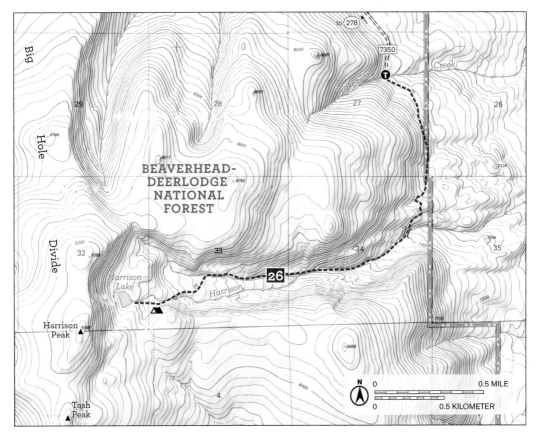

Arnica blooming along Harrison Lake Trail

At about 3.2 miles, traverse the base of a large talus slope then cross the nascent creek one final time. The rocky trail takes you into ever more scenic country as you pass a rugged butte on your left and enjoy nice views of a slightly reddish-tinged ridge to the west. The tread disappears where you cross a large boulder field. The proper course heads due west toward a prominent post marking the route. From there the faint tread crosses a small meadow and then makes a short, steep climb up a grassy swale to the shores of Harrison Lake.

This small lake has no jagged peaks around it, but is still very scenic with the steep talus slopes of Harrison Peak rising directly above its western shore. The lake is stocked with cutthroat trout and gets relatively light fishing pressure, so your chances should be pretty good. Unfortunately, the rocky terrain makes setting up a tent problematic, so it's better to look for a campsite in the forest around the small meadow below the lake.

27 Crescent Lake

Distance: 12 miles roundtrip
Difficulty: strenuous
Hiking time: overnight
Elevation gain: 1600 feet
Season: July through mid-October
Best time: July to early August

Contact: Beaverhead-Deerlodge NF, Wise River Ranger District
Maps: USGS Maurice Mountain, Mount Tahepia
GPS coordinates: N45° 37.639', W112° 56.274'

Getting there: From Melrose, exit 93 off Interstate 15 about 20 miles south of Butte, go 0.3 mile west, and then keep straight at a four-way junction onto Trapper Creek Road After 1.7 miles, bear right at a fork and proceed 4 miles to a junction just past the remains of the Glendale ghost town. Turn right onto Canyon Creek Road, which eventually becomes Forest Road 7401, drive 11.4 miles, and park in a pullout just past the Canyon Creek Trailhead.

In the heart of the spectacular Pioneer Mountains, Crescent Lake is a supremely scenic destination that provides excellent backcountry fishing and camping. For added interest, the access trail visits several additional wonderfully scenic lakes and high meadows in this delightful country. Other nearby lakes offer enough additional superb destinations for several days of hiking fun.

The trail immediately crosses Canyon Creek on a wooden bridge and turns upstream. The grade is very gentle as you wander along a forested hillside above the willow-lined creek enjoying the pleasant scenery of Canyon Creek's wide canyon. At a little less than 0.4 mile you pass through a fence and meet a trail coming in from Canyon Creek Campground. At 0.5 mile a second

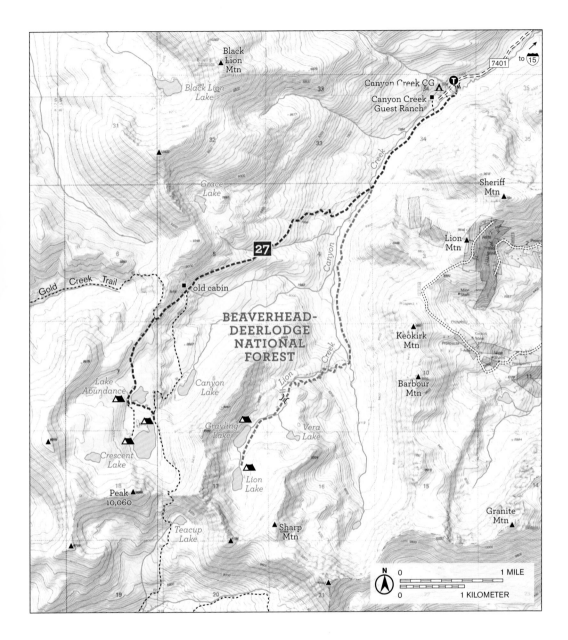

trail comes in from the right, this one from the Canyon Creek Guest Ranch. The ranch uses this trail for horse rides, so you can expect frequent equestrian traffic. Near 1.4 miles the trail forks.

Go right and drop to a calf-deep ford of Canyon Creek, although by searching a bit it's usually possible to locate a convenient log. The trail then climbs an open slope with nice views of the nearby peaks and valleys. An often-steep ascent, including a handful of scattered switchbacks, takes you to the roofless remains of an old miner's cabin, and less than 0.1 mile later, an unsigned split in the trail. Bear right, pass just below an old mine tunnel, and then climb

Angler at Crescent Lake

on often sandy tread to a junction with the faint Gold Creek Trail at 4.8 miles.

Go straight and travel up and down through high-elevation forests and meadows. After a short downhill, you reach Lake Abundance. This very scenic lake offers good fishing, decent campsites, and some exceptionally nice diving rocks for swimmers.

The trail skirts the west side of Lake Abundance, then turns east and comes to a confusing junction. A heavily used horse trail goes right, but you stay on the less obvious hiker's trail that hugs the south shore of Lake Abundance to a second junction. Go right at the second junction and soon come to stunning Crescent Lake. Dotted with rocky islands and backed by the huge bulk of Peak 10,060, this lake is outstandingly scenic. There are good campsites tucked away in hidden niches around the shoreline. The best sites are on the north and west sides of the lake.

Extend your hike: There are several possible alternate destinations in this area, but the best is the trail to Grayling and Lion Lakes. To take it, turn left at the junction at 1.4 miles and gently ascend to a nice little wildflower meadow and a rock-hop crossing of an unnamed creek.

From here you climb two dozen switchbacks to Grayling Lake, which offers very good scenery, better than average fishing, and good camps above the northeast shore. A short additional climb leads to Lion Lake. This stunningly beautiful lake, which sits beneath a row of snow-streaked crags on the slopes of Sharp Mountain, rates a "10" with even the most persnickety scorer. Superb camps near the outlet entice the overnight hiker and there is the possibility of fish for dinner. Look for mountain goats on the crags above the lake.

28 *Gorge Lakes*

Distance: 9.8 miles roundtrip
Difficulty: strenuous
Hiking time: day hike or overnight
Elevation gain: 2200 feet
Season: July through mid-October
Best time: mid-July to early August

Contact: Beaverhead-Deerlodge NF,
Dillon Ranger District
Maps: USGS Mount Tahepia,
Torrey Mountain
GPS coordinates: N45° 29.388',
W112° 53.250'

Getting there: From Apex, take exit 74 off Interstate 15 north of Dillon, then go 4.6 miles west on gravel Birch Creek Road to where the road narrows and becomes Forest Road 98. Drive another 3.8 miles, bear right at a fork, and proceed 1.2 miles to a second fork. Go right again (uphill) onto FR 82, following signs to Willow Creek. This road eventually gets quite rough with many nasty rocks that necessitate a car with good ground clearance. At 6.6 miles from the FR 98 turnoff, a road forks left (downhill) with a sign reading PRIMITIVE ROAD—NOT MAINTAINED BEYOND THIS POINT. Unless you're driving a high-clearance, four-wheel-drive vehicle, park in the small pullout just before this fork.

Rimmed by tall granite peaks, the Gorge Lakes may be the most scenic lakes in the Pioneer Mountains. The road access is rather rough, so take a car that can handle the abuse. However, the trail is in good shape, and your efforts are so amply rewarded at trail's end, I guarantee you won't be disappointed.

Walk down the primitive road to a culvert over Willow Creek, then follow Gorge Creek upstream. Pass a small meadow called Winkley Camp, then reach the signed official trailhead for Gorge Lakes Trail where the jeep road ends at 0.9 mile.

The rocky trail continues upstream, amid lodgepole pine and Engelmann spruce forests and through a hiker's V access across a wooden fence. Soon the trail pulls away from Gorge Creek, climbing at a moderately steep grade

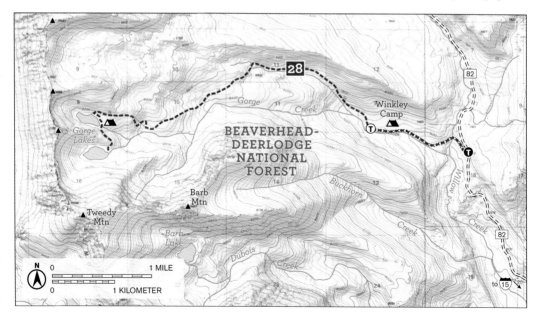

through open forest that offers tantalizing glimpses of the peaks to the west.

At a little less than 3 miles, cross a flattened log over a tributary creek and then climb through an increasingly open forest which offers excellent views of the spiky peaks that rim the Gorge Lakes basin. After a brief downhill, you reach the north shore of Gorge Lake #1 at 4.4 miles.

This lake sits in a spectacular basin of light-colored granite and is supremely photogenic. The lake has cutthroat trout, but they tend to be challenging to catch. There is a good campsite along the northeast shore.

To visit almost equally lovely Gorge Lake #2, take an angler's trail to a campsite near the outlet of Gorge Lake #1, cross the outlet creek, and then follow cairns marking a sketchy footpath that cuts neatly across a steep slope for 0.5 mile to the second lake. The setting for this gem is enchanting, although it may not be quite as dramatic as Lake #1. Camping prospects are more limited here, so backpackers are better off staying at the first lake.

Gorge Lake #1

29 Eighteenmile Peak Loop

Distance: 8-mile loop
Difficulty: very strenuous
Hiking time: day hike or overnight
Elevation gain: 3300 feet
Season: mid-June through October
Best time: late June through mid-July

Contact: Beaverhead-Deerlodge NF, Dillon Ranger District
Maps: USGS Eighteenmile Peak, Cottonwood Creek
GPS coordinates: N44° 28.170', W112° 56.892'

Getting there: From the tiny community of Dell at exit 23 off Interstate 15, cross to the west side of the freeway and follow Westside Frontage Road to the southeast. After 1.8 miles, turn right on gravel Big Sheep Creek Road and drive 17 miles to a major junction. Go left, following signs to Nicholia Creek, and 0.2 mile later go left again. Now on Forest Road 657, drive 6.5 miles and keep left at a fork, after which the road gets noticeably rougher, although it's still okay for passenger cars when conditions are dry. About 0.4 mile later, ford first an irrigation ditch and then Cottonwood Creek (usually not a problem after mid-June) and 0.5 mile later reach a junction. You may prefer to park and walk from this point.

If your car has good ground clearance and decent power, turn right onto FR 3928, a steep and rocky route. Follow this road for 1.3 miles to a signed junction. There is room to park here, if you've had enough of abusing your car. Go right onto FR 8274, ford an irrigation ditch, and climb this rocky road for 0.9 mile to First Harkness Lake.

Eighteenmile Peak is the highest point on the Continental Divide in Montana. Other than ensuring absolutely fabulous views, this qualifies as one of those facts that climbers get all excited about, but causes hikers to say "so what?" What *will* excite hikers, however, is the area's tremendous scenery. The magnificent orange-tinged mountain is surrounded by open country where the views seem to stretch to eternity. The approach hike features a cluster of trout-filled pothole lakes, slopes covered with early-summer wildflowers, and a spectacular alpine lake right at the base of Eighteenmile Peak's cliffs. This remote area also serves as a vitally important wildlife corridor connecting the Yellowstone region with western and northern Montana, so wildlife sightings are common.

From First Harkness Lake, follow a faint ATV track that goes around the south side of the lake and steeply climbs a little hill. All around you is rolling terrain covered with sagebrush and wildflowers, while directly ahead towers Eighteenmile Peak with its striking orange coloration. The faint track follows the top of a little ridge for 0.4 mile to an intersection with a jeep road a little southwest of Second Harkness Lake. Posts mark this road as the Continental Divide Trail (CDT).

Turn right and follow the jeep road past a couple of ponds and through a fence to a hop-over crossing of Cottonwood Creek. From here, skirt the east side of a large meadow that is fenced off as private property. Near 1.5 miles, or about 120 yards after the road makes a sharp left turn, is an unsigned but obvious fork.

The CDT goes right, but you bear left and make a short, steep climb up a ridge. Look for wildlife in this area including moose and large herds of elk. The trail follows a little ridge, taking you ever closer to Eighteenmile Peak and the huge cliff-walled cirque on its northeast side. After not quite 0.6 mile the grassy track ends at a spring with a livestock watering trough.

From here, angle slightly downhill (southwest) going cross-country through open forest. You'll cross a couple of tributary creeks before

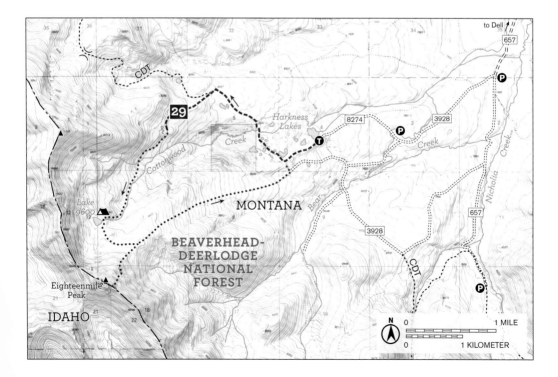

reaching the rushing main stem of Cottonwood Creek. Follow it steeply upstream for almost 1 mile to Lake 9600 (named for its elevation) on the northeast side of Eighteenmile Peak.

This might be the most beautiful lake in Montana that nobody ever visits. Backed by rugged 1500-foot cliffs and talus slopes of orange-tinged rock, and surrounded by heather meadows and small conifers, this is about as idyllic a spot as you can imagine. There are no established campsites, but there's plenty of flat ground for a tent near the outlet.

If Eighteenmile Peak's summit is calling, it's a steep but straightforward scramble from here to the top. The best approach is to climb a moraine south of Lake 9600, then angle uphill to the east-southeast until you reach the peak's northeast ridge. Turn and follow this open and rounded ridge as it heads steeply toward the top. Wildflowers in this harsh environment include alpine buttercup, alpine forget-me-not, lupine,

phlox, sky pilot, and alpine sunflower, none of which are more than 3 inches tall.

Although it's unnecessary for navigation, the intermittent tread of a climber's route proves that others have come before you. The route gets rockier and steeper the higher you go, but it never requires any ability beyond stamina and good judgment about which rocks to step on. At the top, your efforts are rewarded with absolutely breathtaking 360-degree views up and down the sharp spine of the Continental Divide, east to the Lima Peaks and distant Gravelly and Madison Ranges, and west to the rugged Lemhi and Lost River Ranges in Idaho. Take the time to savor this scene, although keep an eye out for thunderstorms.

On the way back, it's shorter and easier to skip Lake 9600 and simply follow the wide, grassy slope going east-northeast from Eighteenmile Peak directly toward the Harkness Lakes, visible below you. Before long you'll encounter jeep roads leading back to your starting point.

Continental Divide stretching north from Eighteenmile Peak

30 *Italian Peaks Loop*

Distance: 19.2-mile loop
Difficulty: strenuous
Hiking time: multiday
Elevation gain: 3500 feet
Season: mid-June through October
Best time: late June through July

Contact: Beaverhead-Deerlodge NF,
Dillon Ranger District
Maps: USGS Deadman Lake,
Eighteenmile Peak, Scott Peak
GPS coordinates: N44° 26.765',
W112° 54.641'

Getting there: From the tiny community of Dell at exit 23 off Interstate 15, cross to the west side of the freeway and follow Westside Frontage Road to the southeast. After 1.8 miles, turn right on gravel Big Sheep Creek Road and drive 17 miles to a major junction. Go left, following signs to Nicholia Creek, and 0.2 mile later go left again. Now on Forest Road 657, drive 6.5 miles and keep left at a fork, after which the road gets noticeably rougher, although it's still okay for passenger cars when conditions are dry. About 0.4 mile later you ford first an irrigation ditch and then Cottonwood Creek (usually not a problem after mid-June) and 0.5 mile later reach a junction.

Bear left, staying on FR 657. Go 0.2 mile, then keep straight where FR 3927 to Deadman Lake goes left. The road soon becomes even rougher, but vehicles with good ground clearance should be okay. After 2.5 miles you reach the road-end trailhead.

The Italian Peaks, the most southerly extension of Montana, are a cluster of 11,000-foot mountains that are only visited by a small cadre of dedicated backpackers every year. That group is keeping a terrific secret because this region hides some of the finest hiking in the state. The peaks are spectacular, the meadows are covered with wildflowers, and wildlife is abundant. If you'd like to join the small group of in-the-know hikers who have explored this stunning region, however, you'll have to drive some mediocre roads and navigate long, often-waterless trails that occasionally disappear in the meadows. But, oh, is it worth it!

The route, which travels along a portion of the Continental Divide Trail (CDT), goes southeast up the valley of Nicholia Creek through open sagebrush meadows with scattered stands of quaking aspens, Engelmann spruces, Douglas firs, and limber and lodgepole pines. Rounded ridges rise on either side of the valley, while far upstream you'll see higher peaks still streaked with snow until about mid-July.

At about 0.4 mile, you meet with willow-lined Nicholia Creek as the trail goes lazily up the wide valley floor. Hop over a side creek at 1.5 miles

(good camps), then pass numerous beaver dams to a prominent junction, and the start of the loop, at 2.1 miles.

A clockwise trip is easier to navigate, so bear left on the CDT, and 0.1 mile later make a bridged crossing of Nicholia Creek. About 0.1 mile after that is a signed junction with a now-abandoned trail up Nicholia Creek.

Go sharply left, following signs for Deadman Lake, and head north across a sage-covered hillside. The trail gradually gains elevation, offering improving vistas to the north-northwest of orange-colored Eighteenmile Peak, west to the sheer cliffs of an unnamed summit, and south to the dark, rugged crags of the Italian Peaks. Near the top of your climb, three well-graded switchbacks take you to a wide, grassy saddle. At the east side of this saddle is a shallow pond near where you cross a fenceline and an abandoned jeep road.

From here the trail remains high, contouring across open slopes for 0.3 mile to a fork where the old CDT (still shown on most maps) goes left. You veer right, following the new CDT, soon top a little rise, and begin a long, gradual downhill. A jeep road below your route (the former CDT)

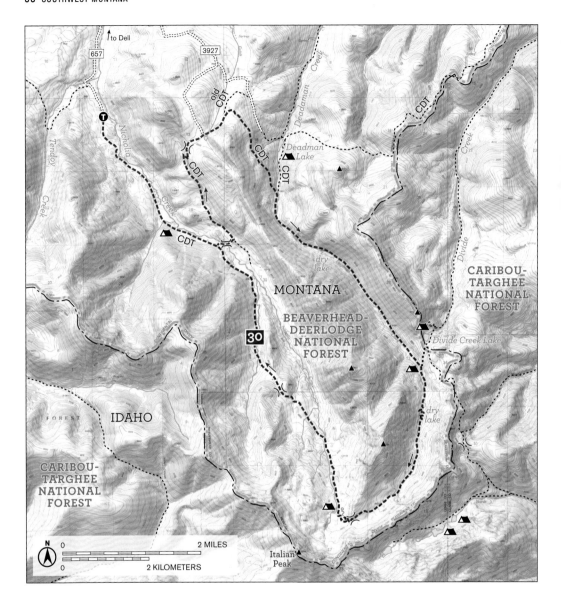

leads down toward shimmering Deadman Lake. Your trail stays well above the lake, gradually descending to a possibly unsigned junction at 6.7 miles, just above Deadman Creek.

The CDT goes left, crossing the creek and heading downstream to Deadman Lake. For this trip, you go upstream and gradually climb through partial forest and tiny meadows. Step over the trickle remaining in the creek and soon find yourself following a dry gully where the creek's water flows underground. Near 7.5 miles the sometimes-obscure trail goes along the bottom of a dry, grassy lakebed and through fields of early-July blooming bluebells and shooting stars.

About 0.3 mile above the lakebed the tread becomes clear once again, traveling along the east side of the canyon. Eventually the

Pass between Deadman and Nicholia Creeks

cheerful creek re-emerges as you meander through meadows backed by tall, partly forested ridges.

Hop over the creek near 8.9 miles, then pass a large, grassy slope coming down from the east side of the canyon. There was once a trail going over this slope to Divide Creek Lake in Idaho. That trail is gone, but boot paths still exist and even without them it's an easy ramble over the slope and down to the lake and its good campsites. You may need that reliable lake water because Deadman Creek disappears once again just above this point and does not return.

The trail up Deadman Creek climbs to another dry lakebed, then gradually ascends through increasingly open terrain to a tremendously scenic high basin ringed by impressive 11,000-foot peaks. Camping here is very inviting, but water is only available from snowfields, which usually remain into early July. Bighorn

sheep and mountain goats are often seen on the nearby slopes.

After topping a nondescript high point at about 11.6 miles, descend toward the basin at the headwaters of Nicholia Creek, which is tucked neatly below the towering north wall of Italian Peak. The descent is initially very steep and rocky but that's over quickly once you pass above a large spring feeding Nicholia Creek. This is your first reliable water since Deadman Creek below the Divide Creek Lake turnoff. There are excellent camping options throughout this extremely scenic basin.

After departing this wonderland, follow cairns and posts past a large rockslide and through a pleasant mix of forest and grassy meadows, with cascading Nicholia Creek on your left and good views in all directions. Hop over the creek about 1.4 miles below the pass, then cross a small tributary shortly thereafter. After about 0.5 mile

97

in forest, you come to a large meadow. The tread disappears here, but just keep going north and you'll pick it up again eventually.

The scenery becomes more subdued as you make your way north over rolling hills with sagebrush and scattered conifers. You'll probably lose the trail once or twice, but if you possess halfway decent navigation instincts this is not a problem.

In the middle of a particularly large meadow about 3 miles from the pass, the route pulls away from Nicholia Creek, climbs to a low rise, and then drops to cross an unnamed tributary creek. (Do *not* go by the USGS map, which shows the old trail that closely followed Nicholia Creek.)

You then parallel the northwest bank of the tributary creek downstream to its confluence with Nicholia Creek and hike north 0.7 mile (about 5.5 miles from the pass) to the signed junction at the close of the loop.

31 *Lima Peaks Loop*

Distance: 7-mile loop
Difficulty: strenuous
Hiking time: day hike or overnight
Elevation gain: 2500 feet
Season: mid-June through October
Best time: mid-June through mid-July

Contact: Beaverhead-Deerlodge NF, Dillon Ranger District
Maps: USGS Edie Creek, Lima Peaks
GPS coordinates: N44° 30.570', W112° 32.807'

Getting there: Take Snowline exit 9 off Interstate 15 south of Lima, cross to the west side of the freeway, and follow Frontage Road to the southeast. After 2.2 miles the road crosses a railroad track and turns to gravel. Drive another 6.8 miles to the national forest boundary, go right on Sawmill Gulch Road (Forest Road 1080), and stay on this narrow gravel road, which at some mysterious point becomes FR 1013, for 5.5 miles to the trailhead at the road's end.

The Lima Peaks are a rugged cluster of mountains just north of the Idaho border along Interstate 15. Despite being easily viewed by thousands of freeway travelers, surprisingly few people hike the trails here. But that oversight is hard to understand because the scenery is excellent—including several peaks over 10,000 feet, high ridges with far-ranging views, mountain meadows carpeted with wildflowers, and relatively easy scramble routes to the tops of the tallest summits.

Although it's hard to discern on the ground, several routes converge at the trailhead. The southbound Continental Divide Trail (CDT) heads east-southeast and is marked with a post. The northbound CDT (shown incorrectly on Forest Service maps) goes directly uphill from the parking area staying on the east side of a little creek. The recommended loop comes *back* that way.

The trail you want is the one incorrectly shown on the Forest Service map as the northbound CDT. It begins beside a large wooden signboard and takes you to a hop-over crossing of a small creek as you head toward the large canyon of Sawmill Creek. Only 10 yards after the creek crossing, angle right on an unsigned but distinct path that goes sharply uphill.

This trail climbs through an extremely scenic landscape featuring the rugged outline of The Thumb to the south and the aptly named Red Conglomerate Peaks to the southwest. On your right, a series of rolling ridges lead up to the Lima Peaks. Alternating between forest and sagebrush-covered meadows, the grassy path goes intermittently uphill, mostly on the south side of the ridge. At

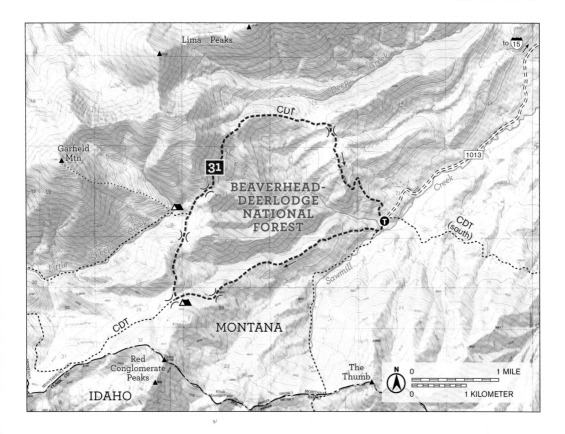

about 1.1 miles you reach and then follow the rolling ridgetop, enjoying wide views, including east to the distant Centennial Mountains.

At 2.3 miles is a prominent post in a grassy saddle. The trail angles to the right here, entering the relatively dense forest on the north side of the ridge. After some up and down, you reach a pass at 2.8 miles with tremendous views to the west of the rugged Italian Peaks. There are good campsites just before this pass, but the only water is from snowbanks or seasonal trickles that usually flow until early July.

A fence crosses the route at this pass and there is a signed junction. Go right on Sawmill-Sheep Creek Trail, which follows the fence uphill. After 0.1 mile, cross the fence and then follow CDT posts along a long-abandoned jeep road that takes you down to a junction on the north side of a wide pass at 3.5 miles. There are terrific views here across a large meadow at the head of

Little Sheep Creek to the tall pyramid of Garfield Mountain. There are possible campsites in the meadows at the headwaters of Little Sheep Creek.

Peak baggers won't be able to resist climbing Garfield Mountain. There is no trail, but it's a straightforward scramble up an obvious ridge on the peak's southeast side. The climb gets steep and rocky but is not technically difficult and the summit views are breathtaking.

The CDT goes right at the junction, heading uphill across an open slope with nonstop views back to distinctive Garfield Mountain. The trail climbs to a high pass, goes through a fence, and then descends one switchback before contouring across open slopes with seemingly endless vistas to the east of the Centennial Mountains and the Yellowstone Plateau. About 0.4 mile into this traverse, you pass above a small spring.

Eventually the trail curves downhill and to the right along a ridge with the trip's best views

Looking west from the ridge south of Lima Peaks

of the Lima Peaks to the north, on your left. At a wide, grassy saddle the trail fades away and an unsigned path bears left. Follow CDT posts to the right, which lead you across the saddle where the tread reappears.

Ignoring several potentially confusing livestock trails, continue following posts that lead you around the left side of a pair of grassy knolls. Wildflowers are abundant on this slope, with lots of flax, wallflower, bluebell, larkspur, Parry's townsendia, locoweed, geranium, phlox, balsamroot, lupine, forget-me-not, salsify, and large white columbine. As expected, the views remain outstanding with a featured attraction being The Thumb to the south. A long well-graded descent over beautiful, mostly open slopes takes you down to a switchback, a fence crossing at a second switchback, then a gentle downhill ramble back to the trailhead.

32 Table Mountain

Distance: 9.5 miles roundtrip	**Contact:** Beaverhead-Deerlodge NF,
Difficulty: very strenuous	Butte-Jefferson Ranger District
Hiking time: day hike	**Maps:** USGS Pipestone Pass,
Elevation gain: 2100 feet	Table Mountain
Season: late June through October	**GPS coordinates:** N45° 46.348',
Best time: late June to mid-July	W112° 29.426'

Getting there: In Butte, take exit 127 off Interstate 90 and go south on Harrison Avenue, which becomes State Route 2. After 3.1 miles, bear left at a junction, staying on SR 2, then drive 5.5 miles to a junction just past milepost 78. Turn right onto paved but usually unsigned Forest Road 84, drive 2.8 miles to a subdivided area where the road forks and bear left. Now on good gravel, you proceed 5.9 miles to a junction beside the Highland Trailhead, turn left, and go 1.2 miles to another junction. Turn left again, drive 1.4 miles to an unsigned four-way junction on a ridgetop, then turn right and carefully drive steep and rocky FR 8514. It's slow going, but possible if your car has decent ground clearance. After 2.1 miles, go left at a junction, drive 0.1 mile, and park in an unsigned turnaround shortly before a gate blocks the road.

The Highland Mountains don't cover much area and have no accessible lakes, but they do feature an outstanding hike to their highest point, Table Mountain. The superb alpine scenery includes wildflower-covered tundra meadows, craggy peaks, and spectacular views that extend across a huge swath of central and southwest Montana. There is no official trail and

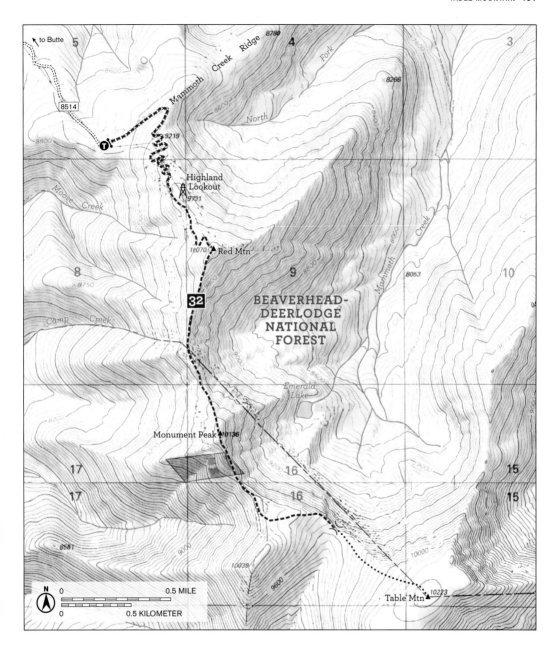

the steep terrain looks intimidating, but a social trail is available for any athletic and reasonably experienced hiker who doesn't suffer from a fear of heights. Wait for a clear day with calm winds to enjoy the views and to avoid getting blown off the narrow ridge.

Walk around the gate and climb the road as it goes through an open forest of whitebark pines, slowly making its way above timberline. The road switchbacks fourteen times, while the views of the Butte area and a host of distant mountain ranges improve with every step. At

Table Mountain and Monument Peak from Red Mountain

1.3 miles you reach the last switchback atop a ridge. The sturdy stone-and-wood Highland Lookout is 120 yards to the left. It's worth a visit, although several electronic and communications towers mar the immediate vicinity.

To continue the hike, pick up an obvious foot trail that steeply ascends the talus slope on the west side of descriptively named Red Mountain. After one fairly long switchback, you return to the ridgeline from which you'll have the unusual perspective of looking *down* on a lookout building. The social trail continues up the steep and rocky ridge for another 0.3 mile to the summit of Red Mountain. Not surprisingly, the view is amazing, including large parts of southwest and central Montana and more mountain ranges and valleys than I could possibly list.

The distinctive flat top of Table Mountain lies about 2 miles southeast of Red Mountain. It's an enticing goal, although reaching it looks difficult since a tall pointed pinnacle (unofficially called Monument Peak) lies along the ridge in between the two. Unless you're afraid of heights, however, it turns out to be mostly a strenuous up-and-down hike

with just a little class 2 scrambling. Travel southeast along the rocky alpine ridge on an intermittent social trail that steeply loses, and then regains, quite a bit of elevation to the base of Monument Peak. The climb over Monument Peak is very steep with some loose talus and scree, but it's no more difficult than countless other unofficial trails in Montana. From the top there is a nice view looking almost straight down to Emerald Lake, which is closed to public access.

Descending the back side of Monument Peak is tricky, but by using your hands for support it can be safely negotiated. This is followed by a rocky section of up-and-down hiking before things get very easy as you wander across a wide tundra-covered ridge down to a saddle and then up to the mesa-like top of Table Mountain. In early July this tundra is carpeted with the yellow blossoms of alpine buttercup.

Once atop Table Mountain, you can enjoy the view and explore the broad tableland to your heart's content. The high point is marked with a large cairn and a solar-powered radio repeater. Return the way you came.

33 *Lewis and Clark Caverns*

Distance: 2 miles roundtrip
Difficulty: easy
Hiking time: half-day hike
Elevation gain: 350 feet
Season: tours run May 1 to September 30

Best time: any time it's open
Contact: Lewis & Clark Caverns State Park
Map: none
GPS coordinates: N45° 50.304',
W111° 52.043'

Getting there: From Butte, drive 29 miles east on Interstate 90 to exit 256 for State Route 359. Go 0.1 mile south, then turn left, following signs to Lewis & Clark Caverns State Park. Drive 7.6 miles, turn left into the state park, and almost immediately reach the lower visitor center where nonresidents must purchase a park entrance pass. To reach the caverns, continue 3.3 miles to the parking lot, gift shop, and upper visitor center. As of 2017, tickets for a cave tour cost $12 for adults, $5 for children between the ages of six and eleven, and free for anyone younger than six.

Montana's most famous state park offers fishing, camping, picnic areas, and several miles of pleasant hiking trails, but most visitors ignore all of that because the star attraction is underground. Lewis and Clark Caverns is one of the largest limestone caves in the western United States and it is filled with countless dramatic and very beautiful formations including sturdy columns, delicate "soda straw" stalactites, intricately patterned flowstones, towering stalagmites, popcorn-like formations, and a host of other wonders. For those not burdened with claustrophobia, this place is definitely a must-see attraction.

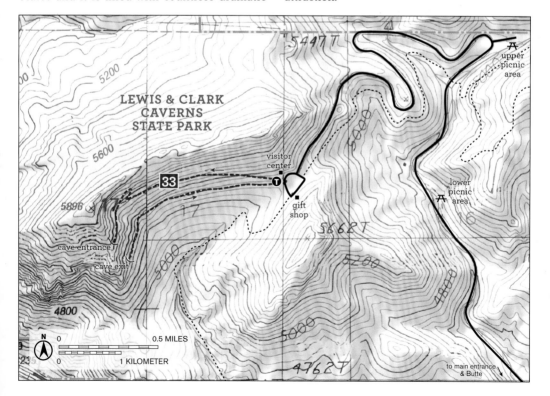

Spectacular cave formations in the Palisades Room

facilities before you leave as there are no further opportunities during the two-hour tour.

The walk begins with a pleasant, gradual uphill stroll on a paved 0.7-mile trail, as the ranger leads your group across relatively open slopes to the cave entrance. The path offers pleasant views and there are a few wildflowers in spring and early summer. Wildlife sightings are also possible, but since you'll be hiking with a group of fifteen or more people, most animals will remain hidden.

Once inside the cave, some of the highlights include: the possibility of seeing bats on the ceiling shortly after you enter the cave; the huge Cathedral Room, where you get the first good look at all the dramatically beautiful formations; the Beaver Slide, where most visitors must slide down a short rock chute on their derrieres; the Crystal Pool, a lovely little pool of clear water where cave formations are growing; the Palisades Room, an enormous opening with many of the cavern's most impressive features; and the Garden of the Gods, an amazing assortment of cave formations in every conceivable shape and size.

The tour concludes with a long walk out of the cave through a human-engineered tunnel. Once returning to the land of sunshine, you'll enjoy a 0.5-mile stroll on a nearly level gravel path back to the parking lot. Overall, this dramatic short "hike" is fun for all members of the family and provides a wealth of amazing and unique experiences.

Keep in mind, however, that this is not a typical hike. First, you are only allowed to enter the cave as part of a ranger-led tour, so you can't set your own pace, and solitude is impossible. Second, unlike most hikes, you'll spend a significant portion of your walk stooped over, walking like a duck, hanging onto handrails, or even sliding on your backside. Finally, forget about packing the "ten essentials" since the only things you're allowed to bring into the cave are a camera, water, and the clothes on your back. Bring a light jacket—the cave remains a rather chilly 48 degrees year-round—and take advantage of the bathroom

34 *Lost Cabin Lake*

Distance: 7.8 miles roundtrip
Difficulty: strenuous
Hiking time: day hike or overnight
Elevation gain: 1550 feet
Season: July through mid-October
Best time: mid-July through September

Contact: Beaverhead-Deerlodge NF, Butte-Jefferson Ranger District
Map: Beartooth Publishing, Tobacco Root Mountains
GPS coordinates: N45° 36.552', W112° 3.325'

Getting there: From Butte, drive 29 miles east on Interstate 90 to exit 256 for State Route 359. Go 5.3 miles south, turn right on South Boulder Road, and proceed 2.8 miles to a

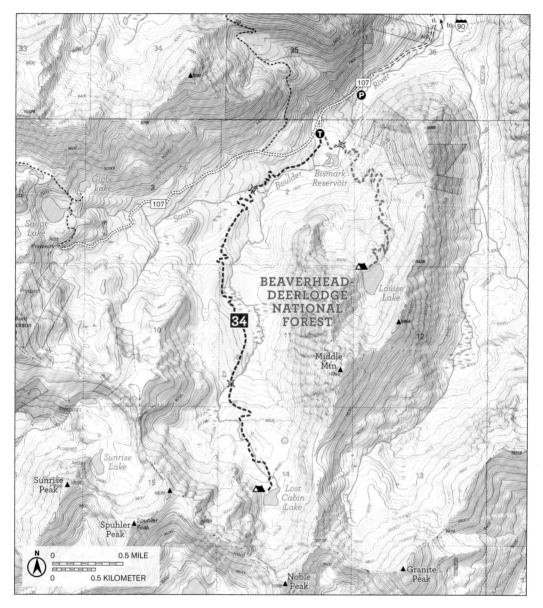

junction at the end of pavement. Go straight and drive 8.5 miles to the remote community of Mammoth. The road, now Forest Road 107, gets noticeably rougher at Mammoth, but it remains passable for most passenger cars. At 3.2 miles from Mammoth, you reach a fork where there is a restroom on the left. Go right and slowly drive 1.4 very rough miles to another fork where there is a nice campsite. If your car lacks good ground clearance, park here.

To reach the official trailhead, keep right, climb this steep and rocky route for 0.25 mile, go left at a fork, and proceed 0.2 mile to the road-end trailhead.

Middle Mountain over Louise Lake

Two very scenic trails depart from this popular trailhead in the Tobacco Root Mountains, both leading to strikingly beautiful alpine lakes. Louise Lake is a shorter hike and the much more popular option, making Lost Cabin Lake a better choice for hikers who prefer a bit more solitude. Fortunately, you won't sacrifice a thing in mountain scenery, because, if anything, the lake is even more lovely than Louise Lake and the access trail passes much better meadows and creekside scenery.

The National Recreation Trail departs from the south side of the parking area and gently climbs through an attractive spruce-fir forest. Hop over a small creek at a little under 0.4 mile, make a couple of lazy switchbacks, then cross a wooden bridge over the headwaters of South Boulder River. From here the well-graded route winds uphill on a course that includes several rounded switchbacks but not much in the way of views.

At 1.7 miles, you pass above a lush meadow backed by jagged Middle Mountain, then walk 0.7 mile to another wooden bridge, this time over an unnamed creek. Near 3 miles you reach higher terrain with open forests and glimpses of several rugged peaks and ridges. Follow a pretty little splashing creek upstream, crossing its flow once along the way, then climb through scenic rocky meadows at the base of a large talus slope where the views really open up and you can fully appreciate the majesty of these mountains.

You reach dramatically scenic Lost Cabin Lake, with its rocky island and tremendous views of several craggy peaks, at 3.9 miles. Mountain goats live on the nearby cliffs and there are numerous good campsites. The fishing for cutthroat trout is generally good, if the scenery alone isn't enough to keep you enthralled.

Extend your hike: For a different destination, hike to Louise Lake. The 3.5-mile (one-way) trail starts from the east side of the same parking area, passes small Bismark Reservoir, then climbs a series of very gentle switchbacks to the scenic pool. Middle Mountain offers a wonderfully photogenic backdrop, but unlike Lost Cabin Lake, you probably won't have the scene all to yourself.

35 *Gneiss Lake*

Distance: 5 miles roundtrip

Difficulty: moderate to strenuous

Hiking time: day hike

Elevation gain: 1400 feet

Season: July through mid-October

Best time: mid-July through September

Contact: Beaverhead-Deerlodge NF, Madison Ranger District

Map. Deartooth Publishing, Tobacco Root Mountains

GPS coordinates: N45° 30.977', W111° 59.460'

Getting there: From the northwest end of Sheridan, turn northeast on Mill Street, following signs to Mill Creek Campground. Drive 2.6 miles to the end of pavement, then go 2.2 miles to where the road enters national forest land and becomes Forest Road 111. This route is bumpy, steep, and occasionally rocky, but it's passable for most passenger cars. After 7.7 miles, reach a junction at Branham Lakes Campground. Go left and 25 yards later park at a small sign for Trail #15.

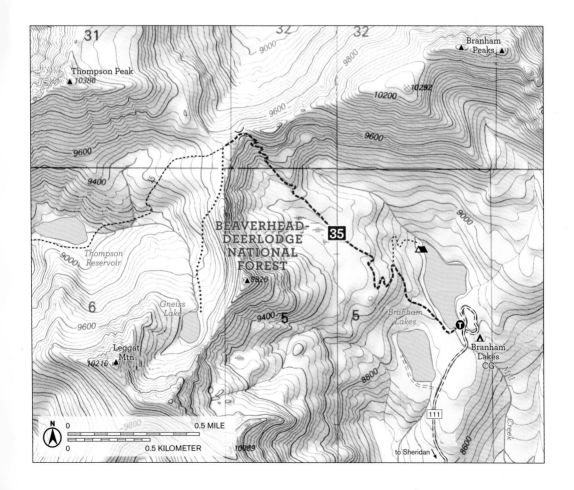

Meadow above Branham Lakes

The Tobacco Root Mountains have hundreds of miles of excellent trails and dozens of scenic alpine lakes, but you'd be hard-pressed to find a destination with a better combination of relatively easy access, solitude, and dramatic scenery than this partly off-trail hike to Gneiss Lake. Every mile of this hike is high and wonderfully scenic—no slogging through viewless forest to reach the good stuff—and while the spectacular destination has no trail, the cross-country portion is relatively short and easy to navigate.

The trail crosses the dam holding back Upper Branham Lake, then curves to the right to follow the lake's shoreline. There are good views across the water toward the colorful and rugged Branham Peaks to the north and Mount Bradley to the east. The path soon pulls away from the lake and climbs steadily through open subalpine fir forests and grassy meadows. At 0.4 mile, the trail switchbacks to the left where a potentially confusing social trail goes straight descending to a campsite at the upper end of the lake.

Two more switchbacks lead to a very scenic subalpine meadow with a seasonal creek, two small ponds, and fine wildflower displays in midsummer. From here, you ascend into the realm of scrawny whitebark pines as the trail steeply climbs up to a windy 9700-foot pass at 1.6 miles. To the southwest you can see bulky Leggat Mountain while the green waters of Bell Lake are visible to the north.

The faint trail, marked with cairns, turns left and then heads downhill toward Thompson Reservoir. Instead of dropping to that lake, leave the trail and head south, going cross-country and gradually losing elevation in the open tundra atop the ridge. After 0.15 mile, veer right and descend a grassy gully, following bits and pieces of a sketchy social trail wherever possible. You lose about 200 feet of elevation, then contour across open meadows and through sparse forest at the base of a large rockslide toward an obvious basin high on the slopes of rugged Leggat Mountain. Once past the rockslide, you'll gain 200 feet before reaching the rocky shores of deep but fishless Gneiss Lake. The dark, jagged mass of Leggat Mountain rises directly above this lake, making for awesome scenery. Camping is difficult on this rocky ground, so make this a day hike.

36 Snowcrest Loop

Distance: 22.5-mile loop
Difficulty: strenuous
Hiking time: multiday
Elevation gain: 4200 feet
Season: mid-June through October
Best time: late June to mid-July

Contact: Beaverhead-Deerlodge NF,
Madison Ranger District
Maps: USGS Antone Peak,
Stonehouse Mountain
GPS coordinates: N44° 50.170',
W112° 11.575'

Getting there: From Dillon, take exit 62 off Interstate 15 and drive 0.6 mile toward town on South Atlantic Street. Turn right near the hospital onto State Route 91S, go 0.3 mile, and then turn left onto Blacktail Road. Drive 6.9 miles to the end of the pavement, then continue another 20.8 miles to a well-signed junction with East Fork Blacktail Road. Turn left, follow this narrow gravel road for 5.5 miles, and then turn right at a junction and immediately cross a bridge over the creek. Proceed 6.2 miles to the turnaround loop and trailhead at the far end of East Fork Blacktail Campground.

The highlight of this loop through one of Montana's most overlooked mountain ranges is a long and glorious ridge walk that will blow you away with its alpine scenery. Actually, several things might get blown away, since this ridge is totally exposed to the weather. Don't make this trip if thunderstorms are in the forecast. Finding water is also an issue because after late June there are usually no reliable trailside sources for almost 11 miles. I recommend starting with several empty containers and filling them at the last available water near the headwaters of East Fork Blacktail Creek. You can then carry enough water the last few miles to a dry camp high on the ridge. The endless views and stunning alpine scenery are worth the extra sweat.

The trail heads up the deep, partly forested canyon of East Fork Blacktail Creek, offering fine views of the high peaks of the Snowcrest Range. At a little over 0.8 mile, make a knee-deep crossing of the sluggish, willow-lined creek. Look for moose, sandhill cranes, and cheerful little dippers near this ford. Near 1.8 miles is a signed junction with the faint Rough Creek Trail. Go straight, and 80 yards later, reach a junction with Lawrence Creek Trail and the start of the loop. Veer left and climb two switchbacks on an open slope covered with grasses, sagebrush, and scattered limber pines. As the trail gradually curves north you'll enter increasingly forested

terrain interspersed with beautiful meadows that provide excellent views to the east of the Snowcrest Divide, south to Antone Peak, and north to Sunset Peak. In a particularly gorgeous meadow near 3.2 miles, make a rock-hop crossing of a small creek and then hike 0.8 mile to a junction with Lodgepole Trail.

Go straight and soon return to the banks of rollicking East Fork Blacktail Creek. At about 4.6 miles is a junction with Two Meadows Trail and a good campsite. Go straight and climb four well-graded switchbacks to a pair of meadows with good views of colorful Sunset Peak to the west. As you approach the diminishing headwaters of East Fork Blacktail Creek, be sure to fill up your water bottles as this is the last reliable source for about 11 miles. You might also wish to camp in this area and there are several potential options for those looking to spend the night. At 7.3 miles you top the divide on an open ridge signed as Honeymoon Park. There is a junction here and superb views looking north to Hogback Mountain and west to Olson Peak.

Turn right on Snowcrest Trail and cross a grassy saddle on an initially sketchy trail marked with enormous rock cairns. The views improve as you steeply climb past a junction with little-used Cook Headquarters Trail, then cross open slopes and go through a ghost forest of beetle-killed whitebark pines. This climb

Along the ridge east of Antone Peak

takes you to the rolling alpine meadowlands of upper Honeymoon Park, where the views are unlimited. In addition to vistas along the peaks of the Snowcrest Range, you can look east across the Ruby River Valley to the Gravelly and Madison Ranges, south to the Centennial Range, and northwest through the deep cleft of The Notch to the distant Pioneer Mountains. Camping here offers amazing scenery and great sunsets, but there is no shelter from the wind and no water after the snow melts in late June or early July.

The trail turns south-southeast following the divide for 0.6 mile before cutting across the steep north face of Stonehouse Mountain. With your head on a swivel taking in all the grand views, you top a ridge on the northeast shoulder of Stonehouse Mountain where there is an unsigned junction. Go right (uphill) then climb across the east side of Stonehouse Mountain to return to the Snowcrest Divide.

Now begins a wildly scenic section of several miles, which go up and down along the treeless divide. The views are breathtaking and the hiking is an absolute joy with numerous tiny wildflowers, rocks covered with colorful lichens, and small but dramatic cliffs dropping off the east side of the divide adding to the scenery. Watch for herds of elk that spend their summers

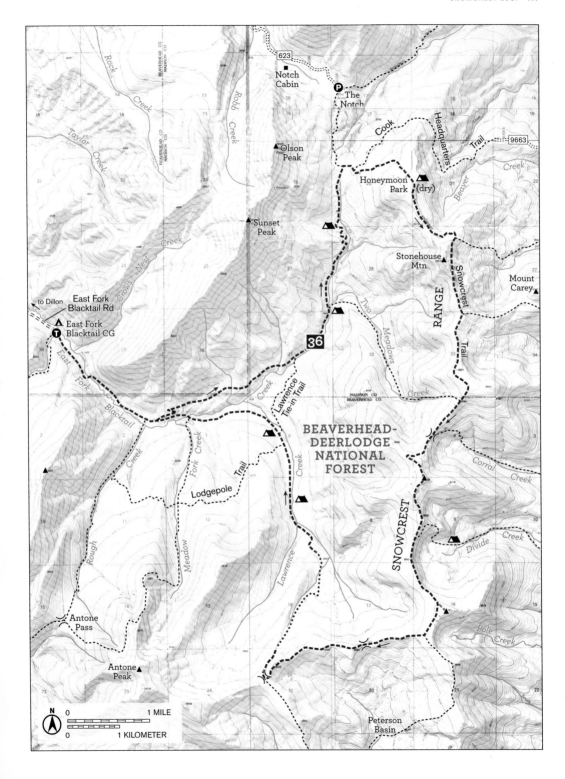

in these high meadows. The trail's tread is frequently nonexistent, but it's also unnecessary as all you have to do is stick with the open ridge and look for cairns.

Some maps show additional trails branching off, but it's not until you reach a saddle at a little over 11 miles that there is a sign for the faint Corral Creek Trail going left. From this saddle the Snowcrest Trail makes a jog to the west before turning sharply east again to climb a spur ridge to the top of the next rounded high point. You then round the tops of the cliffs ringing the scenic basin of Divide Creek. Near 12.5 miles is a junction with Divide Creek Trail, which steeply descends 600 feet into the Divide Creek Basin, where you'll find water and possible campsites.

The contour map shows the Snowcrest Trail climbing to the top of the next high point, but the actual course traverses the west side of this point to the grassy top of a prominent ridge that heads west toward Antone Peak. From here you can look south across Peterson Basin to the distant Lima Reservoir and Centennial Mountains.

Turn west on this ridge and follow cairns marking a faint trail. At the first saddle in this ridge there is a prominent elk trail across your route and often large herds of these ungulates are present as well. Keep straight on the up-and-down official trail enjoying the open terrain and increasingly good views of Antone Peak.

In a wide saddle about 1.7 miles from where you first hit this westward-trending ridge, you'll come to an unadorned wooden post marking an important junction. Turn sharply right, following posts that lead downhill almost directly in line with distant Sunset Peak. The path soon grows very indistinct, so good route-finding instincts are needed as you head north-northeast generally following the right side of a small creek that usually has water for most of the summer—your first trailside water since East Fork Blacktail Creek. Since you're virtually certain to lose the trail, the best advice is to follow a downhill course roughly where the contour map claims the trail to be. Shortly before the bottom of the long descent, you come to a log crossing of Lawrence Creek where the tread rather suddenly reappears where you enter forest.

Now on a good trail, you follow the left side of splashing Lawrence Creek past good campsites and through flat meadows to a junction with the very faint Lodgepole Trail. Keep straight and less than 0.2 mile later come to where the Lawrence Tie-in Trail branches right. Veer left, and hike gently up and down past several small marshy areas to a junction with Meadow Fork Trail just before a calf-deep ford of East Fork Blacktail Creek. From here a 0.5-mile gentle ascent of a sagebrush-covered slope takes you back to the junction at the close of the loop.

Opposite, top: Golden eagle, Glacier National Park

Opposite, bottom: Mount Gould towers above Grinnell Lake.

Glacier National Park

As observed by generations of visitors since the park's creation in 1910, there's just no place like Glacier National Park. Since you're reading a hiking guidebook, you are undoubtedly familiar with this crown jewel park's countless attributes—stunning mountain scenery, abundant wildlife, towering waterfalls, sparkling lakes, sky-scraping peaks—so I won't bore you with the full list. But if you're one of those unfortunate souls who has never been here, then let me assure you that it lives up to every superlative. I should also warn that if you don't come here with *a lot* of extra vacation days, you're going to feel cheated. With over 700 miles of world-class trails and unlimited off-trail possibilities, Glacier tops almost every list of America's best parks for hikers and backpackers. And how could it not? I mean no offense to Great Smoky Mountains, Yosemite, Olympic, Grand Canyon, or any of the other contenders, but you're all just vying for second place.

You need to be prepared for crowds and grizzly bears—Glacier, famously, has plenty of both—and the weather can be iffy, especially on the wetter, west side of the divide, but downsides like these are soon lost in the splendor. As for the bruins, make noise on the trail and carry bear spray. To deal with the crowds, get to day hiking trailheads *very* early in the day and, for backpacking trips, make advance reservations. In 2016 the park started an online reservation system through Pay.gov. Applications can be submitted starting March 15. As of 2017, a nonrefundable $10 fee is charged for each application. A deposit of $30 is charged with the application, but is refunded if you are unable to obtain a reservation. In addition, there is a charge of $7 per person in your group per night in the park regardless of whether the permit is obtained by reservation or on a first-come, first-served basis. For the latest information, visit the park website (see Resources at the end of this book).

So hike here, fall in love with the park, and come back to hike (a lot) more. Because there's just no place like Glacier.

37 Boulder Pass

Distance: 25 miles roundtrip
Difficulty: strenuous
Hiking time: multiday
Elevation gain: 3400 feet
Season: late July to early October
Best time: late July through September

Contact: Glacier National Park
Map: Trails Illustrated, Glacier–Waterton Lakes National Parks
GPS coordinates: N48° 57.487', W113° 53.484' (at Goat Haunt)

Getting there: Two international border crossings and a boat trip are required to reach the trailhead, so the transportation logistics are a little complicated.

First, bring your passport—it's required to get back into the United States after your detour into Canada. Next you'll need a ticket for the boat tour on Waterton Lake. These can be purchased when you arrive, or reserved in advance by calling Waterton Shoreline Cruise Company (see Resources for contact information). If you're returning by boat, you'll need a roundtrip ticket with a different date for the return. Check the website for the latest prices.

Boulder Peak from just east of Boulder Pass

Finally, you must drive to Canada's Waterton Lakes National Park. From St. Mary, drive 13 miles north on US 89, turn left on State Route 17, and go 14 miles to the Canadian border. (*Note:* Although it's illegal to take pepper spray for use against humans into Canada, bear spray is supposed to be okay; check before making your travel plans.) Drive 13.5 miles on Canada Highway 6, cross a bridge over the Waterton River, then turn left and come to the park entrance station. Proceed about 6 miles, then go to the marina in the community of Waterton. Signs direct you to the boat tours office where you can pick up your ticket. Tours leave regularly and it takes about an hour to reach Goat Haunt, in the United States, where you disembark and start your hike.

The dramatic Boulder Pass region, with its tall waterfalls, towering cliffs, high peaks, rock-garden wildflowers, and stunning views is one of the scenic masterpieces of Glacier National Park. The pass can be approached on a steep trail from the west via the Kintla Lakes, and, in fact, if you don't mind a really long car shuttle, that is a highly recommended exit route for this trip. If you're doing an out-and-back hike, however, the Goat Haunt approach is better since the climb from the east is much easier.

You disembark near the Goat Haunt Ranger Station and customs office, the latter of which requires a stop to show your passport and declare anything you're bringing in. Just a short walk to the south is a signed junction. Veer right on Waterton Lake Trail and go 0.3 mile to a junction with the trail to Rainbow Falls. Keep right, cross a swinging bridge over the Waterton River, and come to a spur trail to often-buggy Waterton River Camp.

Go straight, climb two short switchbacks, then turn left on Boulder Pass Trail and climb for the next mile. Things ease off when you round a ridge and enter the valley of Olson Creek. From here the trail has only intermittent uphills until you drop to the shores of scenic Lake Janet. The trail goes around the north side of this large, turquoise-colored lake to Lake Janet Camp on the inlet creek.

The next 2 miles are mostly level, with only a few gentle uphill climbs. The route is viewless and

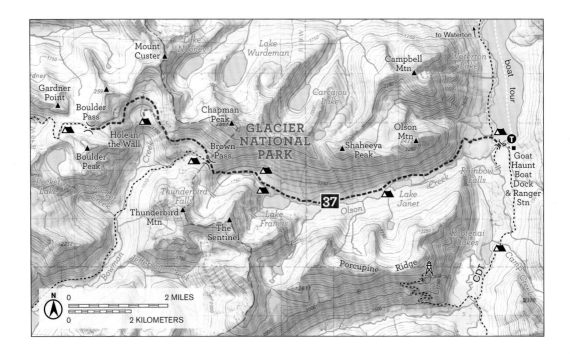

heavily forested, but nicely shaded. Eventually you catch glimpses of greenish Lake Francis on your left shortly before you reach a spur trail to Lake Francis Camp. Highlighting a stay at this excellent location are nice views of a tall veil-like waterfall dropping from the cliffs of The Sentinel to the south. About 0.3 mile past Lake Francis is Hawksbill Camp, a shadeless and brushy site that is less appealing than the camp at Lake Francis.

Above Hawksbill Camp you cross a brushy basin featuring a deep and very scenic unnamed lake. The views across this lake to the dark cliffs and snowfields of Thunderbird Mountain and the long, sliding cascade of Thunderbird Falls are excellent. The climbing resumes as you trudge up a mostly open slope at a moderately steep grade, using thirteen switchbacks to attain a junction at wide and grassy Brown Pass, 8.5 miles from Goat Haunt.

If you are staying at Brown Pass Camp, go straight and walk 0.3 mile to the camp. Although seemingly a perfect base camp for a day hike to Boulder Pass, this site is infamously mosquito infested. In addition, after late July the snowmelt creek beside the camp dries up, so you'll have

to walk almost 0.3 mile beyond the camp to get water. Bring a collapsible bucket if you're scheduled to stay here.

Back at Brown Pass, take the Boulder Pass Trail and make a gradual uphill traverse across open slopes enjoying stupendous views looking south to towering Thunderbird Mountain and down a very deep canyon to fiord-like Bowman Lake. When you round a ridge, the views, almost unbelievably, get even better as you look west to the imposing ramparts of Mount Custer, Boulder Peak, and several unnamed summits. To call this terrain "mountainous" is ridiculously inadequate. This area is vertical in the extreme, with cliffs thousands of feet high, deeply plunging canyons, towering waterfalls, and soaring peaks.

The trail now contours across a steep hillside, taking you to a junction 1.7 miles from Brown Pass with the side trail to Hole in the Wall Camp. This is arguably the most spectacular camp in the Glacier backcountry, so even though snagging a permit to stay here is difficult, it's worth the effort. The main trail keeps right at the Hole in the Wall junction and gradually climbs while making an extended arc across alpine slopes. You'll pass fields of wildflowers and hop over several small creeks along the way, adding to the world-class scenery. You may also have to negotiate a few icy snowfields, so use caution, especially on cold mornings, when they'll be hard and frozen. Most of the trees here are scraggly looking alpine larches, which in late September turn bright gold. As you continue climbing, even the hardy larches give up, leaving you in an alpine land of grasses, tiny wildflowers, and snowfields.

The tread may disappear in the rocky terrain, so follow cairns up to a flat upper basin with small snowmelt ponds that perfectly reflect Boulder Peak in their cold waters. The skinny, permanent snowfield at the base of Boulder Peak is all that remains of once large Boulder Glacier.

A final short uphill over rocks and snow takes you through Boulder Pass, 12.5 miles from Goat Haunt. Immediately in front of you to the north-northwest is the tall, blocky summit of Gardner Point. If you drop down the other side of the pass you can see the tall spire of Kinnerly Peak to the west. For even higher views, climb off trail to the top of an old moraine on the north side of the pass.

38 *Chief Mountain*

Distance: 4.4 miles roundtrip
Difficulty: moderate to strenuous
Hiking time: day hike
Elevation gain: 1100 feet
Season: mid-July to mid-October
Best time: late July through August

Contact: Blackfeet Nation, Fish and Wildlife
Map: Trails Illustrated, Glacier–Waterton Lakes National Parks (access road and trail not shown)
GPS coordinates: N48° 57.323', W113° 36.115'

Chief Mountain from the ridge to the north

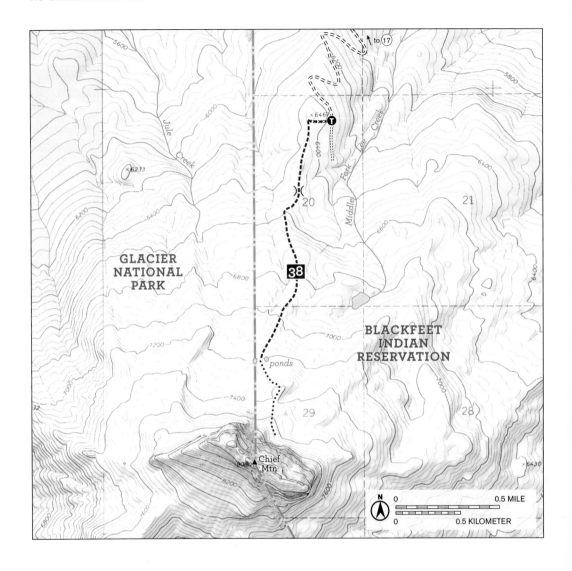

Getting there: From Babb, drive 4.4 miles north on US 89, then turn left on State Route 17. Go 10.1 miles, then turn left on an unsigned gravel road. This road is steep, rocky, and rough but carefully driven passenger cars can usually make it. After 3.5 miles, park in a large clearing where the road splits (and from here, rapidly deteriorates).

Set well east of the main Rocky Mountain divide, the limestone cliffs of dramatic Chief Mountain rise like a misplaced castle above the surrounding rolling hills. Viewed from State Route 17, this landmark is frequently admired and photographed but hikers rarely approach the peak because maps indicate no reasonable access and most of the mountain is on the Blackfeet Indian Reservation. But there is a relatively good trail to the mountain's northern cliffs, and all you need to hike it is a Blackfeet Nation, Fish and Wildlife conservation permit (available at the tribal offices in Browning for $10, as of 2017).

Note: Although access is currently permitted to nontribal members, Chief Mountain is spiritually important to the Blackfeet tribe. You'll see many colorful flags and bits of cloth tied to trees in the area left as religious offerings. Please be respectful and never disturb any religious sites.

Walk uphill on the jeep road to the west, which goes 0.1 mile through high-elevation forest to the top of a ridge. From here, pick up an unsigned but distinct foot trail that follows the ridge to the south through a forest of short subalpine firs. Directly in front of you is massive Chief Mountain, while to the west you can see the main line of peaks in Glacier and Waterton Lakes National Parks.

The circuitous path slowly gains elevation to a minor high point, then drops to a saddle at 0.4 mile. The trail then makes several steep little ups and downs through scrubby forest and rocky areas to reach a cluster of small ponds at 0.9 mile. The view across these ponds to the massive north face of Chief Mountain is amazing.

These pools are a good turnaround spot, or you can continue on the steep and increasingly sketchy climber's route that cuts between the two main ponds and snakes up a rock slide. Eventually you can get all the way to the base of the mountain's monstrous cliffs near 2.2 miles and just soak in the grandeur.

39 *Northern Loop*

Distance: 52 mile-loop (64 miles with side trips)
Difficulty: very strenuous
Hiking time: multiday
Elevation gain: 10,750 feet (11,900 feet with side trips)
Season: late July through early October

Best time: August and September
Contact: Glacier National Park
Map: Trails Illustrated, Glacier–Waterton Lakes National Parks
GPS coordinates: N48° 47.856', W113° 40.715'

Getting there: From St. Mary, go 8.8 miles north on US 89 to Babb. Turn west, following signs to Many Glacier. Drive 11.6 miles, then go straight at the Many Glacier Hotel junction. Exactly 1 mile later, go straight again where a road heads left to the Many Glacier Ranger Station and Campground. About 0.2 mile later, go straight at a fork and park in the enormous (but often full) lot for the Swiftcurrent Picnic Area.

Of all the magnificent backpacking options in Glacier National Park, this loop may be the best. The trip has everything you could want from a backpacking vacation. There are stupendous views of glacier-clad mountains, sparkling lakes in every shape and size, wonderfully scenic high passes and low forested valleys, tall waterfalls and even taller cliffs, abundant wildlife and wildflower-covered meadows, and even several excellent side trips leading to still more wonders. The only downside is that seemingly every other backpacker in the world likes these things too,

so getting a permit is very difficult. Without a reservation your chances of obtaining one of the limited number of first-come, first-served permits are vanishingly small.

From the northwest corner of the parking lot, the heavily traveled gravel trail goes 60 yards to a junction and the start of your loop. The recommended return route of the loop goes left, but for a counterclockwise circuit, go straight, following signs to Iceberg Lake. After 50 yards you reach a road, which you follow for about 80 yards to the Iceberg/Ptarmigan Trailhead.

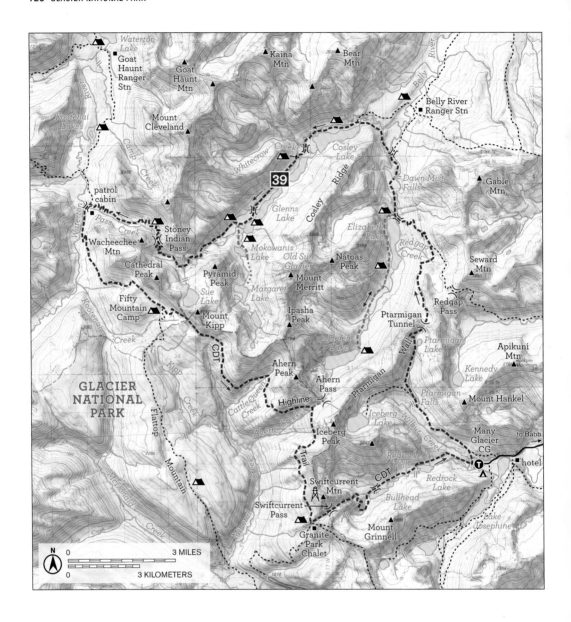

This trail climbs a mostly open, flower-dotted slope for 0.25 mile to where a trail heads right on its way to Many Glacier Hotel. Keep straight and climb gradually through forest and then through open areas on a somewhat brushy slope with midsummer wildflowers and superb views—especially to the west-northwest of the tall cliffs and deeply serrated ridge ringing the cirque of Iceberg Lake. You gradually ascend to pretty Ptarmigan Falls, cross the cascading creek on a bridge just above the falls, and less than 0.1 mile later, reach a junction at 2.8 miles. The trail to the left leads to dramatic Iceberg Lake—a great side trip if you have the time.

Go right, following signs to Ptarmigan Lake and Tunnel, and make a moderately steep climb to the cirque holding deep and beautiful Ptarmigan Lake. From here the trail climbs two long switchbacks on a steep talus slope to Ptarmigan Tunnel, a 200-foot-long hole cut through the top of Ptarmigan Wall. At the north end of the tunnel is a fantastic view of Elizabeth Lake, the Belly River Valley, and the surrounding peaks.

After the tunnel, the trail cuts to the right, crossing a cliff face that is often covered with snow through July. The route then curves north and gradually descends a strikingly red-colored talus slope. On the way down you'll revel in some of the finest views in Glacier National Park, and boy is *that* saying something. Especially outstanding are the vistas looking southwest to Helen Lake and west to Mount Merritt and Old Sun Glacier. After returning to the forest, you cross Redgap Creek and come to a junction with the trail to Redgap Pass at 8.3 miles.

Keep straight and descend ten lazy switchbacks to a swinging bridge over Belly River just below large Elizabeth Lake. About 100 yards after this bridge is the inviting campground at the foot of Elizabeth Lake and a junction.

Side trip: The loop trail goes right, but for a wonderful side trip turn left and follow an up-and-down path along the view-packed west side of Elizabeth Lake (look for trumpeter swans) for 1.6 miles to the end of the lake and a designated campsite. Continue south on a brushy trail up the willow-choked valley of Belly River for 2.7 miles to a bridged creek crossing and Helen Lake. This large and extremely dramatic lake, backed by the towering cliffs of Ahern Peak, is spectacular by any standard. Morning reflections of the peak in the lake's waters are breathtaking.

Back at the junction beside Elizabeth Lake, go north on a mostly flat trail for 1.4 miles to a rocky viewpoint directly above Dawn Mist Falls. This broad waterfall drops into a deep gorge and, true to its name, kicks up plenty of spray. Two quick downhill switchbacks take you to the junction with a short side trail accessing a dramatic photo spot just below the falls.

The main trail soon passes a junction with a horse trail before reaching another junction just above a swinging bridge over Belly River. Go straight, then hike up and down through forest for 2 miles to a ford of the outlet for very scenic Cosley Lake. There is a cable across the stream, although by midsummer this isn't needed as the slow-moving water is only a little over knee deep. Only 50 yards beyond the ford you meet the Stoney Indian Pass Trail.

Turn left, pass the spur trail to Cosley Lake Camp 0.6 mile later, and continue to the far end of Cosley Lake, where you can look east for a view of distant, block-shaped Chief Mountain. You then ascend gradually through a forest of beetle-killed firs, cross a log bridge over Whitecrow Creek, and reach a fork. The trail to the left leads to the popular campground at the foot of long and beautiful Glenns Lake.

The main trail heads right and spends the next couple of miles going up and down in the forest above Glenns Lake to the campground at the head of the lake. Even if you aren't staying here, make the short detour to the camp for excellent views across the water to the tall spire of Pyramid Peak.

The main trail continues up the forested valley to a junction with the Mokowanis Lake Trail (19 miles, without side trips). If you have the time, this trail makes an excellent side trip, climbing gently for about 1 mile to the campground near very pretty Mokowanis Lake. Tough scramble routes lead from there to spectacular Margaret Lake, set beneath the impressive cliffs of Mounts Kipp and Merritt.

The Stoney Indian Pass Trail goes straight, passes Mokowanis Junction Camp, and then begins a steady but gradual ascent, mostly on open, brushy slopes with nice views of a multi-tiered waterfall. Twelve switchbacks lead to the top of the falls and a pretty little basin holding an unnamed, green-tinged lake. Several tall waterfalls thunder off the cliffs of Cathedral Peak into this scenic basin. The trail goes around the north side of the small lake, crosses the inlet creek on a seasonal bridge, and then ascends fourteen switchbacks to the top of the waterfalls. From there you ford a creek (expect *cold* water) and gradually climb a lovely wildflower-covered

Hiker admiring Helen Lake

terrace to an easy rock-hop crossing of a second creek. Just above this crossing is a shallow but stunningly beautiful lakelet with exceptionally photogenic views toward towering Wahcheechee Mountain. A final nine-switchback climb leads to dramatic Stoney Indian Pass.

The switchbacking trail rapidly descends to deep Stoney Indian Lake and the rather exposed designated campground near its outlet. This is a dramatic location, so it's worth trying for a permit to stay here.

The trail continues downhill from Stoney Indian Lake with two dozen irregularly spaced switchbacks to a junction with Waterton Valley Trail (27 miles, excluding side trips).

Go left and walk 0.1 mile to a bridge over Pass Creek and a log patrol cabin. From here, climb two switchbacks and make a long, ascending traverse. As usual, improved views accompany the added elevation, with especially excellent vistas up and down the Waterton River Valley and across the canyon to Kootenai Peak and glacier-clad Vulture Peak. Eventually you'll climb above the trees and come to a spectacular alpine terrace carpeted with wildflowers and offering

outstanding views, especially of Cathedral Peak and the jagged ridge on your left. You'll enjoy almost a mile of this hiking heaven before reaching a junction with the Flattop Mountain Trail and outstandingly scenic Fifty Mountain Camp. **Warning:** Marmots are abundant around this camp, and they're notorious for chewing anything and everything in search of salt. Hang or guard your gear carefully.

The Highline Trail goes southeast from Fifty Mountain Camp ascending the talus and scree slopes on the west side of rugged Mount Kipp. After 0.6 mile, a not-to-be-missed 0.3-mile spur trail goes left to a low point on the divide atop a cliff 800 feet above large Sue Lake. This lake often has icebergs floating in it well into August.

The main trail goes straight, accomplishing a long and gradual downhill over the next couple of miles through a burn zone with continuously fine views. The downhill ends when you make a jog to the east and round the slopes above Cattle Queen Creek.

The trail makes a steep ascent away from this creek to the top of a view-packed ridge then contours to a junction. Don't miss this side trip, which climbs 0.4 mile to Ahern Pass. The view up to Ahern Glacier and down to Helen and Elizabeth Lakes is stupendous.

Back on the Highline Trail, make your way around another basin, where a steep and icy snowfield often blocks the route well into August. Another short uphill takes you around a ridge and then to a junction atop a second ridge. The trail going straight leads 0.25 mile to historic Granite Park Chalet, where you can buy snacks or, with reservations made far in advance, spend the night. Backpackers staying at Granite Park Camp, however, should go right and switchback down past a patrol cabin to the campground. The trail then loops back up to the chalet.

To complete the loop, make your way to a signed junction less than 0.1 mile north of Granite Park Chalet, go east (uphill) toward Swiftcurrent Pass, and climb two switchbacks to a junction. The trail to the left ascends rocky slopes for 1.2 miles to the stupendous views from the lookout building atop Swiftcurrent Mountain.

The main trail goes right and almost immediately crosses the Continental Divide at Swiftcurrent Pass. As you drop over the east side of the pass you'll have fine views of distant Lake Sherburne and a string of smaller lakes leading to it. The trail drops through a stunted subalpine-fir forest, then begins a long downhill. Most of the way is across cliffs or extremely steep slopes and goes past several rocky overlooks with stunning views of shimmering lakes, skyscraping peaks, and numerous waterfalls. After negotiating several long, sweeping switchbacks, you reach the bottom, twice cross a creek on plank bridges, and then come to beautiful Bullhead Lake. The gentle trail goes around the north side of this lake, crosses a side creek on a swinging bridge, and then wanders through willow groves, brushy meadows, and open forest. After 1.5 miles, pass rather disappointing Redrock Falls and then reach scenic Redrock Lake. There are excellent views across this lake to pointed Mount Grinnell.

Another mile of mostly gentle downhill leads to a junction with the short side trail to tiny Fishercap Lake. Stay on the wide and heavily used main trail and just 50 yards later keep right where a horse trail forks left. After another 0.2 mile, the trail leads back to the Swiftcurrent Picnic Area parking lot and the trailhead.

40 *Grinnell Glacier*

Distance: 11.4 miles roundtrip
Difficulty: strenuous
Hiking time: day hike
Elevation gain: 1800 feet
Season: mid-July to mid-October
Best time: late July through August

Contact: Glacier National Park
Map: Trails Illustrated, Glacier–Waterton Lakes National Parks
GPS coordinates: N48° 47.831', W113° 40.111'

Getting there: From St. Mary, go 8.8 miles north on US 89 to Babb. Turn west, following signs to Many Glacier, drive 12.3 miles, then turn left into the Grinnell Glacier Trailhead parking area.

Okay, so this trip isn't exactly off the beaten path. In fact, on a nice summer day, this trail gets beaten more often than my old high school football team—and, believe me, that's saying something. But the booted masses are here for good reason because this is arguably the premier day hike in Glacier National Park. The views are beyond stunning. The wildlife is abundant. And the destination is a large example of the park's namesake geographic feature set under the tall cliffs of scenic Mount Gould. For a more informative trip, ranger-led interpretive hikes occur

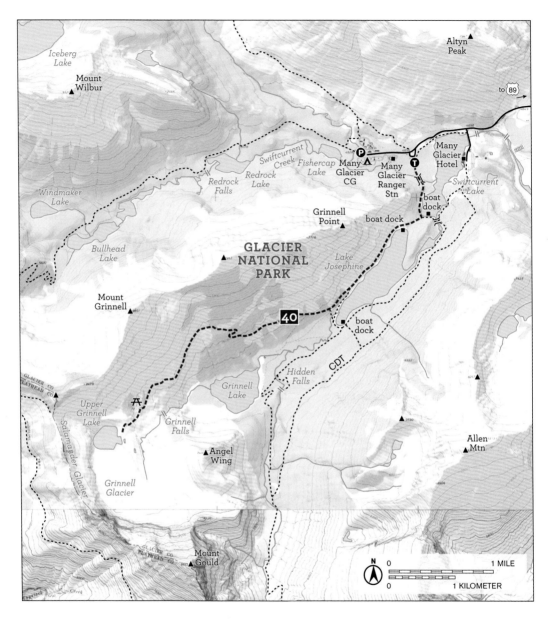

throughout the summer and you can shorten the distance with a two-stage commercial boat ride on Swiftcurrent and Josephine Lakes, which takes 3.4 miles off the roundtrip distance.

The heavily used gravel trail travels gently through forest for 0.2 mile to a bridge over Swiftcurrent Creek, where the surface changes to dirt. The path then skirts the shore of large Swiftcurrent Lake to a junction at the lake's southwest end.

Keep right and go 0.2 mile to a spur trail that leads to the lower boat dock on Lake Josephine. Again, keep right and hug the western shoreline of scenic Lake Josephine for not quite 1 mile to a fork. Bear right and gradually climb away from the lake for 0.4 mile to a junction

Upper Grinnell Lake and the remains of Salamander Glacier

where a trail to the upper Lake Josephine boat dock goes left.

Bear right again and steadily climb an open slope with jaw-dropping views of the surrounding area. Blocky Mount Gould dominates the skyline to the south, while to the southwest you can see Salamander Glacier and Grinnell Falls tucked under the cliffs of the Continental Divide. Milky Grinnell Lake is visible below you. It would seem impossible, but the views and scenery manage to improve with every step. The moderately steep uphill continues unabated all the way to an alpine bench about level with the top of Grinnell Falls. Look for bighorn sheep and mountain goats in this vicinity. Grinnell Glacier can be seen in a deep basin below Mount Gould.

After two quick switchbacks, reach a viewpoint and picnic area with pit toilets and wooden benches at 5.3 miles. This is where ranger-led groups stop for an interpretive talk.

To reach iceberg-clogged Upper Grinnell Lake, wind uphill for 0.4 mile over areas of rock and scrubby willows to the trail's end atop a moraine just above the lake. The views of the rapidly receding glacier and surrounding cliffs are beyond outstanding.

41 *Highline Trail*

Distance: 8.8 miles roundtrip to ridge view;
15 miles roundtrip to Granite Park Chalet
Difficulty: moderate to ridge view;
strenuous to Granite Park Chalet
Hiking time: day hike to ridge view;
overnight to Granite Park Chalet
Elevation gain: 1650 feet to ridge view;
1950 feet to Granite Park Chalet

Season: late July through mid-October
Best time: late July through September
Contact: Glacier National Park
Map: Trails Illustrated, Glacier–Waterton
Lakes National Parks
GPS coordinates: N48° 41.795',
W113° 43.088'

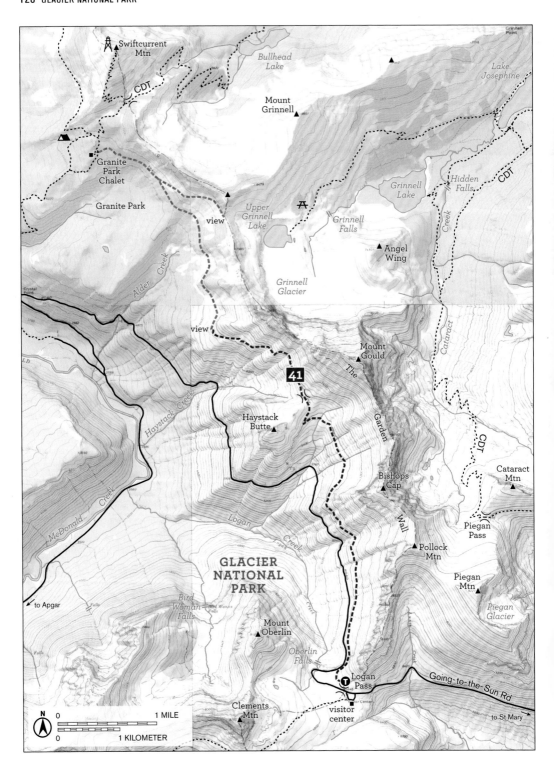

Swiftcurrent Mtn

Bullhead Lake

Grinnell Point

Lake Josephine

CDT

Mount Grinnell

Hidden Falls

CDT

Granite Park Chalet

Grinnell Lake

Granite Park

view

Upper Grinnell Lake

Grinnell Falls

Angel Wing

Cataract Creek

Alder Creek

Grinnell Glacier

Crystal Point

view

Mount Gould

Cataract Mtn

The Garden

41

Haystack Creek

Haystack Butte

Bishops Cap

CDT

Piegan Pass

Piegan Mtn

McDonald Creek

Logan Creek

Wall

Pollock Mtn

Piegan Glacier

to Apgar

GLACIER NATIONAL PARK

Bird Woman Falls

Bird Woman Falls

Mount Oberlin

Oberlin Falls

Logan Pass

Going-to-the-Sun Rd

Clements Mtn

visitor center

visitor center

to St Mary

N

0   1 MILE

0   1 KILOMETER

Looking southwest to Heavens Peak and McDonald Creek valley from north of Haystack Butte

Getting there: Drive Going-to-the-Sun Road to Logan Pass—32 miles from the park's western entrance or 16 miles from the eastern entrance—and park in the huge (but often full) lot on the south side of the highway. Alternatively, to avoid the traffic and parking hassles, use the park's free shuttle bus, which stops at Logan Pass.

Any list of the best hikes in America's national parks inevitably places Glacier's Highline Trail near the top—and justifiably so. The trail travels beneath the cliffs of the Continental Divide offering continuously amazing views of the deep valleys and high peaks of this magnificent park. Wildlife is abundant, including both mountain goats and bighorn sheep. This popular trail also provides the most scenic access to Granite Park Chalet, a historic overnight stop with views to die for.

The trail departs from the north side of the highway and descends slightly across an open slope on the west side of the divide. There are nearly continuous spectacular views of the winding highway and Oberlin Falls backed by the towering pinnacle of Clements Mountain to the southwest and bulky Mount Oberlin to the west.

The trail settles in to a northward traverse paralleling the highway, which follows a descending route on the slope below you. On your right rises a steep ridge called The Garden Wall, forming part of the Continental Divide. The wall shades the trail through mid-morning, and since snow sometimes lingers until late July, visitors may face an icy and dangerous hike in early summer. Ask at the Logan Pass visitor center about the current conditions.

As you travel along this gentle up-and-down trail, the westerly views increasingly feature the tall cliffs on the northeast face of Mount Oberlin and the dramatic summit of distant Heavens Peak. The immediate terrain is a delightful mix of high-elevation trees, grasses, rocky areas, and abundant wildflowers.

Approaching 3 miles, you cross the steep slopes of a basin enclosed by Bishop's Cap and Mount Gould on the east and Haystack Butte to the northwest. It would seem impossible, but the views actually improve as you enjoy new vistas down the deep, glacial canyon of McDonald Creek with immense peaks towering on either side.

At the head of the little basin the trail makes a moderately graded switchback that climbs to a pass near 3.5 miles on the northeast side of Haystack Butte. Watch for bighorn sheep in this area.

From the pass the trail contours beneath rocky buttresses (look for mountain goats), then descends to a spectacular viewpoint at 4.4 miles. This is an excellent place to stop for lunch as well as a logical turnaround point for a moderate day hike.

Extend your hike: Those who want a longer trek should keep hiking along this ridiculously scenic and relatively level route. At 6.3 miles an outstanding side trail goes sharply right and climbs 1 mile to a clifftop viewpoint where you can look directly down on the icy mass of Grinnell Glacier. The main trail goes straight, and 1.2 miles later, reaches Granite Park Chalet. To stay overnight at this historic facility, call months in advance to make reservations.

42 Hidden Lake

Distance: 6 miles roundtrip
Difficulty: moderate
Hiking time: day hike
Elevation gain: 1200 feet
Season: mid-July through mid-October
Best time: late July through September

Contact: Glacier National Park
Map: Trails Illustrated, Glacier–Waterton Lakes National Parks
GPS coordinates: N48° 41.733', W113° 43.069'

Getting there: Drive Going-to-the-Sun Road to Logan Pass—32 miles from the park's western entrance or 16 miles from the eastern entrance—and park in the huge (but often full) lot on the south side of the highway. Alternatively, to avoid the traffic and parking hassles, use the park's free shuttle bus, which stops at Logan Pass.

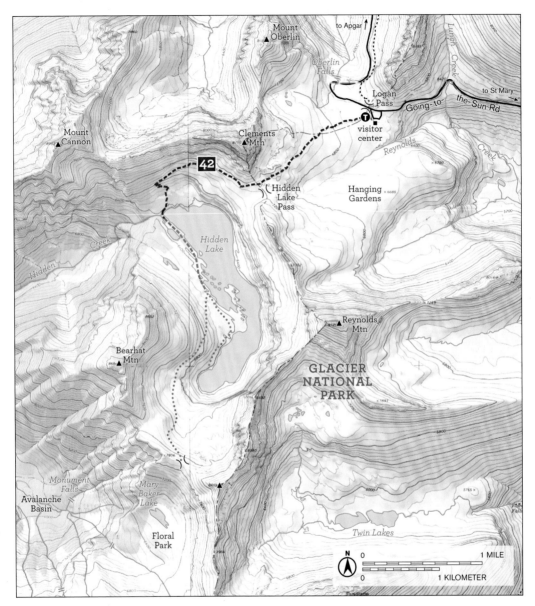

Don't expect solitude on this trip. In fact, Times Square in New York City is a haven of solitude compared to the Hidden Lake Trail on a nice summer day. But the amazing scenery makes this hike worth the parking hassles and the wall-to-wall tourists. And despite the crowds, wildlife is surprisingly abundant. Mountain goats, bighorn sheep, and hoary marmots are all common, and the trail is frequently closed due to grizzly bear activity.

Starting immediately north of the visitor center, the initially paved trail goes west-southwest up the open slopes beneath towering Clements Mountain. This famous view is often depicted in calendars and on postcards, so it will probably look familiar even to first-time visitors. In

Clouds over Reynolds Mountain from the trail above Logan Pass

midsummer, water drips over terraced rocks and wildflowers are abundant, explaining why this slope is called the Hanging Gardens. These alpine plants are extremely fragile, however, so please stay on the trail.

Most of the first 0.7 mile is a boardwalk, to protect the tread and limit the mud on tourist's tennis shoes. As you gain elevation, the surface turns to dirt and you will likely cross a couple of snowfields before leveling out and reaching a shallow pond. Rising across this pond to the west-southwest is square-topped Bearhat Mountain, another much-photographed landmark.

At 1.5 miles is Hidden Lake Pass and one of the most photogenic scenes imaginable. Large, island-dotted Hidden Lake fills the basin below you, while Bearhat Mountain makes a perfect backdrop rising majestically above the water. A viewing platform offers great photo opportunities and is also an excellent place to look for mountain goats, which frequent the ledges of Clements Mountain. When the trail is closed due to bear activity, this pass is as far as hikers can usually go.

If the bruins are cooperating, continue down to the lake on a trail that makes a long, looping descent across open, view-filled slopes, and then descends five steep switchbacks to the lakeshore. As expected, there are very photogenic views across the lake to Bearhat, Reynolds, and other mountains. Since the immediate lakeshore is heavily used, you may want to escape the crowds by fording the calf-deep outlet creek and exploring the much quieter west side of the lake.

Extend your hike: Experienced hikers up for a strenuous adventure can follow a good trail halfway around the lake and search for a sketchy climber's trail angling very steeply up to the right. This leads to an open basin from which you can climb to a high saddle with stupendous views of Avalanche Lake almost 4000 feet below, plus Sperry Glacier, Little Matterhorn, and Edwards Mountain.

43 *Avalanche Lake*

Distance: 4.6 miles roundtrip
Difficulty: easy to moderate
Hiking time: half-day hike
Elevation gain. 600 feet
Season: late May through November
Best time: June through July

Contact: Glacier National Park
Map: Trails Illustrated, Glacier–Waterton Lakes National Parks
GPS coordinates: N48° 40.756', W113° 49.191'

Getting there: From West Glacier, drive 16.5 miles on Going-to-the-Sun Road to the Avalanche Creek Trailhead. Finding parking here is often impossible, so consider taking the park's free shuttle bus, which stops at this trailhead.

This extremely popular hike offers the best relatively easy introduction to the lush scenery on the west side of Glacier National Park. The path travels through cathedral groves of cedars, passes a beautiful slot canyon with small waterfalls, and ends at a very scenic lake surrounded by tall peaks. So while solitude is impossible, the scenery is worth the two-legged company.

From the south side of the road bridge over Avalanche Creek, the trail begins on a boardwalk and heads upstream through a grove of old-growth western red cedars. The trail's surface soon changes to pavement as you pass spur trails to Avalanche Campground on the right and the creek on your left. At 0.3 mile the Trail of the Cedars goes straight while Avalanche Lake Trail heads right (uphill).

Looking down Avalanche Gorge

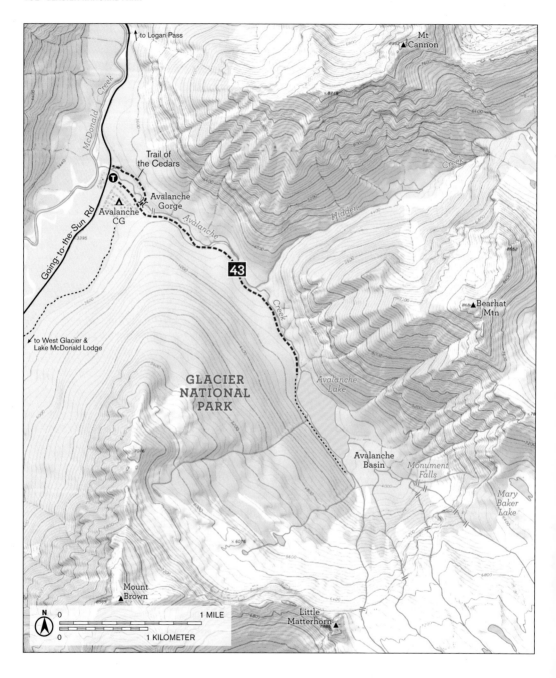

The trail climbs for 25 yards, then goes left at a junction with a trail heading to Lake McDonald Lodge. Soon you pass directly above the waterfalls and dark cliffs of Avalanche Gorge, where you'll want to spend some time admiring the scene before resuming the gentle uphill climb through dense forest. Brief openings in the forest canopy offer views to the north toward the towering summit of Mount Cannon.

After two relatively easy miles, you reach Avalanche Lake. This long, scenic lake has several waterfalls feeding it and a plethora of tall peaks to the east and southeast, dominated by the pyramid of Little Matterhorn. A trail goes around the southwest shore before ending near the head of the lake. Camping is prohibited.

On the return, be sure to take the Trail of the Cedars loop, which crosses Avalanche Creek on a bridge just below the photogenic, waterfall-filled defile of Avalanche Gorge. It then follows a boardwalk trail through a forest of magnificent old cedars back to the trailhead.

44 *Gunsight Pass Traverse*

Distance: 20 miles one-way
Difficulty: strenuous
Hiking time: multiday
Elevation gain: 3500 feet
Season: late July through early October
Best time: August and September
Contact: Glacier National Park

Map: Trails Illustrated, Glacier–Waterton Lakes National Parks
GPS coordinates: N48° 37.015', W113° 52.546' for exit trailhead; N48° 40.645', W113° 39.121' for starting trailhead

Getting there: Glacier National Park's free shuttle bus system makes the transportation logistics simple. From West Glacier, drive 11 miles on Going-to-the-Sun Road and leave your car at the Sperry Trailhead directly opposite the turnoff to Lake McDonald Lodge. Here you board the west side park shuttle to Logan Pass, where you transfer to the east side shuttle and disembark at the Jackson Glacier Overlook/Gunsight Pass Trailhead to begin your hike.

Along the trail east of Gunsight Pass

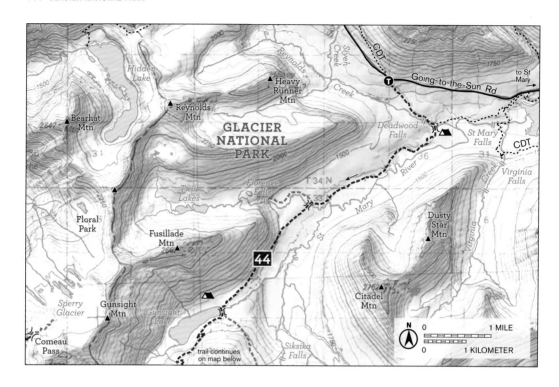

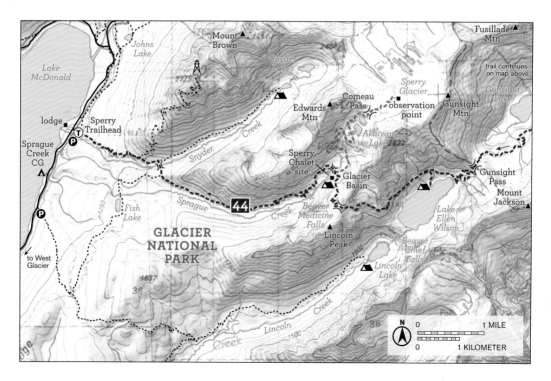

One of the classic hikes in Glacier National Park (and is *that* ever saying something!), this across-the-divide route offers all the park's most famous attributes in one compact package. Here you'll revel in towering waterfalls, tremendous mountain scenery, stunning subalpine lakes, abundant wildlife, and a view-packed high pass. Although the trip is sometimes done as a very long and rushed day hike, a three-day backpacking trip is ideal. Reservations are a must, however, since this trip is deservedly popular.

From the east end of the parking area the trail rapidly loses elevation through a relatively lush coniferous forest. At not quite 1.3 miles, pass picturesque Deadwood Falls, set in a twisting little slot canyon of reddish rock, and reach a junction.

Go right, cross a swinging bridge over Reynolds Creek, and pass the spur trail to Reynolds Creek Camp. The trail now begins a long, gentle uphill that will last all the way to Gunsight Lake. The route first travels through forest as it skirts a large marshy area along St. Mary River, which offers a good chance of seeing moose as well as fine views of nearby mountains. At 4 miles is a junction with the brushy side trail to Florence Falls. This tall, veil-like waterfall amply rewards those who make the 0.6-mile side trip to see its tumbling waters.

The main trail goes straight and immediately crosses an unnamed creek on a log bridge. This is followed by a long traverse of an open hillside from which you'll enjoy excellent views looking south to Blackfoot Mountain and sprawling Blackfoot Glacier. Things level out shortly before you attain Gunsight Lake at 6.2 miles. Fed by waterfalls, this long and wildly scenic lake is backed by the rugged ridge of Gunsight Mountain. The lake has an excellent designated camping area above its northeast shore.

Side trip: The trail soon takes a swinging bridge over the outlet to Gunsight Lake, and comes to a junction. The not-to-be-missed Jackson Glacier Trail goes left, making a steep climb of a brushy hillside, and then follows a scenic up-and-down traverse of an open slope with excellent views and abundant huckleberries.

Hiker approaching Gunsight Lake

Grizzly bears are very common here during the August berry season, so be alert. Although the official path ends well before you reach its namesake glacier, you can easily walk across the wonderfully scenic open slopes and explore as far as you want.

For Gunsight Pass, go right at the junction and steadily climb a brushy and view-packed hillside. Two switchbacks lead to a section of trail that has been chiseled out of a cliff and which is often blocked by snow until early August. Six more irregularly spaced switchbacks take you to the small stone shelter at Gunsight Pass. The views, especially west down to large Lake Ellen Wilson, are superb. A herd of mountain goats hangs around Gunsight Pass and they often approach quite close.

The trail makes several short switchbacks down the west side of the pass, not quite reaching the shores of deep Lake Ellen Wilson. The route then completes an ascending loop to the north, passes a spur trail to a designated camp, and continues across the open hillside with outstanding views of the lake and surrounding peaks. Once past the lake, you'll have great views back to tall Mount Jackson and down to towering Beaver Chief Falls, which at 1300 feet is one of the highest waterfalls in the American Rockies. At the end of the traverse, the trail ascends three quick switchbacks to a saddle beside Lincoln Peak.

Descending the west side of this saddle involves five irregularly spaced switchbacks on a rocky slope with nice views looking north to imposing Edwards Mountain. After about 1 mile, pass a side trail to Sperry Camp, and just 0.25 mile later reach the site of the historic Sperry Chalet. The popular lodge burned down in a 2017 wildfire, and, as of this writing, rebuilding plans are unknown. The trail loops around the right side of the chalet site, then descends 0.2 mile to a junction.

Side trip: The final recommended side trip goes right here on the 3.7-mile Sperry Glacier Trail. This trail makes an uphill traverse on a talus slope, passes below a pair of wispy waterfalls, then switchbacks uphill past Feather Woman and Akaiyau Lakes to tiny Gem Lake sitting right on top of Comeau Pass. The route then

goes intermittently downhill to Observation Point. The views looking up to Sperry Glacier and the steep northwest face of Gunsight Mountain are stupendous.

Back on the main trail, descend through Glacier Basin to a bridged crossing of Sprague Creek, then drop to a smaller lower basin before descending six switchbacks to an open slope where you can see tall and picturesque Beaver Medicine Falls. From here, make your way down the steep canyon of Sprague Creek through increasingly lush coniferous forests. Eventually the trail leaves Sprague Creek and traverses over to a junction beside Snyder Creek.

Go right, make a bridged crossing of the creek, and climb a bit to a second junction, this time with the trail to Snyder Lakes. Keep left, walk 100 yards, and then go straight at a junction with the Mount Brown Lookout Trail.

The final 1.8 miles are all downhill as the trails winds through forest, passes a nice viewpoint of huge Lake McDonald, and finally reaches a junction with the Johns Lake Trail. Go straight and pass a couple of side trails to a horse outfitting facility before reaching the Sperry Trailhead at 20.0 miles (excluding side trips).

45 *Piegan Pass*

Distance: 9 miles roundtrip	**Contact:** Glacier National Park
Difficulty: strenuous	**Map:** Trails Illustrated, Glacier–Waterton
Hiking time: day hike	Lakes National Parks
Elevation gain: 1750 feet	**GPS coordinates:** N48° 42.093',
Season: late July through early October	W113° 40.047'
Best time: August	

Getting there: The trailhead is at Siyeh Bend on Going-to-the-Sun Road, 3 miles east of Logan Pass or about 13 miles west of the eastern park entrance.

E very trail off Glacier's Going-to-the-Sun Road is wildly scenic, but Piegan Pass is a favorite because it's marginally less crowded and offers some of the most stunning views in the park, especially of nearby Piegan Mountain and down

the gaping canyon of Cataract Creek. Most hikers take about a week to wipe the smile off their face after taking this hike.

From the north side of the road, the trail goes down to Siyeh Creek, heads upstream for

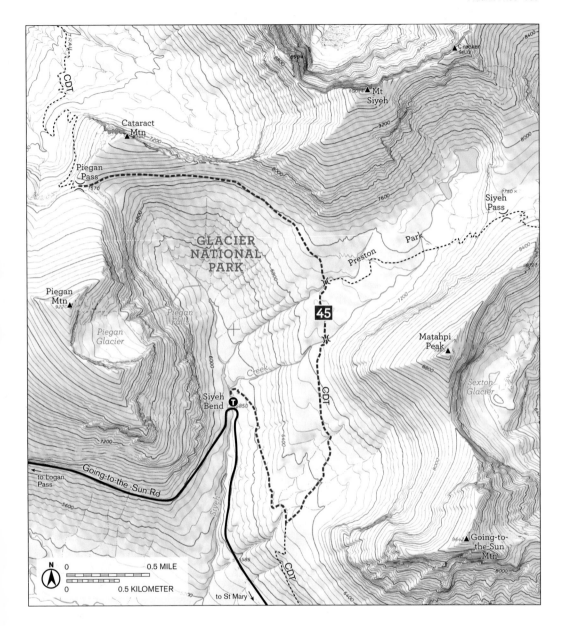

0.1 mile, then turns to the right and gradually ascends. Most of the climb is in forest but there are frequent fine views of Piegan Mountain to the west. At 1.2 miles, go sharply left at a junction and continue the gradual uphill. After crossing small Siyeh Creek on a bridge, hike through a series of gorgeous meadows to a junction at the lower end of Preston Park at 2.7 miles.

Go left and begin a long uphill traverse of the open slope below Cataract Mountain with stunning views, especially southwest to dramatic Piegan Mountain sporting the icy mass of Piegan Glacier in a bowl near the center of the peak. The long and magnificently scenic traverse leads to treeless Piegan Pass at 4.5 miles. Put simply, views just don't get any better than this.

Piegan Mountain and Glacier from the trail up to Piegan Pass

The vista to the northwest, of a stupendous row of towering cliffs and pinnacles culminating in Mount Gould, is especially great, but the views south to Siyeh Bend and north down the canyon of Cataract Creek are also breathtaking. It's possible to exit via a long and magnificent ramble down Cataract Creek to Many Glacier Hotel, but this necessitates a long car shuttle.

46 Otokomi Lake

Distance: 10.4 miles roundtrip
Difficulty: strenuous
Hiking time: day hike or overnight
Elevation gain: 2150 feet
Season: July to mid-October
Best time: July and August

Contact: Glacier National Park
Map: Trails Illustrated, Glacier–Waterton Lakes National Parks
GPS coordinates: N48° 41.690', W113° 31.165'

Getting there: From St. Mary, drive 6.1 miles west on Going-to-the-Sun Road, then turn right at Rising Sun. Go 50 yards, turn right, and park near the Rising Sun Store.

Less heralded than some other destinations in the park, Otokomi Lake is nonetheless a very worthwhile goal with excellent scenery and fine fishing. Although marred by fire damage for the first 3 miles, the access trail passes numerous waterfalls and is well graded throughout. A comfortable designated camp allows backpackers to turn this into an overnight outing.

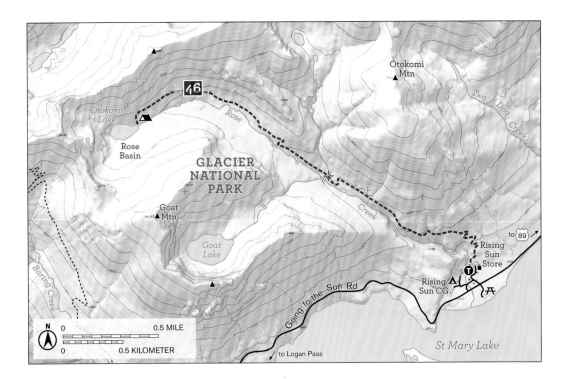

The signed path starts from the west side of the Rising Sun Store and follows boisterous Rose Creek upstream past several guest cabins and outbuildings. The route then pulls away from the creek, ascends a set of moderately graded switchbacks, and steadily climbs a slope that alternates between dense forest and large areas burned in the fires of 2015. Beargrass blooms profusely in early summer.

After a little over 1 mile you begin crossing well above the cliff-edged canyon of Rose Creek, a stream that drops through a series of cascades and small waterfalls. At 2.3 miles you cross a tributary creek on a log bridge then pass several more unnamed waterfalls, a couple of which are impressively large and photogenic.

Two quick downhill switchbacks take you briefly back to creek level. Then it's a long and occasionally steep ascent as the canyon curves to the west offering up dramatic views of the peaks above Otokomi Lake. The deep red color streaking many of those peaks is from argillite, a distinctive rock commonly found in this area.

The last 0.4 mile is mostly level as you cross open scree slopes with great views. A final brief downhill leads to the spur trail to Otokomi Lake Camp just before you reach the lake.

Like nearly every alpine lake in Glacier, Otokomi lies in a spectacular cirque surrounded by tall cliffs and impressive peaks. The fishing is usually good for large cutthroat trout, offering further incentive to linger and enjoy the scene.

Hoary marmot, Glacier National Park

One of many lovely waterfalls along Rose Creek

47 *Triple Divide Pass*

Distance: 14.2 miles roundtrip
Difficulty: strenuous
Hiking time: day hike
Elevation gain: 2400 feet
Season: mid-July to mid-October
Best time: late July through August

Contact: Glacier National Park
Map: Trails Illustrated, Glacier–Waterton Lakes National Parks
GPS coordinates: N48° 36.146', W113° 23.022'

Getting there: From Browning, go 16 miles northwest on US 89 to a four-way junction near milepost 17.3. Turn left on a gravel road and drive 5 miles to the trailhead on the right just before Cut Bank Campground.

Hidden in the relatively little visited Cut Bank area of Glacier National Park, this trip offers all the scenic rewards of other hikes in this famous preserve, but without the crowds. Triple Divide Pass offers not only tremendous views but also geographic interest because it sits next to Triple Divide Peak, the only place in North America that water drains toward three different oceans: Atlantic, Pacific, and Arctic. Nearby Medicine Grizzly Lake offers an easier but still very scenic alternative destination.

The gradual up-and-down trail travels west through a mix of forest and meadows along clear North Fork Cut Bank Creek. As you ascend, you'll enjoy increasingly fine views of the many rugged peaks enclosing this narrowing valley. Wildlife is common, including moose, bugling elk in September, and grizzly bears throughout the summer.

Cross an unnamed side creek on a log bridge at 3.7 miles, then come to a junction. Relatively short but pretty Atlantic Falls lies 0.2 mile down the trail to the left and is worth

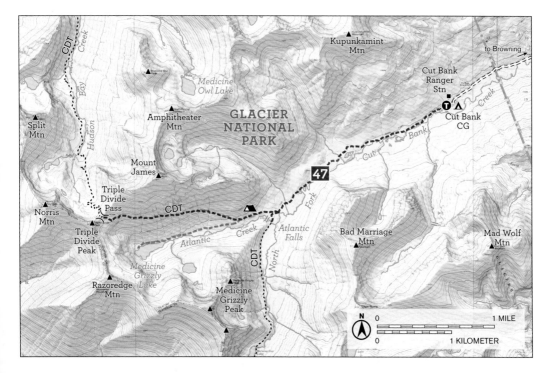

Razoredge Mountain is a backdrop to vivid fall color.

the side trip. The main trail, however, goes right, passes Atlantic Creek Camp 0.4 mile later, and then comes to a junction. Wildly scenic Medicine Grizzly Lake lies 1.4 easy miles down the trail to the left.

For the tougher viewpoint hike to Triple Divide Pass, bear right and make a long, well-graded uphill traverse of an open slope. The views are increasingly awe-inspiring, especially of Razoredge Mountain rising over the Medicine Grizzly Lake basin to the southwest. At Triple Divide Pass the views are stupendous, with pointed Triple Divide Peak and bulky Norris Mountain right beside you, and long views down the scenic valley of Hudson Bay Creek to towering Split Mountain to the north.

48 *Oldman and No Name Lakes Loop*

Distance: 18.8-mile loop
Difficulty: strenuous
Hiking time: overnight or multiday
Elevation gain: 3100 feet
Season: late July to mid-October
Best time: late July and August

Contact: Glacier National Park
Map: Trails Illustrated, Glacier–Waterton Lakes National Parks
GPS coordinates: N48° 29.525', W113° 21.937'

Getting there: From East Glacier, go 4 miles north on State Route 49, then turn left on Two Medicine Road. Drive 8.6 miles, turn right into Two Medicine Campground, and proceed 0.3 mile to the trailhead on the left.

This classic loop is arguably the best short backpacking trip in Glacier National Park. The route is popular, so reservations are advised, but it's well worth the trouble since the loop visits two gorgeous high-elevation lakes connected by a magnificent alpine ridge walk. Strong hikers can do the loop in a day, but the route deserves a slower pace to fully appreciate its charms.

Cross a wooden bridge over Two Medicine River and walk 0.1 mile to a junction at the start of the loop. For a counterclockwise circuit, go right, following the river downstream for 0.3 mile, then climb a hillside and curve left up the canyon of Dry Fork. The trail then descends to a partly forested bench above the creek before heading upstream under the increasingly tall and rugged peaks lining the canyon.

Cross the creek on a bridge at 2.2 miles, go left at a junction, and slowly climb through forest and across an open hillside. After passing a view of a distant, unnamed waterfall, the trail stays on open slopes with ever-improving views of the spectacular pinnacle of Flinsch Peak. The steady uphill

continues all the way to the turnoff for Oldman Lake at 5.9 miles. To visit the lake and its good camps, go left and descend 0.3 mile to its shores. This deep lake is extremely scenic with the spiky summit of Flinsch Peak rising to the southwest and the cliffs of Mount Morgan to the northwest.

The loop trail goes right at the junction and climbs irregularly spaced switchbacks on an open slope with dramatic views of the basin of Oldman Lake. At the top is Pitamakan Pass where you gain spectacular views looking almost straight down to large Pitamakan Lake and the canyon of North Fork Cut Bank Creek.

Bear left at a junction with the Pitamakan Pass Trail, then go left again 0.2 mile later at the junction with Cut Bank Pass Trail. Now above timberline, the trail climbs across the rocky north side of Mount Morgan, then turns south to make a mostly level crossing of the steep and barren slopes on the west side of the peak. The views to the west are outstanding—toward countless tall peaks and deep valleys, much of which burned in the 2015 Thompson Fire.

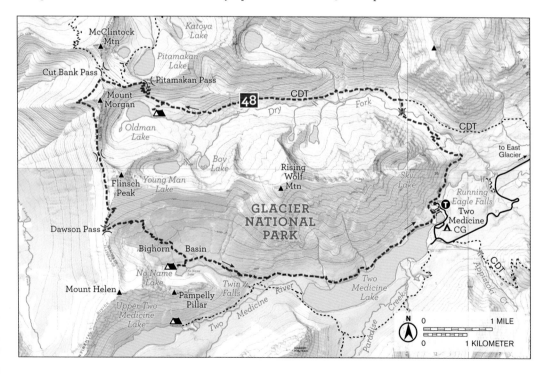

Looking north toward Mount Morgan from the ridge

Near 10 miles, you reach a windy pass almost directly beneath the soaring cliffs of Flinsch Peak and with amazing views down to Oldman Lake. You then traverse the west side of Flinsch Peak and descend seven switchbacks to Dawson Pass.

The trail turns sharply left here and steeply descends a series of traverses and switchbacks taking you back into the forest. At 1.9 miles from the pass, a 0.2-mile side trail goes right to No Name Lake, which is tucked under a tremendous row of towering cliffs on Mount Helen. The campsite here is a scenic spot to spend the night.

To complete the loop, wind steeply downhill for 1.4 miles to a junction, go left, and follow a gentle up-and-down route through forest and across brushy areas and aspen groves around the north side of Two Medicine Lake back to the trailhead.

49 *Firebrand Pass*

Distance: 9.6 miles roundtrip
Difficulty: strenuous
Hiking time: day hike
Elevation gain: 2000 feet
Season: late June through October
Best time: July

Contact: Glacier National Park
Map: Trails Illustrated Glacier–Waterton Lakes National Parks
GPS coordinates: N48° 22.299', W113° 16.771'

Getting there: From Marias Pass on US 2, go 5 miles east to milepost 203 where an unsigned and very short dirt road descends from the north side of the highway to the trailhead beside a set of railroad tracks.

Almost entirely overlooked by park visitors and even most park rangers, this highly enjoyable and very scenic hike explores a beautiful area in the southern reaches of Glacier National Park. The goal is a dramatic alpine pass, but the real joy comes from discovering a

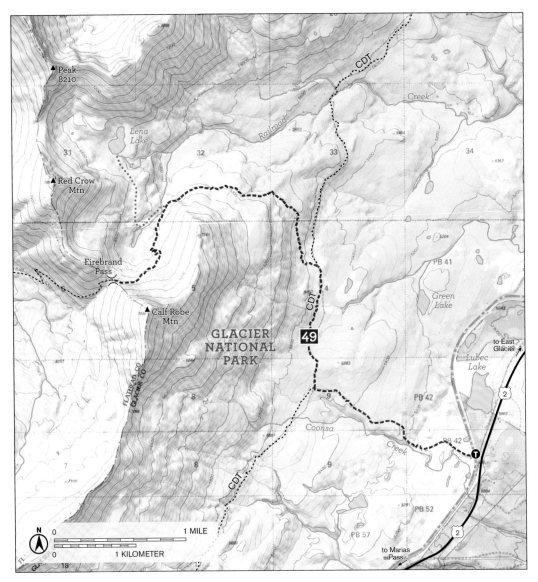

gorgeous on-trail park beauty spot that you may have all to yourself.

Walk a grassy track that heads north over the railroad tracks and through a fenceline toward the bulky mass of Calf Robe Mountain. The tall, pyramid-shaped peak to the southwest is Summit Mountain. Following a long-abandoned jeep track, now covered with grasses and wildflowers, the scenic route goes past a series of beaver ponds (look for moose) then uphill through

forests of quaking aspens and lodgepole pines to a junction at 1.4 miles.

Turn right and make an up-and-down traverse through forest and a series of pretty meadows carpeted with wildflowers in early summer. At 2.4 miles, bear left at a junction and begin an often-steep ascent. Increasingly good views open up to the southwest toward the rugged Bob Marshall Wilderness. Once you reach the top of a ridge, the trail curves left into the broad upper valley of

Alpine wildflowers brighten the view at Firebrand Pass.

Railroad Creek, which is rimmed by a stunning array of high mountains.

The trail gradually climbs over increasingly open slopes dotted with small subalpine firs to a high and very attractive basin below Firebrand Pass at 3.8 miles. From here, climb four switchbacks and make a long traverse up a talus slope to the often-windy pass. This remote grandstand offers outstanding views especially looking southwest to the Ole Creek Valley and adjoining peaks such as Summit, Little Dog, and Brave Dog Mountains.

Extend your hike: To visit this area's prettiest lake, from the basin below Firebrand Pass, head cross-country to the north over open and relatively easy terrain toward castle-like Peak 8210. You'll climb over a little ridge before descending to gorgeous Lena Lake, about 0.8 mile from the trail. The lake is situated in a spectacular and rarely visited cirque between Peak 8210 and Red Crow Mountain.

Opposite, top: Fritillary butterfly, Scapegoat Wilderness

Opposite, bottom: Balsamroot frames butte view along Willow Creek Trail

The Bob Marshall Wilderness Complex

One of the largest wild areas in the continental United States, the adjoining Bob Marshall, Scapegoat, and Great Bear Wilderness areas combine to form a vast area of rugged mountains, towering cliffs, wide valleys, and forested ridges south of Glacier National Park. Usually referred to simply as "The Bob," this enormous area honors the legacy of the great conservation icon and wilderness advocate Bob Marshall.

Widely acknowledged as the crown jewel in America's wilderness system, these three preserves encompass several entire mountain ranges in a vast pristine environment that is beyond parallel in the United States, outside of Alaska. This is the kind of wilderness that Marshall envisioned when he advocated setting aside areas where a person could "spend at least a week or two traveling and not cross his own tracks." Although the scenery is occasionally excellent, especially on the hikes included here, often the main attraction is simply immersing yourself in the enormity of what the untamed American West used to look like.

The wilderness is a stronghold for wildlife, including a healthy population of grizzly bears, so hike and camp accordingly. Massive forest fires regularly burn large portions of this wilderness, so you should expect some trips to include many miles of charred terrain. Finally, most trails here were built for equestrians, so only a few major stream crossings have bridges and the busiest trails are frequently muddy from the churning of hooves. Often the best time to visit is early September, when the trails are at their driest, the river crossings are easier, and neither the hunters nor the winter snows have yet shown up for their seasons.

50 *Jewel Basin*

Distance: 11.6 miles roundtrip
Difficulty: strenuous
Hiking time: day hike or overnight
Elevation gain: 1500 feet
Season: late June through October
Best time: mid-August, September

Contact: Flathead NF, Swan Lake Ranger District
Map: USFS Jewel Basin Hiking Area
GPS coordinates: N48° 09.657', W113° 56.882'

Getting there: From Kalispell, drive 6 miles south on US 93, turn left on State Route 82 and go 7.2 miles, then go right on SR 35. After 0.4 mile, turn left onto SR 83 for 2.7 miles then turn left (north) on Echo Lake Road. Proceed 2.1 miles, turn right on Foothill Road, and drive 1.1 miles to a junction. Go straight on gravel Forest Road 5392 and continue 6.5 steep miles to the Camp Misery Trailhead.

Jewel Basin is an enchanting realm of numerous mountain lakes, wildflower-filled meadows, scenic peaks, and good viewpoints that is set aside for the exclusive use of pedestrians. Deservedly popular with Kalispell-area hikers, this region features many miles of fun, interconnected trails. Arguably the best is this trip to Crater Lake, but other options abound.

Take Trail #8, which passes a small ranger cabin, then climbs two well-graded switchbacks on a rather brushy slope to a junction. Turn sharply right and continue gradually uphill to a

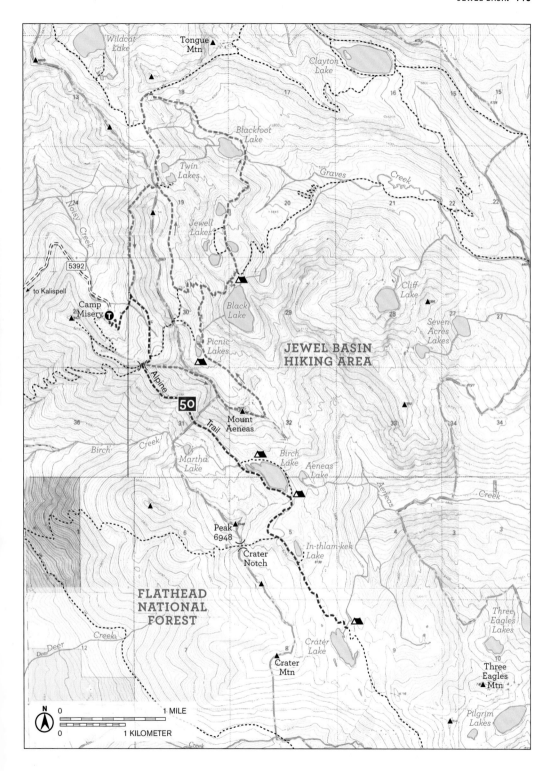

Wildcat Lake

Tongue Mtn

Clayton Lake

13

18

17

16

15

15

Blackfoot Lake

Twin Lakes

Graves Creek

19

20

21

22

22

Toosy Creek

Jewell Lakes

5392

to Kalispell

Camp Misery

30

Black Lake

29

Cliff Lake

28

Seven Acres Lakes

27

27

JEWEL BASIN HIKING AREA

Picnic Lakes

Alpine

50

Mount Aeneas

Trail

36

31

32

33

34

34

Birch Creek

Martha Lake

Birch Lake

Aeneas Lake

Aeneas

Creek

1

6

5

4

3

Peak 6948

In-thlam-keh Lake

Crater Notch

FLATHEAD NATIONAL FOREST

12

Deer Creek

7

8

Crater Lake

9

Three Eagles Lakes

10

Three Eagles Mtn

Crater Mtn

N

0   1 MILE

0   1 KILOMETER

Pilgrim Lakes

Creek

Dramatic clouds over Crater Lake

junction with Alpine Trail at 1.3 miles. Go right for just over 0.1 mile to a multi-way junction in a saddle.

Bear slightly left (south-southeast), staying on Alpine Trail, from which there are excellent views of the Flathead Valley and huge Flathead Lake far below. The path goes mostly downhill across an open hillside with a nice view of Peak 6948 to the south rising over rock-lined Martha Lake. Just a few yards before reaching large Birch Lake is a junction. Both trails loop around Birch Lake, but the main trail goes straight, skirting the west shore of this beautiful lake where you'll have terrific views across the water to Mount Aeneas, the highest peak in this area.

Above a campsite at the lake's southeast end, the two trails reunite and you continue south through gentle and delightful subalpine terrain past a junction with little-used Crater Notch Trail. Soon thereafter you pass above In-thlam-keh (formerly "Squaw") Lake, then descend on rocky tread to the exceptionally attractive rock-lined basin holding large Crater Lake at 5.8 miles. This lake makes a logical and rewarding turnaround point for a day hike or short backpacking trip with some attractive camps along the lake's northeast shore.

Extend your hike: Outstanding alternate or additional destinations abound. Perhaps the best option is a fun loop through the northern part of the Jewel Basin Hiking Area, which starts from the multi-way junction at 1.3 miles and goes over Mount Aeneas, with its expansive views. From there you drop to the two Picnic Lakes and can loop back to Camp Misery on either a short, direct trail, or via a longer and more scenic, but also more difficult, route past Black and Blackfoot Lakes.

51 *Sunburst Lake*

Distance: 18.4 miles roundtrip
Difficulty: strenuous
Hiking time: overnight
Elevation gain: 1400 feet
Season: July to mid-October
Best time: July to mid-October

Contact: Flathead NF, Spotted Bear
Ranger District
Map: Cairn Cartographics, Bob Marshall
Wilderness Complex: North Half
GPS coordinates: N47° 48.102',
W113° 29.221'

Getting there: From Columbia Falls, drive 7 miles east on US 2, then turn right onto paved West Reservoir Road, following signs to Hungry Horse Dam. Drive 4 miles, cross the top of Hungry Horse Dam, and continue another 11.4 miles to the end of pavement. After another 41 miles on this winding road, turn right onto Forest Road 2826 toward Meadow Creek. Stay on this road, which becomes FR 549, for 15.2 miles, then turn left, following signs to Gorge Creek Trailhead. Drive 1 mile, turn left just after a bridge over Bunker Creek, and go 0.1 mile to the road-end trailhead.

Extremely scenic Sunburst Lake sits in a deep basin at the base of glacier-clad Swan Peak. The woodsy hike to this fish-filled gem follows a rollicking creek and offers a smattering of nice meadows and views. Reaching the trailhead, however, requires a long, tedious drive on a gravel road. Ideally, make the drive the day before, sleep in the dispersed camping area below the trailhead, and start your hike in the morning.

The wide trail crosses a densely forested bench above the rocky chasm carved by aptly named Gorge Creek, but after about 0.5 mile you meet up with the creek and more closely follow its clear waters upstream.

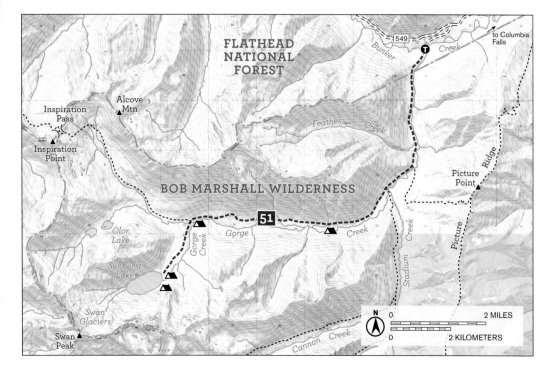

Swan Peak seen from the trail to the northeast

Rock-hop Feather Creek, then continue to the signed junction with Picture Point Trail near 2.2 miles. Go straight, walk 0.6 mile, and then cross the first of several sloping meadows that are cleared of trees by regular avalanches. In the second of these openings is a small cairn marking a faint trail that drops to the left on its way to Stadium Creek Valley.

Keep straight and continue with the pattern of forest mixed with meadow openings. At a strip of trees in the middle of a somewhat larger meadow near 4.9 miles is an unsigned fork where a path angles left to a hunter's camp. Go straight and reach a particularly large and brushy opening at 7.3 miles, where ice-clad Swan Peak rather suddenly makes its appearance to the southwest. Sunburst Lake sits in a deep bowl at the base of this mountain.

At 8.1 miles is a junction marked with an easy-to-miss wooden sign. The faint trail to the right climbs to Inspiration Pass. Take the more travelled route to the left, which in about 100 yards reaches a designated stock campsite. Livestock are not allowed at Sunburst Lake, so equestrians must leave their stock here.

Just past this camp, make a calf-deep ford of Inspiration Creek and then begin climbing beside loudly cascading Gorge Creek. At 9.2 miles you reach a spacious campsite just below large Sunburst Lake. There is another excellent campsite on the other side of a logjam at the outlet of the lake.

Sunburst Lake sits beneath cliffs and tall waterfalls that are fed by the icy remnants of the Swan Glaciers high on the slopes of 9289-foot Swan Peak. The lake is not only extremely scenic, it supports an exceptional cutthroat trout fishery, providing even more enticement for you to set up camp and stay awhile.

52 *Rumble Creek Lakes*

Distance: 8.2 miles roundtrip
Difficulty: very strenuous
Hiking time: day hike
Elevation gain: 3800 feet
Season: mid-July through early October
Best time: late July through September

Contact: Flathead NF, Swan Lake Ranger District
Maps: USGS Condon, Holland Peak
GPS coordinates: N47° 31.412', W113° 38.458'

Getting there: From Seeley Lake, drive 26 miles north on State Route 83 to milepost 40.2, then turn right on gravel Rumble Creek Road (Forest Road 560). Drive 1.1 miles, go left at a junction, and proceed 2.8 miles to the signed trailhead in an old clear-cut.

This trip is not for everyone. The unofficial climber's route is so unrelentingly steep it will severely test your lungs and thighs on the way up and shift the abuse to your knees and toes on the way back down. Then, between the lower and upper lakes, you'll climb a ridiculously steep slope of loose rocks that will stop anyone who is afraid of heights and force all travelers to be extra cautious with their footing.

But for those who can make it, the rewards are off the charts. The two Rumble Creek Lakes sit in spectacular cirques high on Holland Peak, the tallest summit in the Swan Range. Immense tan-colored cliffs rise directly from the upper

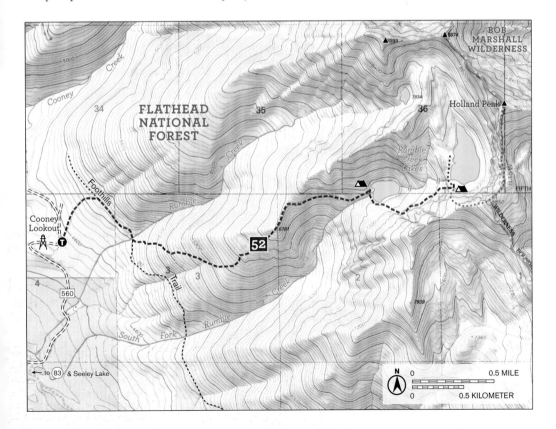

Looking down on Lower Rumble Lake

lake, in a scene that is beyond compare in this part of Montana. And the views stretching west across the Swan Valley to the rugged Mission Range are outstanding as well—all of which makes those gallons of sweat and aching knees worth the price. *Note:* This trail is not shown on the USGS map for this area.

The trail climbs fairly steeply through a shady forest of western larch, Douglas fir, and lodgepole pine for 0.4 mile to a junction with the Foothills Trail. Your route turns right and makes a gentle up-and-down traverse first in forest and then across a relatively open brushy slope. Cross cascading Rumble Creek near 0.7 mile, then just 110 yards later reach an unmarked junction.

Turn left onto a well-defined footpath that ascends a partly forested hillside. This path was built by climbers, a demographic that rigidly adheres to the-shortest-distance-between-two-points

mentality. Do *not* expect switchbacks or any other amenities designed to mitigate the steepness of the slope. Still, even though the trail is unrelentingly steep it remains very distinct, so navigation is not a problem. In addition, the path offers frequent excellent views looking west across the Swan Valley to the scenic Mission Range, so you'll have plenty of good excuses for rest stops.

You reach a high point atop a spur ridge at 2.6 miles (it feels more like 5) after which the trail, frustratingly, steeply loses about 150 feet. You then contour across an open, view-packed slope at the head of South Fork Rumble Creek before making another steep push up the north side of that little stream to the first Rumble Creek Lake at 3.3 miles.

This deep and marvelously scenic lake has high dun-colored cliffs enclosing it on three sides and a tall, sliding waterfall feeding into its eastern shore. A side trail goes left to a nice campsite on the northwest shore.

To see the even more dramatic upper lake, cross the lower lake's outlet and follow a trail around the south shore. After about 150 yards this trail pulls away from the water and climbs extremely steeply to the top of a talus slope. The views from here are superb, especially looking down to the first Rumble Creek Lake and up to the tall cliffs and pointed summit of Holland Peak.

The rocky trail climbs above the waterfall feeding the lower lake, then passes a small upper basin before climbing *ridiculously* steeply up a rockslide that fills a narrow notch in a cliff. You may need to use your hands to steady yourself and you must be careful of your footing on the loose rocks. At the top of this exhausting climb is Upper Rumble Creek Lake. The stupendous cliffs of Holland Peak rise nearly 1600 feet directly above the eastern shore of this deep alpine lake, establishing this as one of the most dramatically scenic lakes in Montana. **Warning:** Be extremely cautious on the steep return hike. There are many places with loose pebbles that create dangerous footing, making it easy to twist an ankle or worse.

Extend your hike: If you somehow have energy to spare, consider expending those calories on a climb of Holland Peak. A steep, but nontechnical scramble route snakes up the rocky slope south of the upper lake to the top of the cliffs. From there the path loops north along the ridge to the summit. As the highest point in the Swan Range, this lofty mountain offers views that are beyond impressive.

53 *Koessler Lake*

Distance: 28 miles (including alternate return route via Sapphire Lakes)
Difficulty: strenuous
Hiking time: overnight or multiday
Elevation gain: 6700 feet
Season: July through October
Best time: mid-July to September

Contact: Flathead NF, Swan Lake Ranger District
Maps: Cairn Cartographics, Bob Marshall Wilderness Complex: South Half
GPS coordinates: N47° 27.176', W113° 36.218'

Getting there: From Seeley Lake, drive 22 miles north on State Route 83 to milepost 36.5. Turn right on gravel Holland Lake Road (Forest Road 44) and proceed 3.8 miles to the road-end trailhead.

Koessler Lake sits in a deep bowl at the eastern base of Ptarmigan Mountain. Although the first part of the trip to Upper Holland Lake is heavily used, very few people make the trek to much more scenic Koessler Lake. Fit hikers can visit the lake as an overnight, but the ideal schedule is a two-night trip, allowing time for a view-packed alternate loop on the return.

The wide and gentle trail sets off through forest composed primarily of Douglas firs and western larches. After 0.1 mile, go left at a junction and travel east almost to the head of large Holland Lake before climbing five switchbacks to a junction. Go right and steadily ascend to a fork at 1.3 miles where the Holland Lookout Trail veers left. This is the recommended return route of the alternate loop.

Bear right and soon cross a hillside with very photogenic westerly views across Holland Lake to the snowy Mission Range. The trail then curves to the east, passes a waterfall, and crosses cascading Holland Creek on a narrow log bridge to a nice campsite. Just above this camp is a lovely mini-waterfall and a junction.

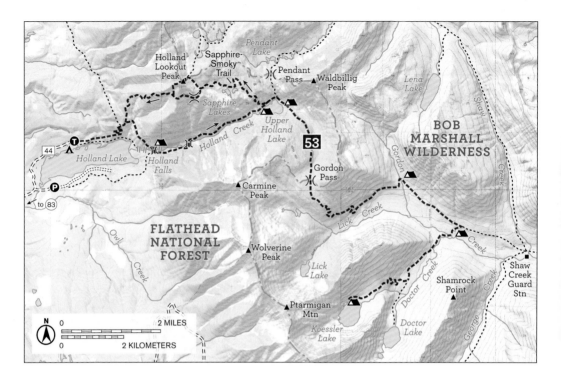

Go left toward Upper Holland Lake and wind your way upstream on an often brushy trail. Climb to a second bridged crossing of Holland Creek, then past a series of confusing old trails (always stay with the uphill option and usually to the right) to Upper Holland Lake at 5.8 miles. There are nice campsites along the north shore of this scenic lake.

The trail soon reaches a signed junction with the Sapphire-Smoky Trail, which goes left. This is the start of the recommended loop on the return hike.

To reach Koessler Lake, go straight, and 0.1 mile later keep right where the Pendant Pass Trail goes left. You pass a large stock camp at the east end of Upper Holland Lake and then begin gradually climbing. After rock-hopping a creek, a steady uphill takes you to Gordon Pass, where you'll enjoy nice views of the rugged east faces of Carmine and Wolverine Peaks.

Descending the east side of Gordon Pass you'll enjoy fine viewpoints overlooking the deep bowl of Lick Lake backed by the tall cliffs of

Ptarmigan Mountain. Eight well-graded switchbacks lead to an easy crossing of Gordon Creek and a nice campsite, a good base for a day hike to Koessler Lake.

From here you gradually descend through forest and brushy avalanche chutes for 1 mile, then turn sharply right on the trail to Koessler and Doctor Lakes. This trail descends to a good campsite shortly before a knee-deep ford of Gordon Creek. The path then ascends the heavily forested valley of Doctor Creek for 0.8 mile to a junction. Go right and climb fairly steeply for 1.5 miles to Koessler Lake. This stunningly beautiful lake has good camps, clouds of mosquitoes in July, and remarkable views of the soaring cliffs of Ptarmigan Mountain rising directly above its western shore. Snowfields usually grace those slopes throughout the summer.

For the highly recommended alternate loop, return to Upper Holland Lake, then turn onto the Sapphire-Smoky Trail and climb a series of switchbacks featuring fine views of red-tinged Carmine Peak rising over the basin of Upper

Snow on the slopes above beautiful Koessler Lake

Holland Lake. From here you ascend a rolling and unusually lovely subalpine plateau to a signed junction about 1.5 miles from Upper Holland Lake. The two sparkling Sapphire Lakes lie a short distance down the trail to the left.

For the loop, keep right and hike through extremely scenic terrain with exceptionally photogenic views across the Sapphire Lakes to Carmine Peak. After a delightful mile you reach a junction and a choice of trails.

If the weather is good and you have the energy, veer right and make the climb over the top of Holland Lookout Peak, with its wide views over the Swan Valley, then steeply descend the peak's west side. For a less strenuous and shorter alternative, go left at the junction, climb briefly over a saddle, and then contour across steep slopes for 0.7 mile to a reunion with the trail coming down from Holland Lookout Peak.

By either route you now face a long downhill accomplished on a mostly forested slope with the aid of twenty-four moderately steep switchbacks. At the bottom, close the loop at a junction with the trail you came in on.

54 *Crescent Mountain Lakes*

Distance: 9.6 miles roundtrip
Difficulty: strenuous
Hiking time: day hike or overnight
Elevation gain: 2400 feet
Season: July through mid-October
Best time: mid-July, late September

Contact: Lolo NF, Seeley Lake Ranger District
Map: USGS Morrell Lake
GPS coordinates: N47° 15.900', W113° 25.894'

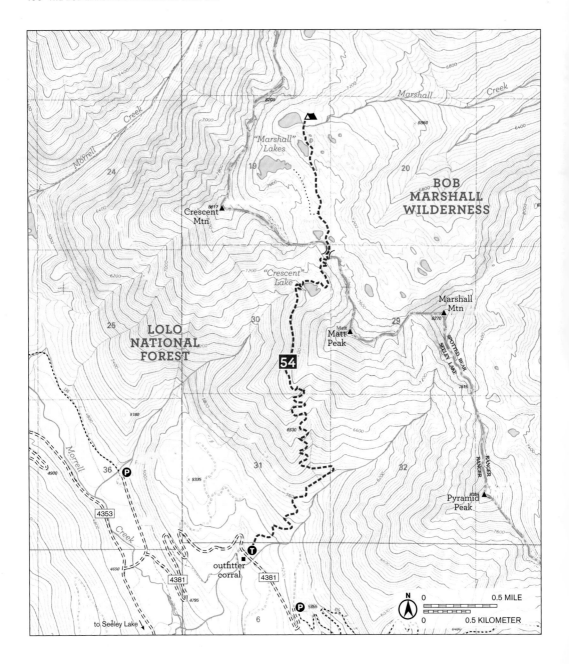

Getting there: From the north end of the town of Seeley Lake, go east on Morrell Creek Road (Forest Road 477), which soon changes from pavement to gravel. After 1 mile go left onto FR 4353, and proceed 5.8 miles to a junction. Turn right on FR 4381, cross a bridge, then keep right at a fork and drive 2.1 miles to the trailhead, marked with a post, immediately before a culvert over an unnamed creek and about 0.1 mile past an outfitter's corral.

View of Crescent Mountain above Crescent Lake

This outfitter's trail isn't shown on any map and only a few local residents even seem to know it exists, but it's well maintained and easy to follow. Best of all, it accesses a cluster of extremely scenic lakes hidden on the back side of Crescent Mountain and is both prettier and much less crowded than the nearby trails to Morrell Falls and Pyramid Lake.

The well-worn trail winds uphill through moderately dense forest, sometimes at a fairly steep grade. The route is viewless and waterless as it steadily ascends dozens of switchbacks until you reach some forest openings offering partially obstructed views to the west of the Mission Range. Soon thereafter the trail performs a series of ups and downs before a final few uphill switchbacks take you to the northwest corner of a shallow lake at 3.4 miles. Locally known as either Crescent or Hoehn Lake, this pool is backed by rugged cliffs on the east and south and by tall and colorful Crescent Mountain to the northwest, making it a scenic spot to eat lunch and enjoy the wilderness.

To see the even prettier lakes on the east side of Crescent Mountain, take the trail around the north side of Crescent Lake, which soon loops to the left and climbs steeply for 0.4 mile to a pass. About 100 yards to your left on the other side of this pass is a lovely pond with very photogenic views across its waters to Crescent Mountain. The trail then passes a smaller pond before heading north over gentle and delightful subalpine terrain with excellent views to the east of the deep, curving valley of Marshall Creek.

About 0.7 mile from the pass you reach a small but gorgeous lake, then it's another 0.3 mile to a somewhat larger lake. This spectacular pool sits directly beneath tall cliffs and rocky slopes and features hundreds of alpine larch trees around its shoreline making it especially lovely in late September. There is a good campsite along the eastern shore. Explorers can find another large and scenic lake on a bench to the southwest. Although none of these lakes is officially named, most people refer to them collectively as the Marshall Lakes.

Looking north across the first Buffalo Lake

55 *Buffalo Lakes*

Distance: 2.8 miles roundtrip
Difficulty: easy to moderate
Hiking time: half-day hike
Elevation gain: 400 feet
Season: mid-May to November
Best time: June, late September

Contact: Helena–Lewis and Clark NF, Rocky Mountain Ranger District
Map: USGS Dancing Lady Mountain, East Glacier Park
GPS coordinates: N48° 22.299', W113° 16.771'

Getting there: From East Glacier drive about 4 miles west on US 2 to an unsigned pullout on the south side of the highway at milepost 204.7.

This short, wildlife-rich outing samples a tiny portion of the Badger–Two Medicine Roadless Area, a very scenic and biologically diverse region south of Glacier National Park. The hike demonstrates why conservationists have long fought to protect this realm, as it offers wonderful views and leads to a pair of marshy lakes used extensively by local wildlife.

Pass through a hiker's V access gate in a barbed wire fence, then follow an old jeep road that is now overgrown with small shrubs and wildflowers. The surrounding forest is mostly lodgepole pines, but they do not block the fine views looking north to the peaks of southern Glacier National Park. More vistas await at the lakes ahead.

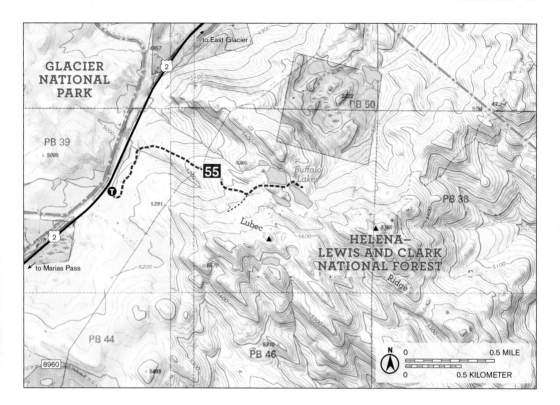

After a brief uphill, turn northeast, paralleling the highway, and remain mostly level for about 0.3 mile. After crossing a seasonal creek, the trail turns right and steadily climbs a partly forested slope with grand views looking north and northwest.

At 1.2 miles is an unsigned T intersection. Go left and travel up and down for a little under 0.2 mile to the first Buffalo Lake. Many kinds of ducks are usually present here, as well as beavers, moose, and grizzly bears. There are great views over the water north to the snowy peaks of Glacier National Park. Expect mosquitoes in early summer. To reach the second lake, simply follow the trail along the south side of the first lake to the beaver dam between the two marshy bodies of water.

56 *Walling Reef*

Distance: 15 miles roundtrip
Difficulty: very strenuous
Hiking time: overnight
Elevation gain: 4150 feet
Season: June through late October
Best time: June through early July

Contact: Helena–Lewis and Clark NF, Rocky Mountain Ranger District
Maps: USFS Bob Marshall, Great Bear, and Scapegoat Wilderness Areas; USGS Walling Reef
GPS coordinates: N48° 09.845', W112° 51.852'

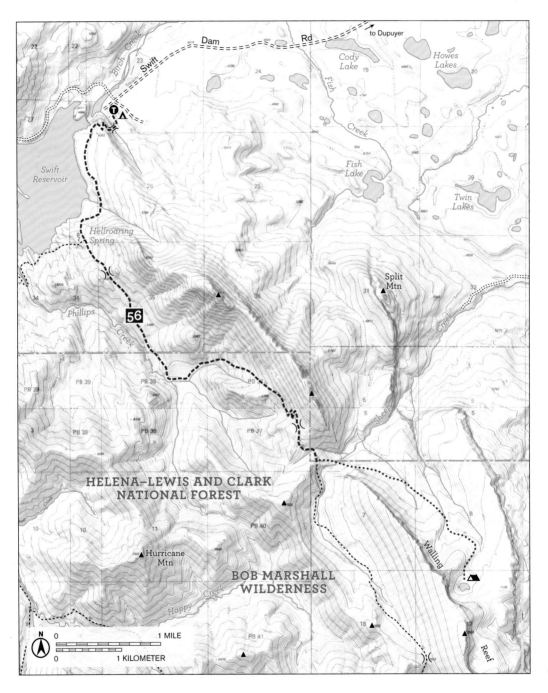

Getting there: From a rest area on US 89 at the north end of Dupuyer, go 18.3 miles west on unsigned but good gravel Swift Dam Road, to the signed county campground below Swift Reservoir Dam. Turn left, drive about 80 yards, and park near a horse loading ramp.

Towering cliffs ringing the basin of Walling Reef Lake

Montana is full of great places that are challenging to reach and any hiker who doesn't visit at least a few of these hidden gems is really missing out. For this hike your destination is a stupendously scenic lake backed by stunning 1000-foot cliffs. And the approach to this gem is over immense subalpine meadowlands covered with wildflowers right beneath the soaring cliffs of Walling Reef.

On the downside, although the majority of this trip is on either maintained trail or through open country that is easy to navigate, there is a nasty off-trail section of a little over 0.5 mile that involves steep travel over rocky terrain and bushwhacking through tough riparian brush. But the reward is *absolutely* worth the effort—although you might not believe it as you beat your way through all that brush.

The trail crosses a culvert over an irrigation ditch, then ascends one switchback on a scrub-covered slope before looping around to a bridge over a trickling creek. Two more switchbacks lead to an open hillside above Swift Reservoir with fine views looking west across the water to Mount Richmond. The route remains well above the reservoir taking you to a hop-over crossing of a little creek then climbing in forest to gushing Hellroaring Spring at 1.9 miles.

Just a few yards past this spring is a signed fork. Bear left on Phillips Creek Trail and make an intermittent climb to a narrow saddle. From here the route contours for nearly 1 mile then makes a short, steep drop to Phillips Creek, which you follow upstream through small meadows and brushy areas. Eventually you turn up a tributary creek then make an extended climb leading to a set of four moderately steep switchbacks shortly before you reach a high pass at about 5 miles. There are outstanding views from here looking south to Walling Reef and a pointed unnamed peak to the south-southeast.

The somewhat indistinct trail now steeply drops to the bottom of a grassy hillside where you cross a gully and then try to follow a basically nonexistent tread that goes downhill as it loops to the south. Since the official trail is impossible to follow, the best plan is to steeply descend a rocky slope to the upper end of a brushy meadow where cascading Sheep Creek enters from a canyon to the south. Maps show a trail going downstream along the north side of Sheep Creek, but that route involves lots of awful bushwhacking. A better plan is to ford Sheep Creek near the head of the brushy meadow and follow game trails that lead generally southeast and uphill. You'll still have to struggle through dense brush, but the going is easier than the route shown on the USGS map.

After about 0.5 mile you'll gratefully reach the open slopes at the eastern base of Walling Reef. There is no distinguishable trail, but it's easy to navigate as you ascend an open slope just east of a tiny creek. The views of Walling Reef's towering cliffs and an unnamed reef to the north are superb.

Eventually you'll reach the headwaters basin of a little creek then go over a low ridge before following a second seasonal creek up to a partly forested basin. The lake is a short walk above and west of this basin. The fishless lake (7.5 miles) has no established campsites, but it's possible to set up your tent in nearby groves of subalpine firs. And you'll want to stay at least one night to enjoy the jaw-dropping scenery and views of the 1000-foot cliffs of Walling Reef.

57 *Volcano Reef Loop*

Distance: 10.4 miles
Difficulty: strenuous
Hiking time: day hike or overnight
Elevation gain: 2750 feet
Season: late May through October
Best time: June

Contact: Helena–Lewis and Clark NF, Rocky Mountain Ranger District
Maps: USFS Bob Marshall, Great Bear, and Scapegoat Wilderness Areas; USGS Volcano Reef
GPS coordinates: N48° 0.553', W112° 42.538'

Getting there: From Choteau, drive 13 miles north on US 89 to Bynum. Turn left on Blackleaf Road, following signs to Bynum Reservoir. Go two blocks, then turn right and stay on this good gravel road for 13.9 miles to a junction where you turn left, following signs for Blackleaf Wildlife Management Area and Forest Road 145. After 1 mile, go straight at a junction, where the road quickly becomes rather rough and narrow. Go 1.6 miles, bear left at a fork, and then continue 2 miles to a usually simple ford of Blackleaf Creek. Proceed 1.7 miles to the road-end trailhead.

The Rocky Mountain Front, a dramatic landscape at the abrupt dividing line between the rolling plains and the Rocky Mountains, is on spectacular display on this wildly scenic, hike around Volcano Reef. Like other outings on "the Front," the landscape is incredibly scenic, featuring tall north-south trending cliffs, known as "reefs," composed of colorful limestone and other sedimentary rocks. Spectacular canyons cut through these reefs offering dramatic travel corridors for hikers. Wildlife is abundant with large populations of grizzly bears and big game species that use the region as critical wintering grounds. *Note:* Although entirely on trails, parts of this loop are hard to follow. The loop

is much easier to navigate when done clockwise, as described here.

The trail goes west up dramatically scenic Blackleaf Canyon—hemmed in by towering cliffs on either side. The first section follows a long-abandoned jeep road, which gently wanders through wildflower meadows, groves of quaking aspens, and spotty forests of limber pines and Douglas firs. On your left, cottonwood trees crowd the banks of small Blackleaf Creek. Take some time to scan the canyon's cliffs, as mountain goats are often seen in this area.

At a little over 0.3 mile, make an easy crossing of Blackleaf Creek then hug the mostly forested south canyon wall as the gorge widens and the tall cliffs disappear. Rock-hop the creek again at

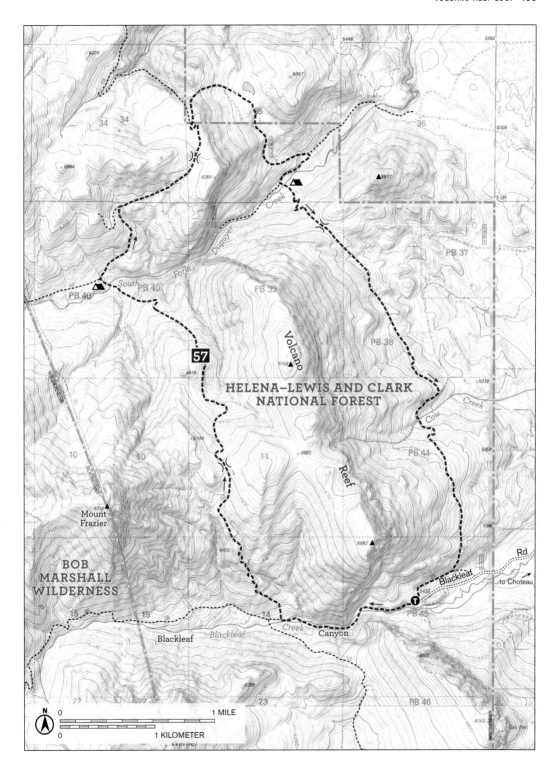

34 34

36

8917

PB 37

PB 40

South PB 40

PB 39

Volcano

PB 38

57

6752

HELENA–LEWIS AND CLARK
NATIONAL FOREST

Cow Creek

10 10

Mount
Frazier

11 6663

Reef

PB 44

BOB
MARSHALL
WILDERNESS

6892

Rd

Blackleaf

to Choteau

T

PB 45

15 15

14

Blackleaf Creek Canyon

Blackleaf

PB 46

N

0   1 MILE

0   1 KILOMETER

The trail up to the pass offers a great view of Mount Werner.

about 0.7 mile then walk 0.1 mile and look for an unsigned trail that goes right (uphill). A small cairn marks this junction.

Turn right and climb fairly steeply on a partly forested slope, with views of Mount Werner to the southwest improving with every step. The trail climbs through a small burned area, then crosses open meadows where you'll be eye to eye with the massive hulk of Mount Frazier rising dramatically on your left.

Complete the ascent at 2.3 miles at a high, windy divide. The views from here are

tremendous: east to the endless rolling plains, south to the cliffs of distant Choteau Mountain, and up close of rugged Mount Frazier to the west. This pass is an excellent goal for a shorter day hike (4.6 miles roundtrip and 1200 feet of elevation gain).

Those doing the full loop follow a good trail that goes steadily down the north side of the pass through dense forest for the next mile before breaking out into lovely meadows. The huge, jagged peak to the north-northwest is Old Man of the Hills and there are also good views of the

NORTH WALL LOOP 167

rounded peaks and ridges at the head of the wide valley. At the bottom is an easy calf-deep ford of South Fork Dupuyer Creek. Although there are no established sites, camping is possible on either side of this crossing.

The indistinct route intersects an obvious trail north of the creek where you go right and angle uphill across an open hillside with tremendous views to the south-southwest of Mount Frazier. Reenter forest, then at about 0.6 mile after the creek crossing look for an obvious trail angling to the right. Take this trail, which gradually climbs a lovely view-packed meadow to a sloping ridgetop. Grizzly bears and bighorn sheep are both commonly seen in this area.

On the other side of the ridge, go through a fence and then gradually descend wind-swept slopes with gorgeous views to the west of Old Man of the Hills and northwest to Walling Reef. About 0.25 mile from the fence crossing is a large cairn marking a junction.

Keep straight and steeply descend for 0.1 mile to another fence crossing. You are now on land owned by the Boone and Crockett Club, a hunter's conservation organization. The club graciously allows public access to this property, but please do not camp or build a fire. At a fork immediately past the fence, go right and steeply descend toward a shimmering lake in the meadow-filled basin below. A little before you reach the lake, the trail's grade lessens and the grassy route angles to the right passing through a lovely meadow.

About 0.25 mile from the lake the trail goes through yet another fence and reenters national forest land. The occasionally obscure route now descends at an inconsistent grade taking you down to an unsigned junction near South Fork Dupuyer Creek. Turn right (upstream) and ascend this scenic valley for 0.4 mile to an unsigned but obvious fork. Go left and make a calf-deep ford of the creek to a nice campsite.

The trail climbs to the top of a minor ridge then begins traversing rolling terrain where you cross a series of small ridges and seasonal creeks. The route is not always obvious, but you'll generally be on the correct course if you keep right on what appears to be the main route where several confusing game trails and old paths lead down to the left. The scenery remains excellent throughout with fine views to the west of the tall cliffs of Volcano Reef and the trip's best vistas to the east of the vast plains of central Montana.

Near the southern end of this traverse, cross the wide valley of Cow Creek, which has several beaver ponds, then go over a ridge and descend toward Blackleaf Creek. About 0.1 mile before reaching the road, bear right at a fork and ascend a grassy swale for 0.2 mile before dropping to the trailhead.

58 North Wall Loop

Distance: 74-mile loop
Difficulty: strenuous
Hiking time: multiday
Elevation gain: 11,700 feet
Season: July through October
Best time: July

Contact: Helena–Lewis and Clark NF, Rocky Mountain Ranger District; Flathead NF, Spotted Bear Ranger District
Maps: Cairn Cartographics, Bob Marshall Wilderness Complex: North Half
GPS coordinates: N47° 50.852', W112° 46.951'

Getting there: From Choteau, drive 4 miles north on US 89 then turn left onto Teton Canyon Road, following signs to Ski Area. Go 16.6 miles, then turn left onto a gravel road, following signs to Ear Mountain Natural Area. After 0.4 mile, go right onto Forest Road 109 and proceed 9.4 miles to the trailhead.

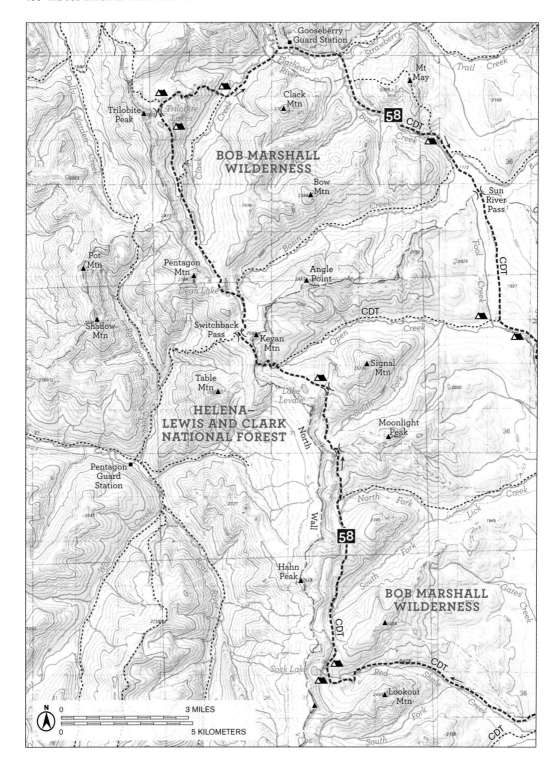

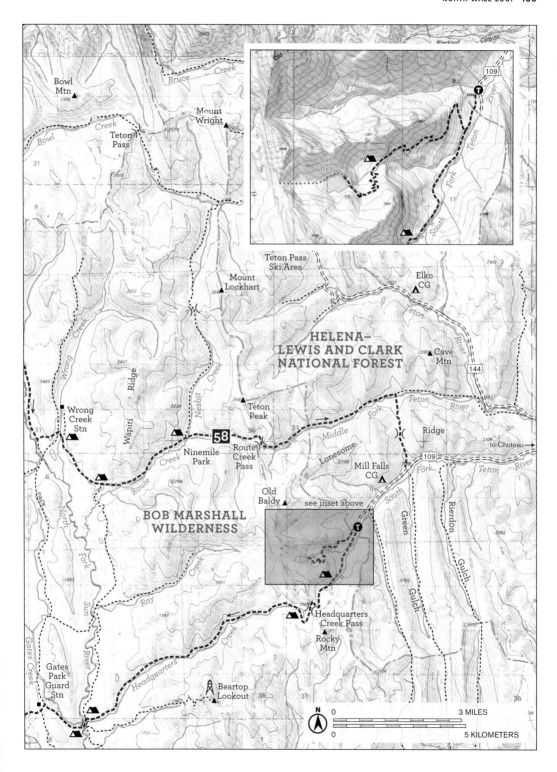

Camping at Dean Lake offers views like this one of Pentagon Mountain.

This trip involves a long but superb backpacking vacation into a remote and strikingly beautiful part of the magnificent Bob Marshall Wilderness. The North Wall, arguably even grander than the Bob's more famous Chinese Wall, offers a stiff challenge, so only hardy hikers should take this trip, but the scenic rewards are great. That statement is especially true when the basic loop is combined with the spectacular peaks and lakes of the Trilobite Range. If you only have the time and energy for a short jaunt, the popular day hike to gorgeous Our Lake starts from the same trailhead and offers a taste of the even greater wonders found on the loop.

The wide trail departs just 20 yards back up the road from the parking area and goes gently uphill through dense coniferous forest to a junction at 0.3 mile. The 2.7-mile one-way side trip to Our Lake (not to be missed, if you have the time) goes right here and switchbacks up to and above a pair of waterfalls on its way to this extremely photogenic lake. Mountain goats are often seen on the surrounding slopes.

For the North Wall, bear left at the junction, soon enter the wilderness, and climb steadily in a spruce-fir forest. A tiring ascent, well above the creek on your left, leads to more open terrain featuring fabulous views of towering Rocky Mountain, the highest point in the Bob Marshall Wilderness. After passing a tall, unnamed waterfall, you cross the creek below a second, veil-like falls and switchback up to a dramatic high basin directly beneath the imposing ramparts of Rocky Mountain. There is a very scenic campsite here, ideal for those who got a late start.

The final push to Headquarters Creek Pass involves eight switchbacks over open and dramatically scenic terrain. Once atop the 7700-foot pass, the views—especially looking west down Headquarters Creek to the distant Lewis and Clark and Trilobite Ranges—are terrific.

Three well-graded downhill switchbacks lead to a beautiful basin west of the pass with a good campsite. Below this point you enter the burn zone of the 1988 Gates Park Fire, which you'll be in and out of for much of the remainder of the hike. A long and shadeless descent down Headquarters Creek takes you into the lower canyon where the terrain is flatter and the trail sometimes muddy. At 11.3 miles is a junction above the gently flowing North Fork Sun River.

Keep left, pass a spacious campsite, then make a rock-hop crossing of Headquarters Creek and keep right at a pair of junctions to cross a large wooden bridge over the river. Just after this bridge is another comfortable campsite. From here you climb gently away from the river for 1.2 miles to a junction with a trail that goes right 0.25 mile to the Gates Park Guard Station.

Turn left, skirting the southern edge of the large meadow at Gates Park, then go straight at a pair of junctions. About 1 mile later, bear right onto the Continental Divide Trail (CDT), which heads northwest up the badly burned valley of Red Shale Creek. After several miles, you pass a tall red-colored mesa, which obviously gives Red Shale Creek its name, to reach the unburned forests and meadows at the base of dramatic North Wall (20 miles). The scenery here is superb with massive limestone ramparts towering 1200 feet above a marvelous campsite. This is truly a spot to savor.

For the next several miles the trail travels north, generally following the base of the wall, climbing over several minor passes and dropping into creek drainages. There are very few campsites, but the scenery is off the charts. After 6.1 miles you reach a junction near North Fork Lick Creek. The trail to the right would shorten the trip, but there is still plenty of fine scenery to come, so veer left (uphill) and climb over the next saddle to the outstandingly scenic basin at the head of South Fork Open Creek. Next up is the more heavily forested valley of Open Creek,

where, after a set of downhill switchbacks, you cross a creek and reach an unsigned but obvious junction. The 0.2-mile trail to the left goes past an excellent campsite to the rocky bowl holding Lake Levale. This gorgeous turquoise-colored lake sits right beneath a towering limestone cliff and is quite spectacular. Camping is prohibited within 500 feet of this lake.

The main trail descends to a junction and a second opportunity to shorten the loop. But having come this far it would be a shame to miss the remote and wildly scenic Trilobite Range, so go left, cross Open Creek, and then make a steep ascent to an unnamed pass on the Continental Divide. Views extend all the way across the Bob Marshall Wilderness.

From the pass you follow cairns to the right across the view-packed slopes of Kevan Mountain down to a junction at Switchback Pass. Go right and descend to possible campsites at the bottom of a bowl-shaped area at the head of Basin Creek. A short climb then leads to super scenic Dean Lake. Towering Pentagon Mountain provides a stunning backdrop to this choice location, and possible campsites allow you to enjoy the magnificent scene at leisure.

Upon leaving idyllic Dean Lake (aw, mom, do we really have to go?) you descend to a simple crossing of Clack Creek then contour along a scenic shelf past a small pond to a junction just after crossing a nameless creek. Veer left and climb 1.4 miles to the fine campsites at Middle Trilobite Lake (40 miles), which feature awesome views up to Trilobite Peak. From here you climb over a minor pass to an unsigned fork. Bear right and drop to beautiful, meadow-rimmed Lower Trilobite Lake, featuring more scenic camps.

Now you face a long downhill to Clack Creek, initially over open slopes and then switchbacking through timber. At the bottom you cross the upper end of a large marshy area as you ford a couple of branches of Clack Creek and come to a junction just beyond a horse-oriented campsite. Go left, ford the main stem of Clack Creek, and travel up and down for 1.9 miles to a knee-deep ford of Middle Fork Flathead River and the small

Gooseberry Guard Station. Just behind this log cabin you turn right, heading upstream.

The trail reenters a burn area (expect deadfall) and gradually gains elevation through an area with an unusually high concentration of bear sign, so stay alert. After 1.3 miles you bear right at an intersection, make a calf-deep ford of Strawberry Creek, and soon walk past an easy-to-miss junction with the Mount May Trail. About 2.3 miles later, at Grizzly Park (possible camps), you go straight at two junctions before splashing across Bowl Creek. About 0.2 mile later watch carefully for a sign for the Basin Creek Trail, which veers right.

Bear left on an initially faint trail that soon grows more distinct. This path climbs to low and unimpressive Sun River Pass (50 miles), taking you back over the Continental Divide. After 3.4 miles of rather monotonous up-and-down hiking, you'll reach a junction with Open Creek Trail. Keep left, soon pass a fair campsite beside Open Creek, then head downstream through mile after mile of burned snags. After about 3.5 miles you turn left onto a poorly signed but obvious trail that gradually ascends through young lodgepole pine forest for 0.6 mile to a four-way junction. Go straight and soon make an ankle-deep ford of Wrong Creek to a nice campsite.

Ignoring unsigned outfitter trails that go left, bear right and contour around a hillside to the drainage of Route Creek where there is a campsite and a junction. Keep left and ascend the valley of Route Creek through lush unburned forest. The often-muddy trail takes you to a large campsite just before a junction (keep straight) and an easy ford of Nesbit Creek.

Again ignoring confusing outfitter trails that go left, keep straight and wind your way uphill on a steady, moderately steep grade onto alpine slopes with many wildflowers and increasingly good views. The climb ends at 7263-foot Route Creek Pass (64 miles), which is a windy notch with tremendous views especially looking south-southeast to nearby Old Baldy. Eight gently graded switchbacks take you down to forested terrain in the narrow canyon of Middle Fork Teton River. After 1.6 miles you pass a tall waterfall, and then continue another 3 miles to a well-signed junction.

Turn right onto Lonesome Ridge Trail, which is open to motorcycles, make an easy ford of Middle Fork Teton River, and climb through dense forest to a grassy pass. A sometimes steep descent of the south side of the ridge takes you back to Forest Road 109, just 1.8 miles from the junction where you started the loop.

59 *Willow Creek Falls*

Distance: 7.8 miles roundtrip
Difficulty: moderate
Hiking time: day hike
Elevation gain: 1500 feet
Season: June through early November
Best time: June

Contact: Helena–Lewis and Clark NF, Rocky Mountain Ranger District
Map: USGS Double Falls, Wood Lake
GPS coordinates: N47° 27.745', W112° 43.483'

Getting there: From Augusta, go 0.3 mile southwest on State Route 435 then turn right on Eberl Street, following signs to Benchmark. This road soon changes to good gravel and goes 14.5 miles to a fork. Bear right on Forest Road 233, drive 1.2 miles, and then turn left at a sign for Willow Creek Administrative Site. This road is fine for the first mile, but then gets so rough you may prefer to walk. At 1.7 miles from FR 233, park at a turnaround in front of an unsigned gate.

Find several mini-waterfalls beyond Willow Creek Falls.

The Willow Creek Trail is arguably the best day hike sampler of the magnificent Rocky Mountain Front. You'll climb through beautiful meadows with great views of towering limestone reefs, pass a series of dramatic waterfalls, and finish at a high pass with expansive views. Strangely, few people hike this trail, so solitude is another bonus for those who make the trek.

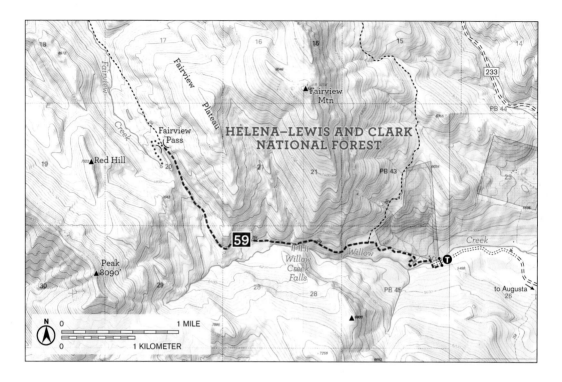

To avoid private property, do *not* go through the green metal gate blocking the road. Instead, make a 40-foot detour to the left, cross the fence, and hike west along the left side of another fenceline. Directly in front of you rise the impressive limestone battlements of an unnamed reef while Fairview Mountain towers to the north.

After less than 100 yards you'll pick up an obvious trail near a lower parking area. Go right at a fork and 30 yards later make an easy ford of Willow Creek. The trail passes a private ranch, heads upstream through a pretty meadow, and then climbs one switchback to an open bench with excellent wildflower displays in early summer and great views at any time of year. You steadily ascend along a fence to a higher bench where you turn west toward the impressive gap in the cliffs carved by Willow Creek.

Shortly after entering a forested area, you pass an easily missed junction with a faint trail that goes to the right. Keep straight and soon begin hugging the cliffs high above cascading Willow Creek. Near 1.6 miles you'll pass viewpoints of tall, two-tiered Willow Creek Falls. The falls makes a good turnaround for a shorter hike.

To see more of this beautiful country, leave the cliffs and pass a series of lovely mini-waterfalls as the trail enters an open and very scenic upper basin. There are fine views looking west to the rounded mass of Peak 8090 and a rugged red rock formation on your right.

The trail goes around the base of the red rock formation, then turns northwest. A steady ascent on mostly open slopes, with an unusual abundance of blue sugarbowl flowers, leads to low and narrow Fairview Pass at 3.9 miles. There are nice views looking north to Sheep Shed Mountain. A short scramble up the rugged hill west of the pass provides a grand viewpoint of misnamed Red Hill and a more distant unnamed summit to the west. You can also scramble down the other side of the hill to visit a scenic little pond.

60 *Scapegoat Mountain*

Distance: 30 miles roundtrip
Difficulty: strenuous
Hiking time: multiday
Elevation gain: 6500 feet
Season: July through October
Best time: mid-July to mid-August

Contact: Helena–Lewis and Clark NF, Rocky Mountain Ranger District
Map: Cairn Cartographics, Bob Marshall Wilderness Complex: South Half
GPS coordinates: N47° 24.264', W112° 44.198'

Getting there: From Augusta, go 0.3 mile southwest on State Route 435 then turn right on Eberl Street, following signs to Benchmark. This road soon changes to good gravel and goes 14.5 miles to a fork. Bear left on Forest Road 235 and proceed 5.5 miles to the Crown Mountain Trailhead where a pair of minor roads go left and downhill. Parking is available a short distance down the first road on the left, while the trail follows the gated second road.

The Crown Mountain Trail provides the most scenic of several approach routes to Scapegoat Mountain, the highest point and undisputed highlight of the Scapegoat Wilderness. But regardless of how you get there, you'll be blown away by this mountain's rim of towering, 1000-foot cliffs. The scenery is overwhelming and demands at least a day or two of exploring to appreciate its enormity and grandeur.

Walk 60 yards down the gated road to a bridge over Ford Creek, then continue 0.1 mile to a junction with Trail #270. Go right and hike

Towering walls above Halfmoon Park

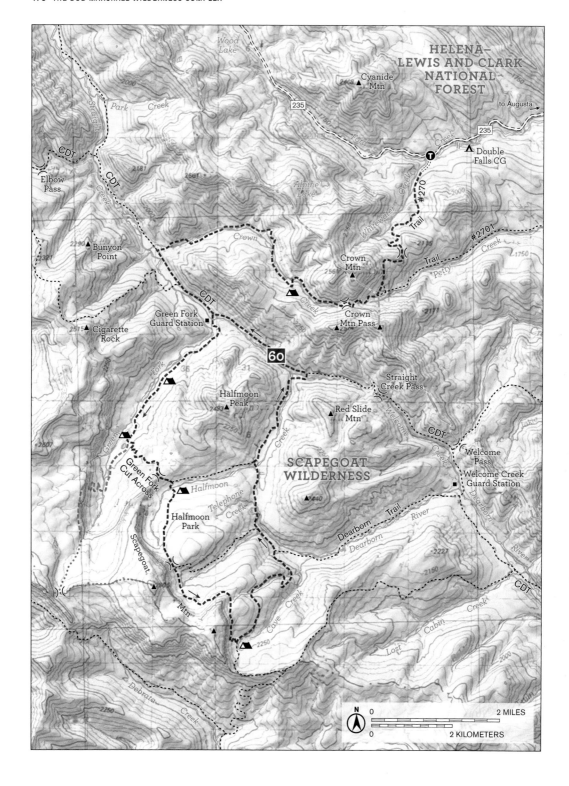

gently uphill through a mixed conifer forest beside small Whitewater Creek as the steady uphill soon takes you away from the creek and toward the amphitheater of dun-colored cliffs forming the summit of Crown Mountain. After gaining 1200 feet, the climb tops out at a pass populated by scrubby whitebark pines and subalpine firs.

From here the trail curves to the right into an exceptionally scenic defile lined on both sides by rugged cliffs and pinnacles. At 3 miles the trail forks, with Trail #2701 veering left. Keep right and walk 0.2 mile to a junction with a different spur of Trail #2701.

Turn sharply right and steeply climb over loose rock to narrow Crown Mountain Pass at 3.6 miles. From here there are excellent views looking east to the sharp pinnacle of Haystack Butte and the endless plains beyond.

The trail now curves northwest and begins a long downhill, first in open forest then through an extensive burn area, where fireweed blooms profusely from late July to mid-August. During the descent you cross the trickling flow of Crown Creek several times. The tread sometimes disappears, but if you just keep going downstream you're bound to find it again. At 7.4 miles you reach the bottom and a junction with Straight Creek Trail, which is also the CDT.

Turn left, gradually ascending a valley of blackened snags for 0.6 mile. Go straight at the junction with Cigarette Rock Trail, and 0.3 mile later reach a fork at the start of the recommended loop for exploring Scapegoat Mountain.

Bear right on Green Fork Trail, soon rock-hop Straight Creek, and come to the Green Fork Guard Station. Somehow this log structure escaped the fire even though everything surrounding the building is charred. Take the route going east-southeast from this cabin heading toward the narrow canyon of Green Fork and follow this trail as it crosses the partly forested slope above this moderate-sized stream.

The burn area finally ends in the wide central valley of Green Fork, where there are excellent views of the ridges and light-colored cliffs all

Gentians in the Scapegoat Wilderness

around. At 2.4 miles from the Straight Creek Trail is a junction. The Green Fork Cut Across Trail goes left (uphill) and is the continuation of the loop.

Side trip: With an extra day, don't miss the climb to the top of Scapegoat Mountain. To do this, go straight at the junction with the Green Fork Cut Across Trail, and almost immediately pass above an easy-to-miss little lake. The trail then goes under the awe-inspiring ramparts of the west face of Scapegoat Mountain and reaches its official end just after a creek crossing. From here take a steep and sketchy climber's route up the west wall of the valley to a sloping bench between two rows of cliffs. The path contours along this bench then disappears as you make your way over tundra and rocks to a wide, alpine ridge on the Continental Divide. From here you follow the long and moderately graded rocky slope to the 9202-foot summit. The views over enormous expanses of wild country are breathtaking.

Back at the junction with the Green Fork Cut Across Trail, turn east and ascend more than a dozen moderately graded switchbacks to a divide, where you briefly reenter the burn zone and lose about 200 feet to a junction with Halfmoon Trail.

Turn sharply right and almost immediately pass a supremely scenic (but horse-oriented) camp at the lower end of Halfmoon Park. An enormous amphitheater of 1000-foot cliffs on the north face of Scapegoat Mountain forms the backdrop to this choice location, providing lasting memories of their grandeur. Cross a creek just past the camp, then climb open, rolling meadowlands, feeling constantly in awe of the enormous cliffs directly in front of you. The trail exits Halfmoon Park via a pass located directly beneath the cliffs. About 0.1 mile down the other side of this pass is a junction with Upper Dearborn Trail.

Go right and make your way up and down around the usually waterless Upper Dearborn Basin, which is enclosed on two sides by dramatic cliffs. The trail crosses a talus slope, then rounds a high ridge before descending to a junction with Cave Creek Trail. This scenic basin has some decent campsites with a tiny creek for water.

The loop trail goes sharply left on Cave Creek Trail and climbs a bit through a silvery ghost forest of snags from the 1988 Canyon Creek Fire. You top a little ridge then begin a long, well-graded descent. **Warning:** Be especially wary of grizzlies here. I was charged by a sow with cubs in this area! Make plenty of noise and have your bear spray handy.

A couple of long switchbacks take you down to a junction (18.5 miles, excluding side trips) with Dearborn Trail where you turn left and climb gradually through a forest of young lodgepole pines. After 0.4 mile, rock-hop the headwaters of Dearborn River and reach a junction.

Go right on Telephone Creek Trail and gradually climb beside the trail's often-dry namesake creek to a high point. From here you descend past a pretty meadow then hop over Halfmoon Creek to reach a junction. There are nice views across a meadow here up to Scapegoat Mountain.

Go straight on Halfmoon Creek Trail and gradually descend to a second crossing of Halfmoon Creek where the trail turns right and goes uphill beside tiny Straight Creek to a junction. Go left on Straight Creek Trail and cross steep, fire-scarred slopes before making an irregular descent to the Green Fork junction at the close of the loop.

61 Anaconda Hill

Distance: 11.4 miles roundtrip
Difficulty: strenuous
Hiking time: day hike
Elevation gain: 1600 feet
Season: June through October
Best time: mid-June to mid-July

Contact: Helena–Lewis and Clark NF, Lincoln Ranger District
Map: USGS Rogers Pass
GPS coordinates: N47° 04.385', W112° 22.235'

Getting there: From Lincoln, drive 17.5 miles east on State Route 200. The trail begins where an unsigned jeep road goes right (southeast) about 0.15 mile before Rogers Pass.

This book describes several outstanding sections of the Continental Divide Trail, which loosely follows its namesake feature through more than 900 miles of western Montana. One of the more easily accessible stretches of this scenic trail goes south from Rogers Pass through the Anaconda Hill Roadless Area. Although this area lacks dramatic peaks and lakes, it features miles of enchanting ridgetop meadows carpeted with early summer wildflowers. A newly rerouted trail,

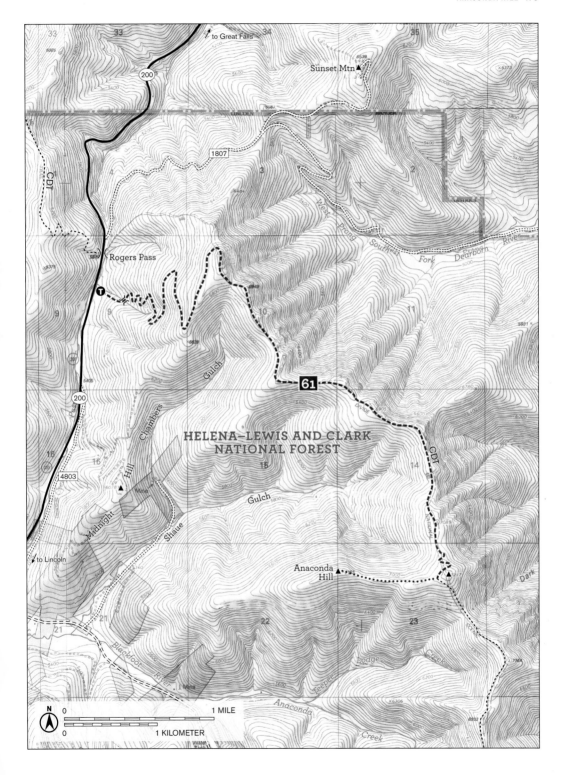

to Great Falls

Sunset Mtn

200

1807

CDT

Rogers Pass

T

West Prong Southeast Fork

Dearborn River

61

Gulch

Chambers

HELENA–LEWIS AND CLARK
NATIONAL FOREST

CDT

Hill

Gulch

Midnight

Mine

Shaue

to Lincoln

Anaconda
Hill

Dark

200

4803

Blackfoot River

Mine

Teepee

Lodge Creek

Anaconda
Creek

N

0   1 MILE

0   1 KILOMETER

A cairn along the Continental Divide Trail near Anaconda Hill

not yet shown on USGS or Forest Service maps, offers relatively gentle access to the high country.

Walk the jeep road through a small meadow for about 0.1 mile to a Continental Divide Trail sign where the route narrows to a foot trail. This recently built path goes up along a small creek, crosses it on a wooden bridge, then climbs a series of seven long switchbacks up a forested slope and past a couple of small springs and seasonal creeks. The grade is never very steep and there are nice views of the Rogers Pass vicinity.

Near 1.8 miles the trail reaches the first ridgetop meadows and goes around the west side of a prominent high point. Once past this butte you begin an extended and highly enjoyable ridge walk that always stays on or near the Continental Divide. The terrain is mostly meadows with superb displays of early summer wildflowers and features excellent views of the vast plains to the east, distant Scapegoat Mountain to the north-northwest, and a myriad of rounded mountains and valleys to the west. The ridge route has only minor ups and downs and provides several close-up views to the tall and colorful cliffs dropping off the east side of the divide.

Near 5 miles, three rounded uphill switchbacks take you into a strip of denser forest shortly before you intersect a westward-trending side ridge. There is no trail, but it's a simple matter to follow this partly forested ridge for about 0.5 mile to the summit of Anaconda Hill. Here there are very nice views to the west of countless forested ridges and valleys and comfortable lunch spots to sit and take it all in.

Opposite, top: Mountain goat, Crazy Mountains

Opposite, bottom: View down the canyon of South Fork Sweet Grass Creek from near Glacier Lake

Central Montana's "Island" Ranges

Mount Brown from the first saddle above the trailhead

East of the Rocky Mountains, Montana flattens out into a rolling prairie that extends all the way to the border with the Dakotas. But in central Montana that flat land is peppered with a dozen or more isolated mountain ranges. These ranges rise thousands of feet above the sea of grass, effectively forming "islands" where the climate is both cooler and wetter than the surrounding prairie. This climate nurtures forests and a fascinating mix of flora and fauna from both the Rocky Mountains and the Great Plains. Although geologically part of the Rocky Mountain uplift, these ranges are well to the east of the main divide and sit in the rain shadow of that lofty mountain massif. This allows for somewhat drier conditions and trails that open weeks before the higher mountains to the west and south. The somewhat drier climate also explains why, with the spectacular exception of the lofty Crazy Mountains, most of these island ranges were never extensively glaciated, meaning they are more rounded in appearance and have fewer lakes than in the ice-carved Rockies.

Hiking in these island ranges is a joy. The abundance of wildflowers makes for some of the finest color shows in the state. The drier climate leads to open forests with less underbrush, offering both unobstructed views and easier off-trail hiking. And while the scenery is generally less dramatic than in the mountains to the west, there are also fewer other hikers, so solitude is a bonus.

This region presents very few difficulties for hikers. The area gets a few thunderstorms, but not that many. Grizzly bears do not live in most of these mountains. And the drier conditions mean that there are fewer mosquitoes than in the wetter parts of Montana.

62 Sweetgrass Hills: Mount Brown

Distance: 7 miles roundtrip
Difficulty: strenuous
Hiking time: day hike
Elevation gain: 2750 feet
Season: mid-May to mid-November
Best time: late May through June

Contact: Bureau of Land Management, Havre Field Office
Maps: USGS Bingham Lake, Hawley Hill, Haystack Butte
GPS coordinates: N48° 54.552', W111° 07.422'

Getting there: First, drive to tiny Whitlash, about 35 miles north-northwest of Chester along good gravel roads. From the middle of "town," go 3.8 miles west on Blackjack Road, then keep straight, still on Blackjack Road, although the road that goes left is more heavily traveled. Stay on this narrow and rough dirt-and-gravel road, which can become impassable when wet, for 4.4 miles to where the road makes a sharp left turn. Park here in the spacious pullout beside a large sign stating SWEETGRASS HILLS AREA OF CRITICAL ENVIRONMENTAL CONCERN.

The Sweetgrass Hills are a dramatic landform that may have no equal in the United States. Located just south of the Canadian border, these misplaced buttes abruptly rise fully 3000 feet above gently rolling plains, making them visible for over 100 miles in every direction. The hills offer outstanding biological diversity with a relatively cool and wet "island" ecosystem that mixes plants and animals from both the Great Plains and the Rocky Mountains.

The isolation, along with sometimes difficult access over private lands, means that hikers rarely visit the Sweetgrass Hills. But it's worth making the effort because the hills are not only fascinating, they are also very scenic. This hike takes you to the top of Mount Brown, the second highest of the three main hills, on a route that is entirely over public land. And while there are no formal trails, that's not a problem because the open, grassy terrain offers unobstructed travel.

Warning: It can be extremely windy along this open ridge, so carry a windbreaker, strap down your hat, and wear sunglasses to protect your eyes from wind-driven dust.

Two fencelines converge beside the parking area. Go through the gate on your left that is oriented on a northeast-southwest line. There is no official trail, but right from the start you can see the hulking summit of Mount Brown to the south, so navigation is simple. The easiest approach is to follow a very faint and grassy jeep track that initially goes southeast for 0.25 mile to the top of a wide draw. The route then bends to the right before following the top of a rolling ridge that climbs toward the north side of Mount Brown.

The grass- and wildflower-covered landscape is absolutely enchanting, especially for hikers who feel claustrophobic when walking in a forest. While trees are nonexistent, wildflowers are amazingly abundant. In fact, in early June these hills host some of the best displays of blossoms in Montana. Just a sampling of the most abundant varieties includes sticky geranium, yellow locoweed, bladder-pod mustard, shooting star,

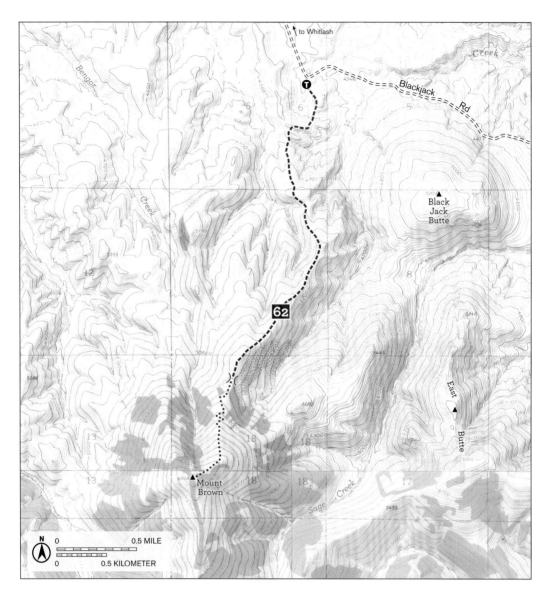

prairie star, field chickweed, lupine, lomatium, pasqueflower, larkspur, American bistort, golden pea, long-plumed avens, and gromwell. It's a color show that would make Van Gogh jealous.

At about 2.4 miles you reach a saddle at the northern base of Mount Brown. There are a few low-growing junipers here, as well as a small forest of limber pines, Douglas firs, and Engelmann spruces hiding on the wetter and more protected north side of the ridge. Small snow patches sometimes remain on this slope into early June.

The next 0.8 mile gets much steeper, as you ascend first over grass and then up a talus slope. You top out on the partly forested summit ridge of Mount Brown, where the views are stupendous. On clear days you can see more than 100 miles in all directions. The vast plains, dotted with ponds to the east, are fascinating while to the west rise the other major summits of the Sweetgrass Hills—the narrow pyramid of Gold Butte and the bulky mass of West Butte—and the distant crags of the Rocky Mountains. To the south you can see the Highwood, Little Belt, and Bears Paw Mountains.

Turn right (west) on the summit ridge and ascend at a more moderate pace through partial forest and a small burn area for 0.25 mile to Mount Brown's high point. Trees block the view, but with a bit of searching you'll find openings where you can sit and enjoy unparalleled vistas while eating your lunch.

63 *North Fork Highwood Creek Loop*

Distance: 10-mile loop
Difficulty: strenuous
Hiking time: day hike
Elevation gain: 3100 feet
Season: late May to early November
Best time: June

Contact: Helena–Lewis and Clark NF, Judith Ranger District
Map: USGS Arrow Peak
GPS coordinates: N47° 28.170', W110° 35.058'

Getting there: From Great Falls, go east on US 89/87 to a junction about 3 miles past the eastern outskirts of town. Turn left onto State Route 228, following signs to Highwood, and drive 19 miles to a junction where the road makes a prominent left turn. Bear right onto Upper Highwood Creek Road and follow this bumpy gravel road for 6.5 miles to a T intersection, where you go left. Proceed 7.4 miles to the national forest boundary and just 20 yards later go left on Forest Road 8841, following signs to North Fork Trailhead. Drive 1 mile, then turn right and continue 0.6 mile to the road-end trailhead.

The Highwood Mountains lack craggy mountain scenery, but they still offer attractions such as miles of well-maintained trails, splashing creeks, wildflower-covered meadows, and view-packed ridges. Vistas from the highest summits extend across vast prairies to the distant Rocky Mountains. This trip to Prospect Peak, with a return loop along a very scenic ridge, offers a superb sampling of this range's many charms and may be the finest hiking option within an hour's drive of Great Falls. *Note:* These trails are popular on weekends with mountain bikers and motorcyclists; hikers seeking quiet and solitude should visit on a weekday. Some trails are not shown on the USGS map.

From the southeast end of the parking lot, go around a gate, keep right at a junction with a trail to Thain Creek Campground, then cross a log bridge over North Fork Highwood Creek. From there the route follows a long-abandoned jeep road that is now so overgrown with grasses it has effectively reverted to a trail. The surrounding landscape soothes your senses with a gentle beauty featuring lovely meadows rimmed by cottonwoods and quaking aspens. Rounded ridges rise on either side with the sunnier south-facing slopes covered with sagebrush and grasses, while the shadier north-facing slopes are cloaked in evergreens.

The Center Ridge Trail goes right 100 yards after the first bridge, but you keep straight passing through lovely meadows beside the rushing creek. Cross the creek again at just shy of 0.4 mile, then walk another 0.4 mile to a junction with White Wolf Trail and the start of the recommended loop.

Go straight and at 1 mile rock-hop North Fork Highwood Creek where a small side creek comes in from the left. A second easy rock-hop crossing comes just 0.2 mile later, after which you remain faithful to the left (northeast) side of the creek. Birds are everywhere in this environment, including ruffed grouse, yellow-breasted chats, flycatchers, and various warblers and vireos. Flowers are also abundant with golden pea, desert parsley, blazing star, flax, sticky geranium, American bistort, chokecherry, pussytoes, serviceberry, larkspur, long-plumed avens, death camas, and several other species putting on a fine show in June. Finally, beaver activity is often visible along the creek and lucky hikers may see one of these large, flat-tailed rodents.

The gentle trail follows the creek upstream, reaching a reunion with the Center Ridge Trail at 2.6 miles. Continue straight and soon begin a steady ascent, always remaining on the mostly treeless hillside on the left side of the drainage. At 3.1 miles is a junction with Kirby Creek Trail #486. The recommended return loop goes sharply left.

Side trip: For the side trip to Prospect Peak, continue straight, cross the trickle that remains of North Fork Highwood Creek, then climb in forest and across open hillsides for 0.7 mile to a large meadow just below a forested pass. Leave the trail at this meadow, angling uphill to the northeast, and soon pick up a ridge that heads almost directly toward Prospect Peak. This open ridge has few trees so navigation is not a problem. As you approach the peak there is a short but very steep and rocky section. The best plan is to follow a game trail that angles steeply uphill to the right, which takes you around the worst of the rocks. Once at Prospect Peak's summit you'll enjoy wide vistas of the folded Highwood Mountains, with the two most prominent summits being Highwood Baldy to the west and Arrow Peak to the south.

To do the loop, return to the Kirby Creek Trail and climb an open hillside to a junction in a wide saddle. Turn left onto Marie Spring Trail and climb at a moderate grade over slopes with fine views of Prospect Peak and Arrow Peak. In early June, arrowleaf balsamroot blooms profusely, covering this sunny hillside with large

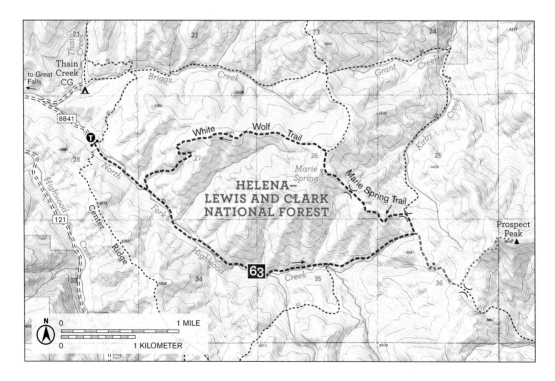

Highwood Baldy from the Marie Spring Trail

yellow blossoms. After attaining the ridgetop, the scenic trail goes up and down, passing a side trail to Marie Spring stock tank and coming to a cluster of very colorful lichen-covered rocks.

Just shy of 0.2 mile past these rock formations is a signed but easy-to-miss junction. Go left (downhill) on the White Wolf Trail, which stays near the top of a mostly open ridge serving up splendid views of Highwood Baldy and the plains beyond. After a very scenic 1.2 miles, the trail descends three well-graded switchbacks to the junction at the close of the loop beside North Fork Highwood Creek.

64 *Missouri River Canyon*

Distance: 9.8 miles roundtrip
Difficulty: strenuous
Hiking time: day hike or overnight
Elevation gain: 2000 feet
Season: April to November
Best time: May to June

Contact: Helena–Lewis and Clark NF, Helena Ranger District
Map: USFS Gates of the Mountains Wilderness & Recreation Area
GPS coordinates: N46° 49.097', W111° 53.898'

Getting there: In Helena, take Custer Avenue exit 194 off Interstate 15, go 1.2 miles east, and then turn left on York Road (State Route 280). At 10.4 miles from Helena, or 0.3 mile past a bridge across Hauser Lake, is a junction at the tiny community of York. Turn left on gravel Nelson Road and proceed 8.1 miles to a T intersection at the settlement of Nelson. Turn left, drive 4.6 miles, and then turn right on FR 1812. Slowly drive this rough road (in wet conditions it may be impassable) for 2 miles to a junction on top of a grassy hill. Turn right, following signs to Missouri River Canyon Trailhead, and proceed 0.4 mile to the road-end turnaround.

Over countless millennia the Missouri River has carved a dramatic canyon through the deep layers of limestone in the northern Big Belt Mountains. This impressive defile, at the transition point between the mountains of western Montana and the rolling plains to the east, is not only extremely scenic, but also offers interesting history. In 1805 Lewis and Clark named this place the Gates of the Rocky Mountains. You can visit their campsite and imagine the awe they felt gazing up at towering canyon walls and heavily forested mountains, instead of the endless plains that had greeted them every day for months before.

Like Lewis and Clark, most people today reach this place by water, taking commercial boat tours up Holter Lake, a reservoir on the Missouri River. Hikers sometimes take this boat, walk the canyon trails, and catch a return boat later in the day. (Contact Gates of the Mountains Boat Tours for reservations; see Recommended Resources.) For those with the time and energy, however, it's more satisfying to hike into the canyon by climbing over a high ridge and descending grassy slopes with dramatic views of both the surrounding mountains and the canyon below.

The trail begins beside a large signboard on a grassy hillside with scattered ponderosa pines. In May and early June, arrowleaf balsamroot, death camas, phlox, western gromwell, and lomatium brighten this sunny slope with color. For added interest, both elk and mule deer are often around, especially in the morning.

The grassy path climbs gradually across the delightfully open landscape, skirting a parcel of private property before reaching rocky Grant Gulch. Here you turn sharply uphill and make a shadeless ascent that is best tackled in the cool of the morning. After gaining 840 feet, you top out at a wide saddle marked by a tall cairn. This pass has excellent views both straight ahead into the Missouri River Canyon and behind you across the Helena Valley to the jumbled Elkhorn Mountains.

From the pass you make a long 1100-foot descent to the river. This north-facing slope is cooler and wetter than the other side of the pass, with relatively dense Douglas fir forests. Notable wildflowers here include shooting star, buttercup, pasqueflower, Oregon grape, and yellow fritillary. The sometimes obscure trail makes six moderately long downhill switchbacks and offers up marvelous views of the limestone crags and forested hills across the canyon.

At the bottom is the Missouri River, which here is backed up behind the slack waters of Holter Lake. There are superb campsites on grassy benches a little above the water. The scenery will argue in favor of camping, as you can look across to forested slopes and tall limestone ramparts rising majestically above the water.

Looking across the Missouri River from the Meriwether Picnic Area dock

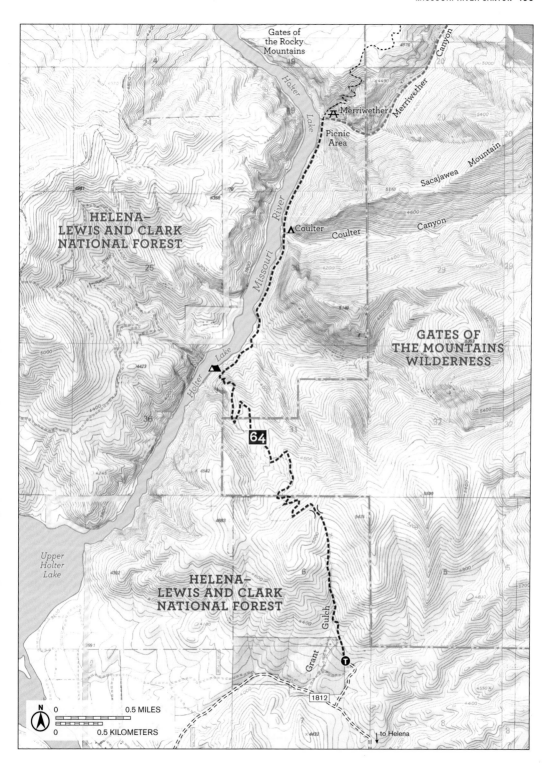

Gates of
the Rocky
Mountains

Holter Lake

Merriwether Canyon

Merriwether

Picnic
Area

Sacajawea Mountain

HELENA–
LEWIS AND CLARK
NATIONAL FOREST

Missouri River

Coulter

Coulter

Canyon

Holter Lake

GATES OF
THE MOUNTAINS
WILDERNESS

64

Upper
Holter
Lake

HELENA–
LEWIS AND CLARK
NATIONAL FOREST

Grant Gulch

T

1812

to Helena

N

0   0.5 MILES

0   0.5 KILOMETERS

While still about 80 feet above the river, the faint trail turns downstream (right) and follows the partly forested slopes beneath the dramatic cliffs on either side of the canyon. After about 0.8 mile you reach boater-oriented Coulter Campground with picnic tables, an outhouse, a boat ramp, garbage cans, and a not-always-functional water pump.

Beyond Coulter Campground the trail crosses forested slopes for 0.8 mile to Meriwether Picnic Area at a small alcove across from a huge rock buttress. In addition to the jaw-dropping scenery, this picnic area offers a modern shelter, cut firewood, picnic tables, a boat ramp, and a water fountain. Historical plaques commemorate the Lewis and Clark expedition, which camped at this site in 1805, and thirteen firefighters who lost their lives fighting the nearby Mann Gulch Fire in 1949.

Extend your hike: For those seeking additional exercise, a trail goes up Meriwether Canyon with a side trail leading to the solemn gravesites of the firefighters who died in the Mann Gulch blaze.

65 *Trout Creek Canyon*

Distance: up to 6 miles roundtrip
Difficulty: easy to moderate
Hiking time: day hike
Elevation gain: 650 feet
Season: May to October
Best time: mid-May to early July
Contact: Helena–Lewis and Clark NF,

Helena Ranger District
Maps: USFS Gates of the Mountains Wilderness & Recreation Area; USGS Hogback Mountain, Snedaker Basin
GPS coordinates: N46° 46.020', W111° 39.061'

Getting there: In Helena, take Custer Avenue exit 194 off Interstate 15, go 1.2 miles east, and then turn left on York Road (State Route 280). At 10.4 miles from Helena, or 0.3 mile past a bridge across Hauser Lake, is a junction at the tiny community of York. Go straight and drive 6.6 miles to where the road makes a sharp right turn into Vigilante Campground. The Trout Creek Trailhead is immediately ahead of you just before the road makes this turn.

In the Big Belt Mountains east of Helena lies a spectacular landscape of deep canyons, towering limestone cliffs and pinnacles, and heavily forested hills. The remarkably gentle Trout Creek Trail explores the bottom of this region's most impressive canyon, following a small creek that flows past the base of multi-colored cliffs and towers, which soar several hundred feet above you.

The heavily used trail follows an old road, which was closed after being damaged by floods once too often for the tastes (and budget) of the Forest Service. The first mile is an easy wheelchair-accessible nature trail with bridges

Colorful tower in upper part of Trout Creek Canyon

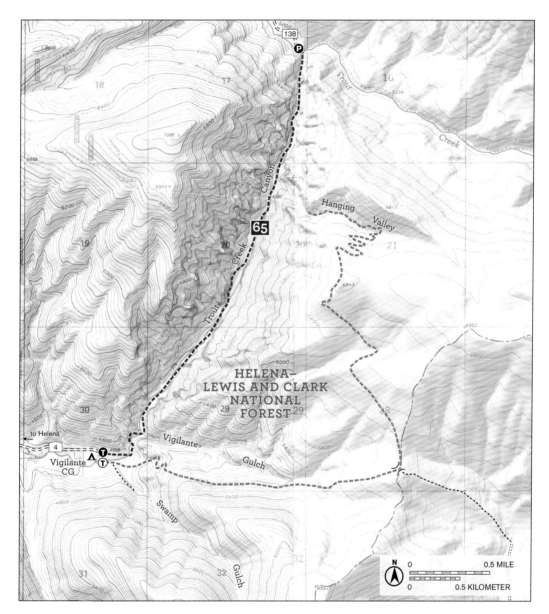

over the creek and a gravel surface. Once the nature trail ends, the dirt path wanders through open forest and includes several short, steep sections as well as a dozen or so creek crossings requiring wet feet, rock-hopping skills, or the ability to long jump up to 10 feet. The total elevation gain is minimal, however, so the hiking is not difficult.

What *is* difficult is prying your eyes off the absolutely staggering views of the immense cliffs rising on either side. The canyon is narrowest and the scenery is most impressive between about 1 mile and 2.5 miles from the trailhead, so go at least that far to enjoy the best this trail has to offer. The trail ends at a little over 3 miles where it meets Forest Road 138.

Extend your hike: For a much stiffer hiking challenge, try the nearby Hanging Valley Trail. It starts near campsite #9 in Vigilante Campground and climbs almost 3000 feet to a ridgeline before dropping into its namesake valley—a narrow, forested gully with numerous tall rock spires on either side. From here you hike through this rocky wonderland, go under a small natural bridge, then carefully pick your way down a couple of rock chutes to the abrupt end of the trail at a metal fence blocking the chasm. Immediately on the other side of this fence the valley drops off a dizzying 1000-foot cliff to the bottom of Trout Creek Canyon.

66 Mount Baldy Basin Loop

Distance: 18-mile loop
Difficulty: very strenuous
Hiking time: overnight
Elevation gain: 4400 feet
Season: mid-July through mid-October
Best time: late July to September

Contact: Helena–Lewis and Clark NF, Townsend Ranger District
Map: USGS Mount Edith, Gurnett Creek East
GPS coordinates: N46° 29.708', W111° 15.345'

Getting there: From Townsend, drive 2.2 miles east on US 12, then turn left on State Route 284. After 10.9 miles turn right on Duck Creek Road, which eventually becomes Forest Road 139, and climb 12.8 miles on this increasingly rough gravel road to a junction at Duck Creek Pass. The signed Hidden Lake Trailhead is at the end of a 0.2-mile loop road on your right.

The most impressive lakes and scenery in the Big Belt Mountains are at the southern end of the range around Mount Baldy. This peak boasts dramatic cirque basins filled with gorgeous little lakes that beckon Helena-area pedestrians with fine scenery and good fishing. This trip includes the best of the lakes and, for experienced hikers, offers an optional return route along a rugged off-trail ridge with tremendous views.

The trail heads south from a small wooden sign, climbing a hill just to the east of a jeep road. After 120 yards the trail angles away from the road and begins an extended climb. As you gain elevation, subalpine firs dominate the surroundings amid millions of silvery snags from beetle-killed pines. Near 2.4 miles, and again at 2.8 miles, keep left when unsigned spur trails from the end of the jeep road intersect your route. After the second junction the trail descends fourteen gently graded switchbacks to a junction with the Gipsy Lake Trail. Go straight, gradually climb over a rounded spur ridge, and then descend to a creek crossing and a very pretty

lake with a good campsite. *Note:* This lake is not shown on the USGS map.

At the southeast end of this lake is a junction at 5.8 miles. To reach Hidden Lake, turn right and walk 0.1 mile to this deep and scenic lake backed by a tall cliff. Rocks limit the camping options but there is a good spot above the southeast shore.

You could turn around at Hidden Lake, perfectly content with your hike. But this lake also makes a convenient location for a base camp to explore the numerous other nearby lakes. The most dramatically scenic ones are tucked away in high alcoves to the west and southwest. Grace Lake (reached by a signed trail from the southeast end of Hidden Lake), Upper Baldy Lake (accessed via a sketchy footpath from the upper end of Grace Lake), and Lake 8530 (a steep and challenging off-trail scramble west of Hidden Lake) all make outstanding destinations.

If you're an experienced hiker up for an off-trail loop on the return trip, hike back to the small lake below Hidden Lake and go south on the signed trail toward Edith Lake. After 0.5 mile

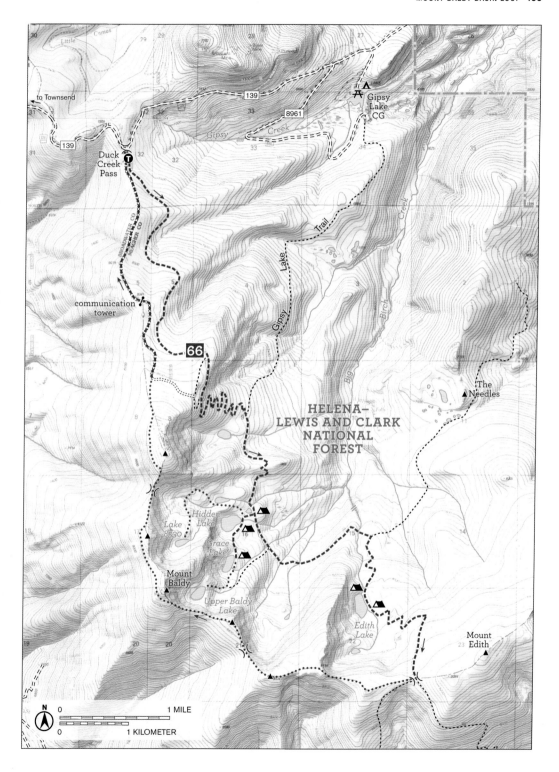

to Townsend

139

8961

Gipsy   Creek

139

Gipsy

Lake

Gipsy   Lake   CG

Duck
Creek
Pass

communication
tower

66

Gipsy

Lake

Trail

Big

Birch

Creek

HELENA–
LEWIS AND CLARK
NATIONAL
FOREST

The
Needles

Hidden
Lake

Lake
8530

Grace
Lake

Mount
Baldy

Upper Baldy
Lake

Edith
Lake

Mount
Edith

BROADWATER CO

MEAGHER CO

N

0   1 MILE

0   1 KILOMETER

Upper Baldy Lake

you pass a marked but little used path to Upper Baldy Lake, then cross a series of small creeks and traverse around a ridge to a junction. Turn right and steadily climb for 0.8 mile to Edith Lake. This forest-rimmed gem has good fishing and is backed by a tall, partly forested ridge. There is a fine campsite near the outlet complete with a wooden picnic table.

Beyond Edith Lake the rocky trail passes a decent campsite beside a tiny creek, then makes six switchbacks as it ascends to a high ridgetop on the divide of the Big Belt Mountains. The views are tremendous looking east to the Smith River Basin and west to the Elkhorn Mountains.

Your route leaves the trail at the ridgetop and turns west, beginning a 5-mile cross-country jaunt along the view-packed ridgeline. There is some tricky rock scrambling, so novice hikers shouldn't try it, but navigating is simple and the scenery is superb. The most technically challenging section is the climb over a rocky knoll south of Mount Baldy. The steep climb over Mount Baldy itself is tiring but not dangerous. After rounding a large high point about 1 mile north of Mount Baldy, you descend to a jeep road and follow it for 2 miles, past a gate and communications tower, back to the trailhead.

67 Big Baldy Mountain

Distance: 10.2 miles roundtrip
Difficulty: moderate to strenuous
Hiking time: day hike
Elevation gain: 1900 feet
Season: July through October
Best time: mid to late July

Contact: Helena–Lewis and Clark NF, Belt Creek and Judith Ranger Districts
Map: USGS Yogo Peak
GPS coordinates: N46° 54.942', W110° 35.008'

Getting there: From US 89 at the Kings Hill summit, go 1.9 miles north, then turn east onto dirt Forest Road 3328. Drive 1.9 miles, turn sharply right at a sign for South Ridge, and proceed 2 miles to a ridgetop junction. Bear left on FR 251 and carefully drive this

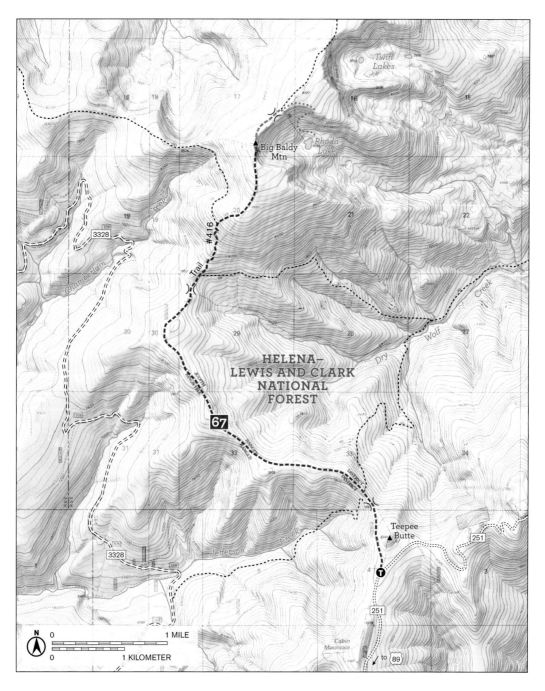

rocky road, which has some terrible mud holes when wet and requires better than average ground clearance. After 3.4 miles the road forks in front of Teepee Butte. Park here since driving farther requires four-wheel drive. *Tip:* Mountain bikes are a great option for traveling the next 3.6 miles of ATV road.

The forested and sprawling Little Belt Mountains aren't known for lakes or dramatic alpine scenery. But the range's highest point, Big Baldy Mountain, offers expansive views, wildflower-covered alpine meadows, and an impressive cirque on its eastern flank that holds a small, scenic lake. The final descent to the lake is only for experienced hikers confident on steep, off-trail routes. Others should stop at the summit, still enjoying a great hike.

Take the left fork and walk this rugged road downhill for 0.7 mile across the west side of Tee-pee Butte to a junction in a grassy saddle. Keep straight on the up-and-down ridgeline route, enjoying marvelous views in all directions. Wide and bulky Big Baldy Mountain dominates the scene to the north. In July the open meadows come alive with wildflowers and attract thousands of butterflies. Even though your route is technically an ATV road, it feels more like a wide trail and is a highly enjoyable hike, especially on weekdays when motorized users are rare.

At 3.6 miles, just above a saddle on the south side of Big Baldy Mountain, the ATV route ends at a signed junction. Mountain bikes are allowed beyond this point, but it soon gets too steep for them, so it's better to leave your bike here.

Go left (uphill) on Trail #416 and steeply climb first in open forest then across view-packed scree slopes and alpine meadows. After 0.4 mile, keep right at a junction and continue steeply uphill, soon reaching timberline amid rolling alpine meadows. Hardy wildflowers here include stonecrop, alpine buttercup, American bistort, locoweed, phlox, dwarf lupine, and yarrow. After a couple of false summits, reach the top with amazing views that extend up to 100 miles in all directions. There is a small solar-powered weather station at the summit and bighorn sheep are sometimes seen on the nearby slopes.

Big Baldy Mountain over Rhoda Lake

Extend your hike: Immediately east of the summit is a cliff-walled basin holding sparkling Rhoda Lake. Reaching this goal requires some very steep rock scrambling, which is only recommended for experienced hikers. To tackle this challenge, descend on good trail to a saddle northeast of Big Baldy. The USGS map shows a trail to the lake from here, but that isn't accurate. The safer option is to hike uphill along the rim another 0.3 mile, leaving the trail and following the edge of the cliff to a point on the southeast side of the next rounded high point. Look carefully here for a narrow ledge that angles sharply right descending across the steepest parts of the cliff. The route is fairly steep, rocky, and narrow, but reasonably safe, and is obviously used by both people and animals. By the time the ledge disappears the slope is still steep, but less so than before, and can be carefully descended over rocky areas to Rhoda Lake.

This gorgeous pool holds both arctic grayling and cutthroat trout and offers great scenery since the lake is surrounded by 850-foot cliffs. Camping is possible, but the shoreline is fragile, so it's not recommended.

68 *Collar Peak Loop*

Distance: 5.6-mile loop
Difficulty: moderate to strenuous
Hiking time: day hike
Elevation gain: 1300 feet
Season: mid-May to early November
Best time: late May through mid-June

Contact: Bureau of Land Management, Lewistown Field Office
Map: USGS Judith Peak
GPS coordinates: N47° 12.522', W109° 12.889'

Getting there: From Lewistown, go 10.5 miles north on US 191 then turn right on Maiden Road, following signs to Warm Spring Creek Canyon. Drive 8.7 miles to the end of the pavement at Maiden, continue 1 mile on good gravel, then turn left, heading for Judith Peak. Drive 2.1 miles and park in the signed pullout on the right for the Collar Peak Trail.

If you tell a typical Montanan that you are going hiking in the Judith Mountains they are likely to ask, "Where's that?" Needless to say, this isolated range is not on the radar screens of most Treasure State pedestrians. But these forested mountains offer several fine trails (many not shown on maps) that provide good scenery, lots of wildflowers, and plenty of solitude. The best is this scenic circuit to the top of Collar Peak, which features wide-ranging views, open meadows, a pretty creek, and miles of attractive forests.

From the trailhead a jeep road angles to the east-southeast and your loop will come back on this road. For now, take the hiking and mountain biking trail that goes northeast and contours across a hillside forested with lodgepole pines. The understory is rather sparse, with just a few ground-hugging junipers, various grasses, grouse whortleberries, and scattered wildflowers.

The trail stays high with only tiny ups and downs for almost 1 mile to where you cross the trickle of water in the upper reaches of Collar Gulch.

From here, you climb briefly, then follow a rolling wooded ridge south toward Collar Peak. At 1.6 miles is a saddle with good views to the southwest of Big Grassy Peak. The trail then steadily climbs the east side of the ridge to the top of a small meadow covered with arrowleaf balsamroot blossoms in early June, before reaching a saddle on the north slopes of Collar Peak.

A fairly steep 0.4-mile climb leads to the open summit at 2.5 miles. There are wonderful views here of the Judith Mountains, especially south to rounded Crystal Peak, west to well-named Big Grassy Peak, and northwest to Judith Peak, which is topped with several radio, cell phone, and other towers. You can also see the long ridge of the Big Snowy Mountains to the

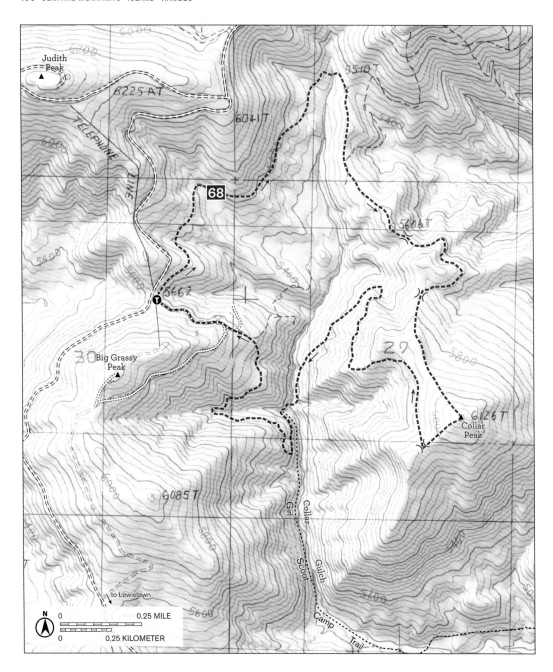

south-southwest and the vast plains of eastern Montana all around.

From the top of Collar Peak the indistinct trail angles southwest following low cairns and a rock-lined path that rapidly descends to a saddle where the trail leaves the ridge and drops to the right back into forest. Here a distinct path goes north, staying on the west side of the ridge you came in on, then descends to the left and crosses a very scenic open slope with excellent views of Big Grassy Peak across Collar Gulch. After this attractive section, the trail cuts to the right, going through forest and across a series of small talus slopes to a switchback beside a little gully. More downhill leads you to the creek in Collar Gulch, which you follow downstream for about 0.4 mile. You rockhop the creek and about 50 yards later reach a junction. The faint Girl Scout Camp Trail goes left (downstream).

You keep right, make one switchback, then ascend the south side of a usually dry drainage coming in from the west. Eventually you cross this rocky gully then make a gradual uphill traverse of a partly forested hillside with good views back to Collar Peak to trail's end at a switchback on a jeep road. Take the left (uphill) road fork and keep straight 50 yards later when another jeep road goes sharply left. Follow this level road for another 0.25 mile back to the trailhead.

Crystal Peak as seen from atop Collar Peak

69 *Big Snowy Crest*

Distance: 35.5 miles roundtrip (including the Ice Cave Loop on the return)
Difficulty: very strenuous
Hiking time: multiday
Elevation gain: 4300 feet
Season: mid-June through October
Best time: late June

Contact: Helena–Lewis and Clark NF, Judith Ranger District
Maps: USGS Crystal Lake, Half Moon Canyon, Jump Off Peak
GPS coordinates: N46° 47.657', W109° 30.540'

Getting there: From Lewistown, drive 10 miles southwest on US 87/191, then turn left on gravel Crystal Lake Road. Go 5.4 miles, turn left at a junction, and proceed 3.9 miles to another junction. Still on Crystal Lake Road, go left and drive 7.1 miles to where you enter national forest land and the road returns to pavement. Now on Forest Road 275, drive 4.9 miles to Crystal Lake and follow the road around the eastern shore for 0.7 mile to the Ice Cave Trailhead turnoff. Turn left to reach the spacious trailhead parking lot.

The Big Snowy Mountains sit at the geographic center of Montana, and on clear days, the views from the alpine ridgeline that forms the backbone of these mountains extend from Canada to the Wyoming border. But the trails here offer more than just seemingly endless vistas. There are also interesting limestone caves with impressive ice formations inside, plenty of wildlife, lots of wildflowers, enormous alpine meadows, and deep and dramatic canyons. The only drawback is a lack of water. Backpackers must rely on snowbanks, which typically remain in sheltered places along the ridgetop until early July.

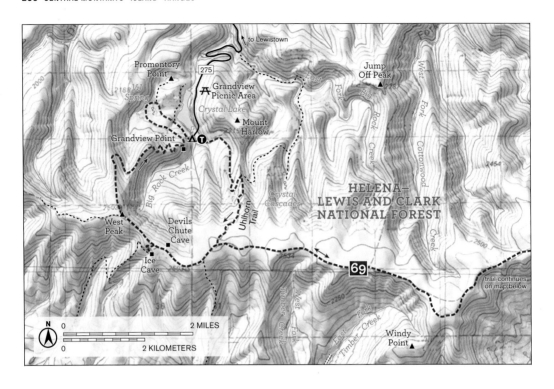

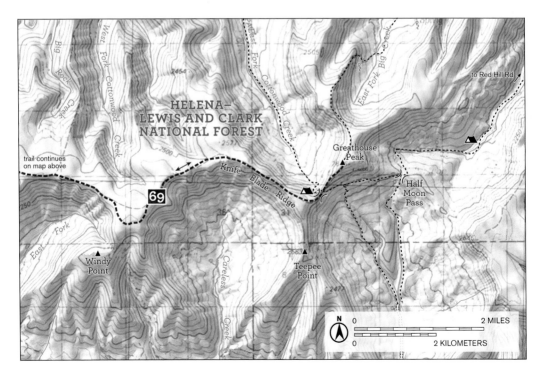

Crystal Lake from Grandview Point

Go southeast on Uhlhorn Trail, heading gradually uphill through a forest of lodgepole pines, Douglas firs, and Engelmann spruces. From mid-June to early July, wildflowers are abundant, including American bistorts, bluebells, lupines, pasqueflowers, fairyslipper orchids, baneberries, Oregon grapes, and prince's pines. After just 40 yards, keep left at a junction with a stock bypass trail, then gradually ascend in two long switchbacks to a ridgetop junction at 1.2 miles.

Your trail goes right, staying on the increasingly open and rocky ridgetop that offers nice views of the tall ridgeline to the south. The well-graded trail makes several switchbacks that take you across open scree slopes with fine unobstructed views of the Crystal Lake basin and the distant Highwood, Judith, Moccasin, and Bears Paw Mountains. Eventually you top out at a signed junction at 3.1 miles on the main, east-west divide of the Big Snowy Mountains. For a day hike that just does the loop to Ice Cave, go straight.

Backpackers won't want to miss the trip to the east along the spectacular alpine crest of the Big Snowy Mountains. To do this, turn sharply left, following signs to Half Moon Pass, and hike a faint trail marked with low cairns. The wide and lightly forested ridge offers easy walking as it intermittently gains elevation and there are frequent excellent views up and down the scenic ridge and off to distant plains and mountains.

At 2.7 miles from the junction you reach an overlook of the gaping bowl on the south side of the divide formed by East Fork Timber Creek. The trail makes a circuit around the top of this bowl before finally gaining enough elevation to reach the treeless alpine meadows that characterize the central and eastern parts of the Big Snowy Mountains. From here the views extend for over 150 miles while at your feet tiny alpine forget-me-nots, alpine buttercups, Jones columbines, and other high-elevation wildflowers offer bits of color. **Warning:** Although this is wildly scenic country, it is no place to be when it's particularly windy (frequently the case) or when thunderstorms threaten (also common).

The faint tread continues east through this gentle, alpine wonderland passing several dramatic canyons on both sides of the divide. At one point the trail skirts the south (right) side of a low limestone escarpment before returning to the wide alpine ridge.

Near 10.5 miles the ridge narrows at the western end of Knife Blade Ridge. Here the divide squeezes down to just a few feet wide with drop-offs of several hundred feet on either side. Things remain wide enough that people with any normal fear of heights won't have a problem, but it's exciting nonetheless. The trail skirts the first narrow section of Knife Blade Ridge on the south then climbs to a somewhat wider hill. Here you have a fine view looking east of tall and sloping Greathouse Peak, the highest point in the Big Snowy Mountains. A second even narrower section of Knife Blade Ridge forces the trail to the north side, giving you nearly constant superb views down the wide canyon of East Fork Cottonwood Creek.

Once past Knife Blade Ridge, the trail descends past a couple of very scenic campsites, although the only nearby water is from snowbanks that *might* last until early July, to a long saddle on the west side of Greathouse Peak. There are no signs, but several trails intersect at this point.

A well-defined trail starts at a prominent cairn in the saddle and drops down the south side of the ridge descending to just above a couple of tiny ponds before continuing on to Half Moon Pass. The trail going straight ahead leads up an exposed ridge to the top of Greathouse Peak, from which you'll enjoy what is probably the most expansive view in the state of Montana.

Greathouse Peak makes an excellent turnaround point. If you prefer a one-way adventure, it's possible to hike to Half Moon Pass and then take a very scenic trail down Half Moon Creek to the newly developed Uhlhorn Trailhead on Red Hill Road. This trip requires a fairly long car shuttle, however, so most hikers return to the junction on the ridge above Crystal Lake the way they came, more than happy to re-hike the wildly scenic alpine ridge in the opposite direction.

Back at the junction 3.1 miles above Crystal Lake, go west, following signs to Ice Cave, and wander across gentle partly forested terrain. Cairns mark the route, but the tread is well defined. After 0.3 mile there is a signed junction with the little used East Fork Blake Creek Trail heading to the left.

Keep straight and soon cross an extended section of alpine terrain with only a few scattered trees and wide-ranging views. Along the way you pass Devils Chute Cave on your right. This cavern is carved directly into the limestone at the top of the ridge and is difficult to explore without specialized equipment.

About 0.2 mile past Devils Chute Cave, the side trail to Ice Cave goes left. Follow this trail for 0.3 mile to the second of two downhill switchbacks. Here a short spur trail goes straight and soon reaches the dual entrances of Ice Cave. You don't have to go far into these caverns to see interesting ice formations, but if you want to really explore them you'll need a headlamp and spelunking skills.

Back on the main trail, continue westnorthwest on your ridgetop ramble, which takes you a little more than 0.5 mile to a junction atop bulky West Peak. Go straight on Grandview Trail, walk along the top of a high ridge with far-ranging views to the north and west, then switchback to the right and begin a long, gradual descent. After an interlude in forest, the trail follows a rugged but mostly open ridge that offers fine views up and down the Big Snowy Mountains including most of the route of this hike.

Now begins a series of long and very gentle downhill switchbacks, all well shaded under the canopy of conifers. At the fourth switchback a signed trail goes straight for about 80 yards to aptly named Grandview Point with dramatic views of a nearby rock pinnacle and Crystal Lake almost directly below.

Six more very gentle switchbacks take you past spur trails to VJ Spring and Promontory Point before reaching a junction with Shoreline Trail just above tranquil Crystal Lake.

Bear right and follow this popular route to the head of Crystal Lake, where a prominent trail heads right toward the car campground. You go straight and less than 0.1 mile later, just after the trail crosses usually dry Big Rock Creek, turn right on an obvious but possibly unsigned trail. This path parallels the road for 0.2 mile to a point directly across from the turnoff for the Ice Cave Trailhead access road.

70 *Sacagawea Peak*

Distance: 5.8 miles roundtrip
Difficulty: strenuous
Hiking time: day hike
Elevation gain: 2100 feet
Season: July through October
Best time: mid-July through September

Contact: Custer Gallatin NF, Bozeman Ranger District
Map: USGS Sacagawea Peak
GPS coordinates: N45° 54.411', W110° 57.619'

Getting there: From Bozeman, go 20.5 miles north on Bridger Drive (State Route 86), then turn left onto Fairy Lake Road (Forest Road 74). Climb this somewhat rocky gravel road for 6.2 miles to the busy Fairy Lake/Sacagawea Pass Trailhead on the left.

The Bridger Mountains' narrow line of colorful peaks is a familiar landmark to Bozeman residents and the range is a popular destination for area hikers. The tallest summit is Sacagawea Peak and reaching the top is a goal of many local pedestrians. The summit views include many distant landmarks or you can simply look almost straight down at the amazing limestone cliffs on the mountain's eastern face. **Warning:** Avoid this exposed peak on summer afternoons if thunderstorms are in the forecast.

From the signboard on the south side of the parking turnaround, go right on the popular Sacagawea Pass Trail as it climbs gradually through a subalpine-fir forest with occasional views of the colorful and very scenic peaks of the northern Bridger Mountains. July wildflowers are abundant, including arnica, aster, yellow

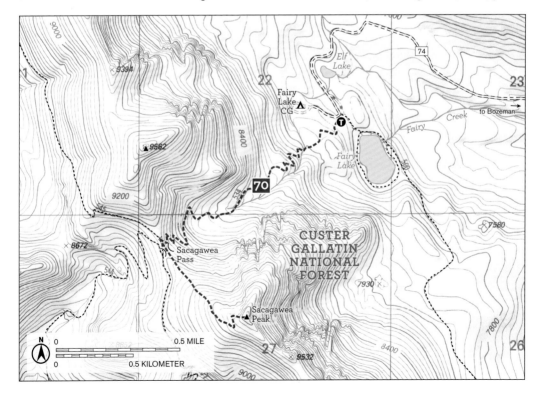

Nannie and kid mountain goat atop Sacagawea Peak

columbine, cow parsnip, yarrow, and paintbrush. The well-graded trail ascends eight switchbacks into more open terrain where there are excellent up-close looks at the rugged limestone cliffs and fins on the nearby slopes. From here you hike through a striking subalpine bowl, then ascend an open slope on thirteen switchbacks to a junction at Sacagawea Pass at 1.7 miles.

Your route turns sharply left and follows the top of an alpine ridge directly toward the summit of Sacagawea Peak. The winding trail steeply ascends the west side of the mountain, reaching the top at 2.9 miles. Mountain goats live here and are often seen by lucky hikers. But these animals are temperamental and have sharp horns, so don't approach too closely. The views from the summit are amazing! Cliffs drop thousands of feet off the east side of the peak and far-ranging vistas extend over the Shields and Gallatin River Valleys, up and down the spine of the Bridger Mountains, and to distant ranges such as the Beartooth and Crazy Mountains.

71 *Sunlight Lake*

Distance: 8.4 miles roundtrip
Difficulty: strenuous
Hiking time: day hike
Elevation gain: 2900 feet
Season: mid-July through October
Best time: late July to September

Contact: Custer Gallatin NF, Yellowstone Ranger District
Map: Beartooth Publishing, Crazy Mountains
GPS coordinates: N46° 08.508', W110° 25.818'

Getting there: From US 89 at the north end of Wilsall, go east on Shields River Road and proceed 16.2 miles to a junction just before the end of pavement. Keep straight, drive 3.8 miles, then turn right on Forest Road 6630, following signs to Sunlight Creek. Take this narrow and rough road for 2.3 miles to the road-end trailhead.

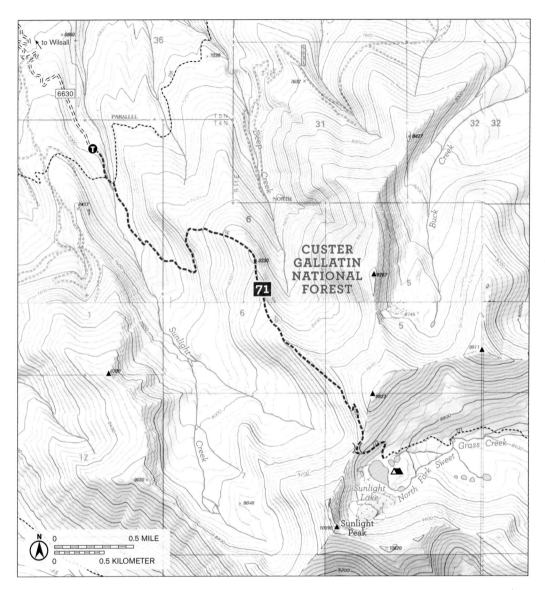

Perched in a cirque beneath the towering walls of Sunlight Peak, Sunlight Lake is a dramatically scenic destination that is well off the beaten track. The lake can be reached by a long hike up Sweet Grass Creek, but that trail has no reasonable public access. The much shorter route described here, however, remains entirely on public land and sneaks into the lake basin by climbing over a view-packed pass.

The trail heads south through a decades-old clear-cut now re-growing with 20-foot-tall lodgepole pines and subalpine firs. There are nice views directly ahead to Sunlight Peak and the other high crags of the northern Crazy Mountains. Follow the long-abandoned road for 0.3 mile to a junction, keep straight, and less than 100 yards later make a simple ford of Sunlight Creek. Almost immediately after this crossing is a signed junction.

marked with small cairns that climbs an open, wildflower-covered hillside. The ascent becomes steeper as you reenter forest and make one long switchback to the top of a ridge.

The trail now turns southeast to follow the ridge, steeply ascending into a land of whitebark pines and alpine meadows. As you would expect, the views of rugged Sunlight Peak to the south as well as the Shields River Valley and pointed Loco Mountain to the north are superb.

As you approach a tall flat-topped mountain, the trail cuts to the right and makes a gradual uphill traverse of a steep talus slope. This takes you to the ridge a little above a rocky pass between the unnamed flat-topped mountain and Sunlight Peak. Sunlight Lake is visible in the basin below you. The trail drops to the pass, then descends a section of narrow and badly sloped tread across a steep hillside to the lake.

Sunlight Lake is a grand spot. The lake usually has ice floating on it through late July and Sunlight Peak rises dramatically above the southwest shore. Camping is possible, but is rather exposed, and the alpine terrain is fragile, so a day hike is a better option. Look for mountain goats around the lake and consider bringing your fishing gear to try your luck with some of the lake's hungry cutthroat, brook, and rainbow trout.

Looking down on the basin of Sunlight Lake

Turn right and steadily climb to an unsigned fork at 0.75 mile. The old road you've been following veers right, but you bear left on a trail

72 Blue and Twin Lakes

Distance: 8.2 miles roundtrip to Blue Lake; 8.6 miles roundtrip to Upper Twin Lake
Difficulty: moderate
Hiking time: day hike or overnight
Elevation gain: 1840 feet to Blue Lake; 1650 feet to Upper Twin Lake
Season: July through October

Best time: mid-July through September
Contact: Custer Gallatin NF, Yellowstone Ranger District
Map: Beartooth Publishing, Crazy Mountains
GPS coordinates: N46° 2.544', W110° 14.382'

Getting there: From Big Timber, drive 11.5 miles north on US 191, then turn left on gravel Wormser Loop Road (County Road 25), following signs to Big Timber Canyon. Drive 2 miles, then turn right onto what eventually becomes Forest Road 197. This road is rutted and rather rough but is maintained for passenger cars. After 13.5 miles you reach the signed trailhead just before entering Half Moon Campground.

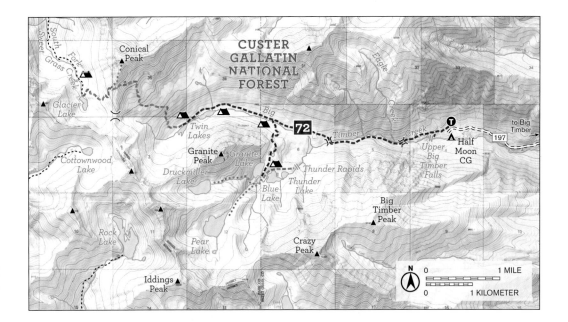

Of all the "island" ranges in central Montana, the Crazy Mountains are the highest and the most spectacular. People driving from the east across the Great Plains often have their first introduction to "real" mountains with their views of the towering peaks of this range. And "real" mountains they are, complete with dense coniferous forests, huge wildflower-covered meadows, sparkling cirque lakes, scenic 11,000-foot peaks, and even a few small glaciers. The only significant downside of hiking here is the checkerboard pattern of ownership of private and public lands (a legacy of railroad land grants), which leaves hikers facing confusing rules for camping and travel.

The trail goes west following an old road that is rapidly reverting to a foot trail. The surroundings are quite dramatic as you stay on the partly forested hillside above rushing Big Timber Creek and walk beneath canyon walls that rise up to 4000 feet on either side.

After 0.4 mile a signed path goes left to Upper Big Timber Falls. It's well worth the 0.1-mile side trip to view this thundering cataract, which twists down a rocky chute in an impressive display of hydropower.

In order to keep pace with cascading Big Timber Creek, the very rocky main trail maintains a steady, rather relentless uphill pace, mostly in forest. At about 1 mile you cross the creek on a large bridge then do so again in another mile. After passing some meadows with fine views of towering Crazy Peak to the south, you reach the junction with Blue Lake Trail at 2.9 miles.

Those heading for Blue Lake should go left (downhill). After a log crossing of Big Timber Creek, the trail switchbacks up a forested hillside for 0.8 mile, passes a couple of shallow ponds, then goes gradually uphill for 0.4 mile to the peninsula between very scenic Granite and Blue Lakes. Part of the shoreline of Granite Lake is on private property, so make sure you camp on public land. Campfires are prohibited in the Blue Lake Basin.

If you're up for some exploring, take an obvious social trail that heads northeast from Blue Lake to small Thunder Lake and the top of aptly named Thunder Rapids. Adventurous types can scramble up to either Pear or Druckmiller Lakes, both large and gorgeous.

For Twin Lakes, go straight at the junction along Big Timber Creek and soon pass a good

Lower Twin Lake, one of several beautiful and popular spots in the area

campsite before resuming your steady, rocky ascent. Not quite 0.5 mile after the Blue Lake junction, you leave the old road and follow a foot trail the remaining distance to Lower Twin Lake. The shores of this lake are very marshy but it's worth slogging down to the water for the classic reflections of a row of jagged, gray-brown peaks to the west.

The trail then climbs to Upper Twin Lake, another drop-dead gorgeous body of water even closer to those aforementioned peaks. Camping prospects are better here than at the lower lake but part of the eastern shore is private land, so be careful about where you put your tent. Both lakes are very popular, so don't expect solitude. Campfires are prohibited in the Twin Lakes Basin.

Extend your hike: If you're still bursting with energy, consider making the stiff climb over a high ridge to starkly scenic Glacier Lake. The trail begins near the northwest shore of Upper Twin Lake and abruptly switchbacks away from the water beginning an arduous 2000-foot ascent. The trail forgoes an enticing-looking pass, the approach to which is blocked by cliffs, and instead crosses the divide on a ridge high on the side of Conical Peak. The view from here is tremendous, including not only the tall cliffs and deep canyons close at hand, but the vast prairies and distant mountains to the north, east, and west.

To see Glacier Lake, descend twenty-eight well-graded switchbacks, losing 1250 feet on a sometimes obscure trail to reach the shore of this stunning lake. Aptly named Glacier Lake sits beneath towering peaks and often has icebergs floating in its waters until early August, so forget swimming unless you're trying to break the world record for the largest goose bumps. Camping here is not recommended due to the fragile and rocky terrain, but there are some decent campsites less than 0.5 mile north where the trail starts its descent into the meadows at the headwaters of South Fork Sweet Grass Creek.

Opposite, top: Cow moose, Beartooth Mountains

Opposite, bottom: Koch Peak over Tumbledown Basin

South-Central Montana

Montana's highest mountains tower into the blue skies of the south-central part of the state. The adjoining Madison, Absaroka, Gallatin, and Beartooth Ranges are the highlights of this dramatic region, which offers some of the best mountain hiking in North America.

Although close together, these four ranges are quite different in character. The Madison Range, farthest west, offers jagged peaks and tranquil lake basins. This range is heavily developed, especially around the Big Sky Resort, but it also enjoys partial protection in the Lee Metcalf Wilderness.

The Gallatin Range stretches from Bozeman all the way south into Yellowstone National Park. This long mountain divide has few lakes but includes numerous petrified forests, enormous flower-covered meadows, and the finest extended alpine ridge walk in Montana.

The lofty Absaroka Range southeast of Livingston has porous soils and relatively few lakes. This mostly forested range has a fine trail system, but outside of hunting season, most of these trails see only light use. As a result, this range is great for solitude seekers.

Most famous of all is the Beartooth Range, southwest of Billings. This wide mountain expanse consists of a huge, above-timberline granite plateau that contains thousands of lakes and some of the oldest rocks on Earth. Some trails are very popular but the enormity of this range spreads visitors out and allows for plenty of options for solitude lovers. The highest mountains and the largest glaciers in Montana help to make this area wildly scenic. The abundance of lakes offers great fishing, but also lots of mosquitoes, at least until late summer.

These ranges are home to some of Montana's densest grizzly bear populations, so hikers must carry bear spray and be alert. The area also gets lots of thunderstorms, especially on summer afternoons, so keep an eye on the sky and stay away from alpine ridges late in the day. Finally, the air is noticeably thinner at these altitudes. Take a few days to get acclimated before attempting any longer backpacking trips in these mountains.

73 *Spanish Peaks Loop*

Distance: 21.5-mile loop (including side trips to Lower Jerome Rock Lake and Spanish Lakes)
Difficulty: strenuous
Hiking time: multiday
Elevation gain: 4200 feet
Season: July through mid-October

Best time: mid-July through early September
Contact: Custer Gallatin NF, Bozeman Ranger District
Map: USFS Lee Metcalf Wilderness and West Yellowstone Vicinity
GPS coordinates: N45° 26.886', W111° 22.637'

Getting there: From Bozeman, drive 19 miles south on US 191 to a junction with Spanish Creek Road (Forest Road 982). Turn right on this good gravel (then paved) road, and drive 9.5 miles to the large developed trailhead.

The Spanish Peaks, a cluster of dramatic sky-scraping summits at the north end of the Madison Range, host dozens of starkly beautiful alpine lakes and include some of Montana's best mountain scenery. These attributes, along with close proximity to Bozeman, make the range popular, so don't expect solitude. *Do* expect tremendous views and some of the state's best

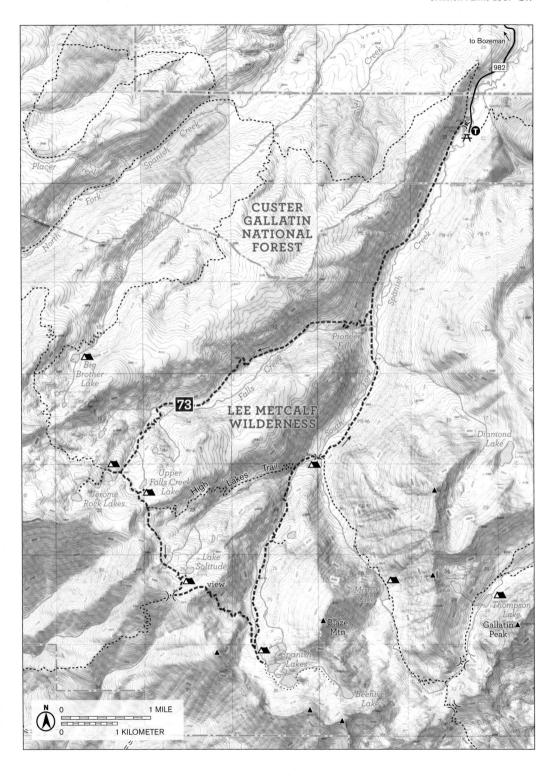

to Bozeman

982

CUSTER
GALLATIN
NATIONAL
FOREST

Placer
Creek

North
Fork

Spanish
Creek

FP3

Camp
Creek

Spanish
Creek

Pioneer
Falls

Big
Brother
Lake

73

LEE METCALF
WILDERNESS

Falls
Creek

South
Fork

Diamond
Lake

Upper
Falls Creek
Lake

High   Lakes   Trail

Jerome
Rock Lakes

Lake
Solitude

view

Mirror
Lake

Thompson
Lake

Blaze
Mtn

Gallatin
Peak

Spanish
Lakes

Beehive
Lake

N

0   1 MILE

0   1 KILOMETER

From the viewpoint above Lake Solitude, enjoy views of the craggy peaks.

hiking. This loop takes you past a thundering waterfall, most of the range's finest scenery, and many of the area's prettiest lakes.

The heavily used Spanish Creek Trail leaves from the northwest end of the parking lot and soon crosses a bridge over clear South Fork Spanish Creek to a junction. Go left (upstream) and for the next 0.5 mile walk through forest near the edge of a meadow. You then enter the Lee Metcalf Wilderness and hike beneath the partial shade of lodgepole pines and Engelmann spruces as the trail makes several minor ups and downs and crosses a series of seasonal tributary creeks. At 2.8 miles there is a signed junction and the start of the loop.

Turn right and switchback uphill for 0.7 mile to a point near the thundering cataract of Pioneer Falls. A short side trail leads to an excellent view of the falls where the frothing waters of Falls Creek tumble 40 feet over a dark cliff face. Above the falls you ascend a tributary creek taking you to another set of switchbacks. After a crossing of Falls Creek, a final set of switchbacks leads to a junction at 8.5 miles. To visit Lower Jerome Rock Lake, go right and climb 0.1 mile to the popular campsites near this pretty mountain lake. For solitude and more dramatic scenery, follow social trails that go southwest to either of the two upper lakes in the Jerome Rock grouping.

For the recommended loop, return to the junction below the Jerome Rock Lakes and go southeast on a trail that takes you mostly uphill for 0.3 mile to Upper Falls Creek Lake, where you'll find good campsites. The main trail does a bit more uphill to the top of a ridge, and then goes 50 yards down to a junction with High Lakes Trail.

Go right on Lake Solitude Trail, descend to a lovely but mosquito-infested meadow, then travel up and down through forests and wet meadows to a forest opening a little above the small basin holding Lake Solitude. It's well worth taking the short side trip to this lake for its fish and nice campsites.

The main trail turns right and quickly gains 500 feet to a junction on a windswept ridge-top. The views, especially looking south and southwest are tremendous, with towering Lone Mountain and the busy Big Sky Resort being the highlights. Go left at the junction, crossing an open slope with fine views to the north of the Bozeman area, then round a ridge and enjoy an outstanding bird's-eye view of the dramatic crags at the heart of the Spanish Peaks. Only Blaze Mountain, with its distinctive long snow-field, has a name, but the many nameless mountains are just as grand. To the east-southeast you can see several glistening members of the Spanish Lakes.

The trail switchbacks steeply down from the ridge, then goes up and down across meadows and rocky areas and around a promontory to a series of very scenic marshy ponds and a signed junction.

For a mandatory side trip, take the trail to the right, which in 0.4 mile climbs gradually to the lowest of the Spanish Lakes. Surrounded by jagged peaks, this deep lake is extremely scenic, but camping is limited by the rocky terrain and some sites are closed for rehabilitation, so it's better to camp elsewhere. Hardy hikers can explore the rocky terrain above this lake to the other Spanish Lakes or scramble up to stark but dramatically scenic Beehive Lake.

Returning to the junction 0.4 mile below the lowest Spanish Lake, bear right on the heavily used Spanish Lakes Trail, soon ford a creek, and then hike a steady but moderately graded downhill section. After 1.3 miles, and shortly after you hop over a tributary creek, is an unsigned junction with a trail that goes sharply right. This unofficial trail goes to an unnamed lake about 0.25 mile to the east.

You keep straight and continue mostly downhill to a calf-to-knee-deep ford of the main creek. About 0.3 mile later, hop over a tributary creek and immediately thereafter reach a junction with High Lakes Trail.

Go right and travel gradually downhill for 0.3 mile to a bridged creek crossing. There are two spacious campsites between this crossing and a log crossing of South Fork Spanish Creek just 0.1 mile later. Less than 100 yards after this second creek crossing is a junction.

Bear left and stay in the forest as you follow South Fork Spanish Creek downstream. The walk is gentle and pleasant, but doesn't offer much in the way of dramatic scenery. You cross the creek after about 1.4 miles then continue downstream to a crossing of Falls Creek and the close of the loop at the junction below Pioneer Falls.

74 *No Man Lake*

Distance: 16.2 miles roundtrip
Difficulty: very strenuous
Hiking time: overnight
Elevation gain: 3650 feet
Season: mid-July through mid-October
Best time: late July to early September

Contact: Beaverhead-Deerlodge NF, Madison Ranger District
Map: USFS Lee Metcalf Wilderness and West Yellowstone Vicinity
GPS coordinates: N45° 06.047', W111° 34.326'

Getting there: From Ennis, go 14 miles south on US 287 to milepost 29.7, turn left (east) on gravel Indian Creek Road (County Road 44), and drive 4.1 miles to a junction. Turn right at a sign for Indian Creek Trail #328 and go 0.4 mile to the large trailhead parking lot.

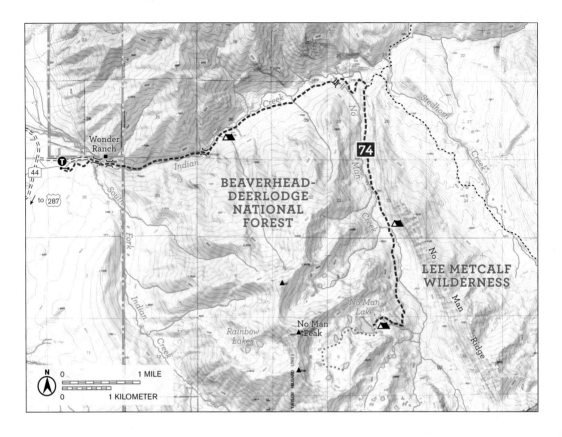

Note: This trailhead is on private land. Do not camp here. Remain strictly on the public-access roads and trails until you enter Forest Service land about 0.7 mile into the hike.

True, the name of this place is less than welcoming for males of our species. But a careful examination of the map made this lake seem so inviting I simply had to take a look. And I'm glad that I did. I was pleased to discover just what the map promised: a beautiful mountain lake, fine lakeside campsites, and some excellent exploring into a nearby alpine basin with outstanding scenery and abundant wildflowers.

Go through a gate on the south side of the parking area and immediately turn left heading uphill across relatively dry terrain with fine views looking west to the Gravelly Range. At 0.3 mile you go through a second gate, then drop into the forested canyon of Indian Creek where you meet a jeep road. Turn right and immediately take a bridge over cascading South Fork Indian Creek.

You soon cross another bridge, this time over the main branch of Indian Creek, and pass a pair of quaint log cabins that are part of the privately owned Wonder Ranch.

From here you leave civilization behind and enter the Lee Metcalf Wilderness. The trail's route takes you upstream along lovely Indian Creek, hugging the north bank of this good-sized stream with several interesting rock formations holding your interest along the way. Churned by horse's hooves, the trail is often muddy, but the grade is gentle and the hiking is easy. You cross Indian Creek on another bridge at 1.8 miles, then pass a series of small meadows with good campsites.

At 3.2 miles, ford an unnamed side creek, rarely more than ankle deep, and just 0.6 mile later cross a bridge over No Man Creek. The trail then briefly goes up the east side of this stream to a rocky overlook of a tall waterfall. From here you ascend, steeply at times, for 0.2 mile to a possibly unsigned junction just 50 yards after the second of two short boardwalks. If you reach a well-signed junction with the Stedhorn Creek Trail, you've gone about 0.2 mile too far.

Turn right (uphill) onto No Man Creek Trail, which is lightly used but still easy to follow. This route goes steeply up a forested gully to a nice overlook of Indian Creek Canyon, then travels up and down as it works its way up the deep canyon of No Man Creek. Most of the way is in forest, but there are several openings where you can admire the colorful rocky peaks to the west. At about 1.9 miles from the Indian Creek Trail turnoff is a pleasant little meadow with a good campsite.

The trail makes an unbridged crossing of No Man Creek beside this meadow then heads upstream. You soon pull away from the creek and about 0.7 mile later begin a long and some-times steep ascent of the west canyon wall. After passing a pretty little subalpine basin with some small meadows and a shallow pond, you make a final short climb to No Man Lake at 8.1 miles.

This deep, scenic, and relatively large moun-tain lake is situated beneath tall reddish-tan peaks and ridges and offers good swimming and some nice campsites under the pines and firs south of the outlet. The outlet creek is partially blocked by an old rock dam, which artificially raises the lake's water level, but the lake retains its natural character and feel.

Extend your hike: Pretty as No Man Lake is, the really terrific scenery is in the off-trail basin west of the lake. To see this area, make your way around the south end of the lake, then follow the first small inlet creek steeply uphill. This takes you to a series of ponds and lovely meadows in a multi-tiered alpine basin beneath the crags of No Man Peak. The highest tier of the basin houses the largest pond and offers arguably the best scenery. It's only a little over a mile to this highest pond, but you'll want to linger awhile and enjoy the scenery, so schedule at least a couple of hours to do this side trip.

Don't miss the beautiful alpine meadows above No Man Lake.

75 *Tumbledown Basin*

Distance: 9.8 miles roundtrip
Difficulty: strenuous
Hiking time: day hike or overnight
Elevation gain: 2650 feet
Season: mid-July through mid-October
Best time: late July through mid-August

Contact: Custer Gallatin NF, Hebgen Lake Ranger District
Map: USFS Lee Metcalf Wilderness and West Yellowstone Vicinity
GPS coordinates: N45° 02.805', W111° 22.479'

Getting there: From Big Sky, go 14.5 miles south on US 191 to the junction with Taylor Fork Road (Forest Road 134). Turn right and drive this rocky gravel road for 4.1 miles to a fork. Go right, drive 3.8 miles, then keep left at a fork and continue 3 miles to the Upper Taylor Fork Trailhead.

Tumbledown Basin is a scenic paradise in the Taylor Peaks region of the central Madison Range. Although rarely visited, this alpine basin offers better scenery than many locations that receive far more visitors. The reasons for the lack of crowds include relative remoteness, a healthy grizzly bear population, a cold stream crossing, and a fairly stiff climb. For the discriminating mountain lover, however, those are small prices to pay for such scenic wonders.

The trail goes upstream through meadows and open forest with tantalizing views of the tall and multi-colored Taylor Peaks to the west. After 0.1 mile a sign informs you that you are entering private lands, so please do not camp for the next 0.75 mile and stay on the trail with its public easement.

At just under 0.4 mile the trail splits. Go right on Taylor Falls Trail, pass a memorial sign, and 0.1 mile later come to a cold, knee-deep ford of

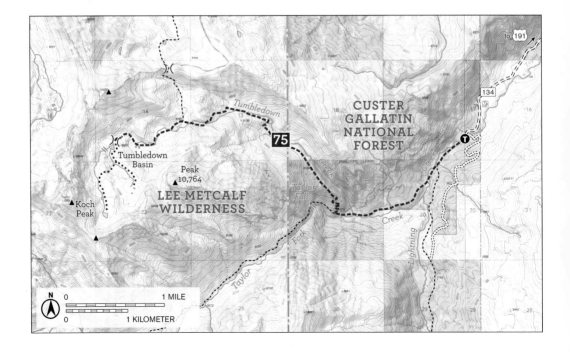

Woodward Mountain over a meadow along Taylor Fork

Taylor Fork. In early summer this ford may be difficult or even dangerous. Turn around if it looks too intimidating.

Near 0.9 mile you pass the first of two gorgeous meadows featuring grand views looking southwest to Woodward Mountain and west to pointed Peak 10,764. Look for moose in these lush meadows. At 1.5 miles is a signed junction.

Turn sharply right onto Tumbledown Trail and steeply climb a series of tight twists and turns under a shady canopy of conifers for 0.5 mile before the grade eases and you gently ascend through pretty wildflower meadows. You enter the Lee Metcalf Wilderness and then begin climbing more steeply on a couple of switchbacks with good views to the southwest of a light-tan-colored mountain.

Hop over small Tumbledown Creek at about 3.3 miles, then climb to a second crossing 0.4

mile later. From here it's a short hike through lovely subalpine meadows to a signed junction, where you go straight on Tumbledown Basin Trail.

From here, every step is a joy as you gradually ascend through the scenic masterpiece that is Tumbledown Basin. Alpine wildflowers abound, adding color to the impressive views of Koch Peak and an array of rugged 11,000-foot mountains that enclose the basin. After 0.8 mile the trail ends at a shallow and wildly scenic pond. The pond's inlet features a small waterfall, while the outlet disappears at a fascinating underground sink.

Potential off-trail explorations abound and the camping prospects are magnificent. The terrain is fragile, however, and grizzly bears are common, so camp on rocky areas and keep the bear spray handy.

76 *Hilgard Basin*

Distance: 19.6 miles roundtrip
Difficulty: strenuous
Hiking time: multiday
Elevation gain: 3650 feet
Season: July through mid-October
Best time: mid-July through early September

Contact: Custer Gallatin NF, Hebgen Lake Ranger District
Map: USFS Lee Metcalf Wilderness and West Yellowstone Vicinity
GPS coordinates: N44° 55.627', W111° 21.623'

Getting there: From the junction of US 287 and State Route 87 about 99 miles south of Bozeman, go 7.7 miles east on US 287, then turn left (north) on gravel Beaver Creek Road (Forest Road 985). Drive 4.5 miles to the Potamogeton Park Trailhead at road's end.

Hilgard Basin is one of the prettiest back-country destinations in Montana, and given the competition, that's quite a recommendation. Supremely beautiful alpine lakes and meadows, numerous outstanding campsites, excellent fishing, plenty of exploring, and some of the most scenic mountains anywhere combine to make this place increasingly popular. You'll probably have to sacrifice solitude, but this slice of mountain heaven is worth it.

Start on the Sentinel Creek Trail, which leaves from the southwest end of the road's turnaround loop. The trail descends to a log bridge over Beaver Creek, then begins an extended uphill that's never steep but continues almost without letup for the next 8 miles.

You remain well away from Sentinel Creek for the first 3 miles before finally coming close to the creek and rock-hopping two unnamed tributaries at 3.5 and 4.3 miles. The higher you

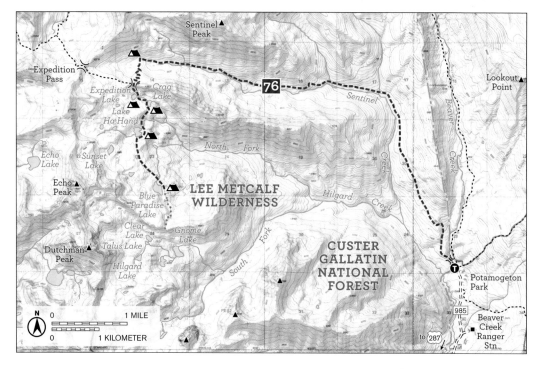

Sentinel Peak from the pass above Hilgard Basin

get the more the forest opens up and the larger and more frequent the meadows become. These meadows offer ever improving views, especially of Sentinel Peak to the north and an unnamed jagged ridge to the south. By the time you reach the upper basin at around 7 miles the scenery is truly outstanding. With a meandering spring-fed creek, sliding waterfalls, rolling meadows, and 11,000-foot peaks on three sides, it just doesn't get much better than this. A couple of magnificent camps near a pond that is a bit west of the trail invite an overnight stay.

The Sentinel Creek basin would be more than enough to recommend this hike, but on this trip you're just getting started. The trail turns south, switchbacking up a slope to a signed junction with a trail that goes west to Expedition Pass—an excellent side trip. Go straight, and 20 yards later, top a divide offering superb views of rolling Hilgard Basin with its many lakes and the dominating summit of Echo Peak in the background. After snapping several photographs, follow a rerouted trail down seven short switchbacks to reach first Expedition and then Crag Lake, each with wildly scenic but rather horse-impacted campsites. Less than 0.5 mile later is Lake Ha Hand, which also has superbly scenic camps, although these receive less horse traffic, and thus are more to the liking of backpackers.

But don't stop yet! The trail now climbs about 200 feet, passes a gorgeous but unnamed pond, then gradually drops to Blue Paradise Lake, at least as spectacular as the earlier lakes but with fewer people and terrific campsites. The early morning light across this lake on Echo Peak is absolutely breathtaking. The official trail ends at Blue Paradise Lake.

Extend your hike: If you've scheduled an extra day or two for exploring (and you'll kick yourself if you haven't), spend it on finding any of the several off-trail lakes in Hilgard Basin, fishing or swimming in the lake of your choice, day hiking to Expedition Pass and the beautiful high country beyond, or climbing Echo Peak (a class 2 scramble). You can also take an unofficial, but easy-to-follow, social trail up the ridge south of Blue Paradise Lake to an excellent view of the stark but beautiful basin that holds Clear, Talus, and Hilgard Lakes.

77 *Sheep Lake*

Distance: 11.4 miles roundtrip
Difficulty: strenuous
Hiking time: day hike or overnight
Elevation gain: 2700 feet
Season: mid-July through October
Best time: late July to early September

Contact: Custer Gallatin NF,
Hebgen Lake Ranger District
Map: USFS Lee Metcalf Wilderness and
West Yellowstone Vicinity
GPS coordinates: N44° 48.609',
W111° 25.833'

Getting there: From the junction of US 287 and State Route 87 about 99 miles south of Bozeman, go 1.4 miles south on SR 87, and then turn left on gravel Sheep Creek Road (Forest Road 6905). Drive 2.6 miles to the road-end turnaround and trailhead.

Sheep Lake is a highlight of the little-known Lionhead Mountains at the southern end of the Madison Range. These peaks offer all the usual delights of mountains in the Yellowstone region—abundant wildlife, colorful wildflowers, impressive scenery, and fine views—but they have fewer visitors than other nearby ranges. Sheep Lake is a favorite in part because this route has fewer grazing cattle than the nearby trail into the popular Coffin Lakes. The Coffin Lakes do have better fishing, however, if that is your goal.

Sheep Lake

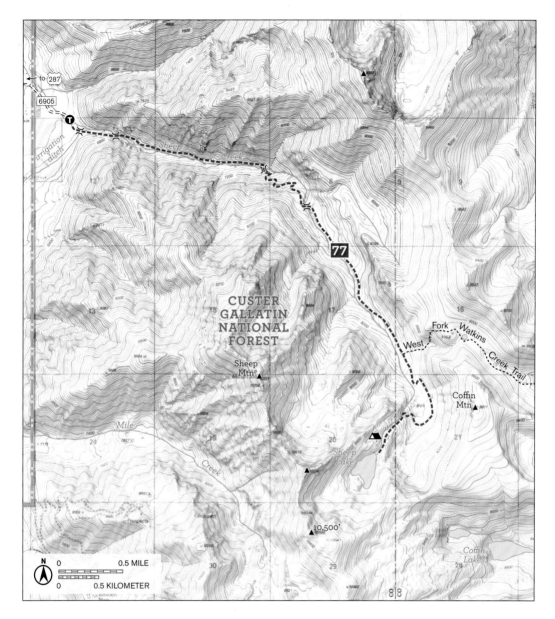

In its first 0.1 mile, the trail passes through meadows and aspen groves as it leads hikers over log bridges across first Sheep Creek and then two irrigation canals. From there it travels through open Douglas fir forests before taking another log bridge over the creek and passing through a gate.

Now closely paralleling the north bank of the rushing creek, the trail ascends at an intermittent grade often passing at the base of talus fields and cliffs. Abundant growths of thimbleberry, fireweed, coneflower, and tall grasses combine to make the route brushy in places. Near 1.5 miles the trail makes another bridged crossing of Sheep Creek then climbs a series of seven well-graded switchbacks.

At 2.7 miles is another bridged creek crossing in a very attractive area of meadows and partial forest with lots of wildflowers and good views of the nearby peaks. After climbing through this enchanting landscape for 1.5 miles, you reach a signed junction with the West Fork Watkins Creek Trail, which goes sharply left.

Go straight and continue gaining elevation as the trail makes a wide loop around an upper basin on view-packed slopes reaching Sheep Lake at 5.7 miles. A bulky 10,500-foot mountain rises above this very scenic lake's southwest shore, while a second unnamed summit fills the sky to the west. It's a dramatic scene, only slightly marred by a stone dam that artificially raises the lake's level by several feet. There are good campsites along the creek just below the lake.

78 Emerald and Heather Lakes

Distance: 11 miles roundtrip
Difficulty: strenuous
Hiking time: day hike or overnight
Elevation gain: 2000 feet
Season: mid-July through October
Best time: late July to early September

Contact: Custer Gallatin NF, Bozeman Ranger District
Map: Beartooth Publishing, Bozeman, Big Sky, West Yellowstone
GPS coordinates: N45° 27.491', W110° 55.257'

Getting there: From Main Street (US 191) in Bozeman, turn south on 19th Avenue (State Route 345). Go 7 miles, then turn left on Hyalite Canyon Road (Forest Road 62). Proceed 10 miles to Hyalite Dam, where the pavement ends. Drive 1.5 miles, then go left at a fork onto FR 6280 and continue 2.2 miles to the road-end trailhead.

Waterfall on East Fork Hyalite Creek

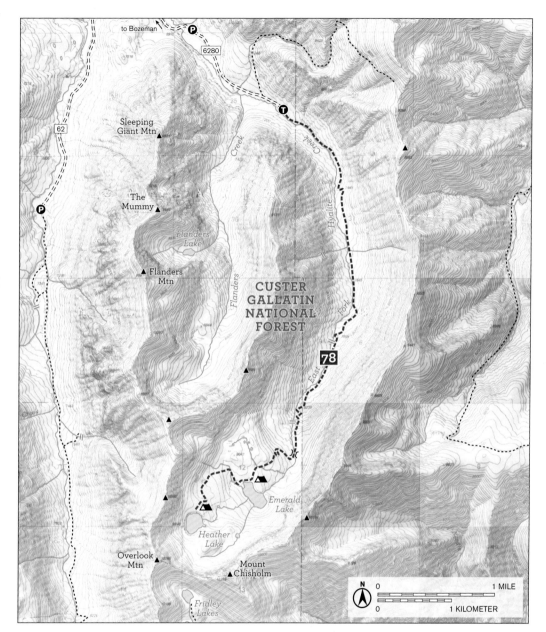

merald and Heather Lakes are popular destinations for Bozeman area hikers—high praise, given the embarrassment of riches offered to local pedestrians. These high mountain lakes sit in wildflower-covered meadows beneath tall cliffs and are extremely scenic. Campsites are available at both lakes, but the area is popular and fragile, so a day hike is the

better choice. *Note:* This is a "timeshare" trail that is always open to hikers, but also open to motorcycles Wednesday through Saturday. To avoid the machines, plan to hike Sunday through Tuesday.

The moderately graded trail climbs through relatively dense forest never far above East Fork Hyalite Creek on your right. Occasional breaks in the forest offer good views of the craggy peaks to the southwest. At 2.2 miles you go through a pretty little creekside meadow, then ascend a dozen switchbacks past a small but very photogenic veil-like waterfall.

Above the falls the grade eases off as you travel through open forest and rolling meadows with terrific views of the tall craggy ridges on either side of the canyon. A log bridge ushers you across the creek, then three switchbacks climb to a second level of even more scenic meadows holding Emerald Lake at 4.9 miles. A

dramatic line of rugged cliffs topped by Mount Chisolm rise just southeast of this beautiful lake and numerous very good campsites tempt the overnight hiker.

The trail circles around the west side of Emerald Lake, then turns away from the water and climbs through delightful wildflower meadows to the trail's end at Heather Lake. This lovely oval lake offers outstanding views of Mount Chisolm and red-tinged Overlook Mountain, decent fishing, and a couple of nice camps above its north shore.

79 *Gallatin Divide Loop*

Distance: 27-mile loop
Difficulty: very strenuous
Hiking time: multiday
Elevation gain: 7000 feet
Season: mid-July to mid-October
Best time: late July to mid-August

Contact: Custer Gallatin NF, Yellowstone Ranger District
Maps: USGS Lewis Creek, Ramshorn Peak, The Sentinel
GPS coordinates: N45° 18.284', W110° 56.342'

Getting there: From Livingston, drive 28.5 miles south on US 89 to milepost 24.2, where you turn right onto gravel Big Creek Road. Go 3.6 miles, bear left at a fork, and proceed 2.5 miles to the road-end trailhead. Although this narrow road has lots of potholes, it's passable for passenger cars.

The long alpine crest of the Gallatin Range offers stupendous views and a haven for many species of wildlife. The Gallatin Divide Trail follows this ridgeline for its entire distance and is one of the finest high-elevation ridge walks in Montana. The entire hike from Hyalite Reservoir to Yellowstone National Park is a magnificent backpacking adventure, but requires several days and a rather long car shuttle to accomplish. This loop is a shorter alternative, which features many of the trail's finest miles and most of the best views from this dramatic high divide.

For the recommended counterclockwise loop, backtrack on the road about 120 yards, then pick up the signed Lewis Creek Trail shortly before a bridge over Big Creek. This path follows the north side of Big Creek on a partly forested

hillside for 0.9 mile, passes above the Mountain Sky Guest Ranch, then curves into the forested canyon of Lewis Creek.

Cross the creek on a log bridge at 1.3 miles, then follow the brushy trail upstream under the shade of tall Engelmann spruces for 0.1 mile to a confusing junction. A heavily used horse trail goes steeply up the hill to the right, but you take the less distinct lower trail that goes straight and stays near the creek.

The next few miles are rather miserable and represent the price you must pay to reach the good stuff. Instead of traveling on the relatively open hillside just above the creek, the trail frustratingly stays in the dense riparian brush by the stream. You'll have to beat your way through this heavy, wet brush as well as wade across Lewis Creek *fourteen times* in about 3.2 miles before

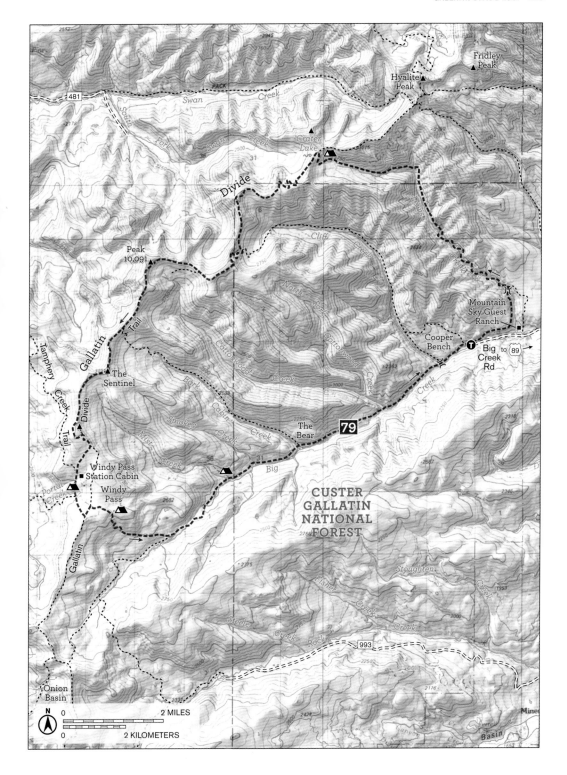

Along Gallatin Divide near The Sentinel

you finally switchback away from this mess and travel across higher terrain. In addition to giving you a break from the wet brush, this higher section provides nice views of the volcanic cliffs and rock outcroppings that characterize the upper portion of Lewis Creek's canyon.

Your respite ends after less than 1 mile as you return to the brush along the creek, although now it is less dense and maddening. Near 7 miles you hop over a fork of Lewis Creek then follow the canyon as it turns west. The trail steeply climbs a narrow meadow along the creek, which is lined with water-loving wildflowers, then takes you to a rock-hop crossing of a side creek just below a small, sliding waterfall. From here you climb a bit more to a scenic basin with a lush little meadow at 9 miles. A short but steep climb through increasingly open terrain takes you to Crater Lake, in a tiny bowl just below the Gallatin Divide. You'll want to take advantage of the good campsites here as this is the last reliable water for many miles. In a grassy saddle just 50 yards west of the lake is an unsigned junction with Gallatin Divide Trail.

Tip: Crater Lake makes a good base camp for a side trip to Hyalite Peak, about 3 miles to the northeast.

Go southwest on the Gallatin Divide Trail, which initially loses almost 250 feet before passing a spring and turning south to traverse a partially forested basin. At the south end of this basin seven switchbacks steeply take you up to the view-packed alpine ridgetop.

For the next several miles the trail remains faithful to the open and wildly scenic ridge. Views seem to extend forever, but beware of thunderstorms, as this exposed ridge is dangerous when lightning is in the area. Occasional cairns or posts mark the route, but the tread is generally obvious and easy to follow.

The up-and-down trail jogs to the west, then climbs over a high point before turning south and reaching a junction with the Cliff Creek Trail, 4.1 miles from Crater Lake. Keep straight and ascend five switchbacks to the top of a rounded mountain (with more amazing views) before following the rolling ridgetop in another jog to the west. Ignore an obvious game trail that angles downhill to the left about 0.5 mile from the rounded mountain, then make a high traverse on the east face of Peak 10,091. Look for mountain goats on the crags and cliffs in this area.

More gloriously scenic hiking takes you down into saddles and over several unnamed high points to a signed junction with the very faint Bark Cabin Creek Trail. Keep straight and climb to the top of The Sentinel, where the views to the west of Lone Mountain and the Madison Range are spectacular.

From here you loop around the west and south sides of an unnamed peak, pass an unsigned spur trail that goes to the top of the unnamed peak, and then gradually descend a beautiful meadowland known as Windy Pass to a trail fork.

The Gallatin Divide Trail veers left, but for the most reliable water and campsites, bear right on Portal Creek Trail. This path goes gently downhill for 0.5 mile to the log cabin at Windy Pass Station, which is open for nightly rentals with advanced reservations through www.recreation. gov. Here is a junction with the Tamphery Creek Trail; keep left and descend briefly to the crossing of a reliable little creek. There are no established sites, but camping prospects are good in this vicinity. Less than 0.1 mile after the creek crossing is a junction.

Tip: The Windy Pass vicinity is excellent for a layover day, with a fun side trip south to Eaglehead and Fortress Mountains through a portion of the Gallatin Petrified Forest.

To complete the loop, turn left (uphill) at the junction and gradually ascend through meadows and open forest for 0.3 mile to a signed reunion with the Gallatin Divide Trail. Turn left (north) and wander across open, grassy terrain where the tread is virtually nonexistent for about 0.25 mile to a signed junction with Windy Pass Trail.

Turn right and follow posts across a grassy expanse to a shallow, meadow-rimmed pond (possible camps). The obvious tread resumes where the trail drops into the trees just south of this pond. Hike through a mix of forest and steep, wildflower-covered slopes as the trail descends a series of switchbacks and wide turns offering good views of Big Creek Canyon and the ridges to the southeast. At about 2 miles from Windy Pass, you meet the Big Creek Trail and turn left.

Now on a good, if sometimes muddy, forest trail, you steadily lose elevation, always accompanied by the pleasant sound of the cascading creek on your right. At 0.5 and again at 1.1 miles down from the junction, you cross the creek. Both crossings usually have logs nearby, but if not, they are easy fords. Next you carefully rock-hop Mist Creek and pass a good campsite on your right. The trail then leads you across a grassy bench dotted with sagebrush and wildflowers to a hop-over crossing of Smokey Creek before descending through lovely meadows to an easy rock-hop of Bark Cabin Creek and a signed junction with the trail of the same name.

Go straight and gradually descend past interesting rock formations (including one descriptively titled "The Bear") and a steep-walled gorge on Big Creek to a gate just before the simple crossing of Cottonwood Creek. You then pass a series of impressively tall rock formations, many with strikingly red walls, to a bridged crossing of Cliff Creek and a junction with Cliff Creek Trail. Keep straight and hike 0.8 mile to a gate across the trail and a junction with the Cooper Bench Trail. Go through the gate and descend the last 50 yards back to the trailhead.

80 *Sky Rim Loop*

Distance: 21.5-mile loop (excluding 4-mile road walk)
Difficulty: very strenuous
Hiking time: multiday
Elevation gain: 5400 feet
Season: mid-July through mid-October
Best time: mid-July through mid-August

Contact: Yellowstone National Park
Map: Trails Illustrated, Mammoth Hot Springs/Northwest Yellowstone National Park
GPS coordinates: N45° 02.910', W111° 08.376' for exit point; N45° 0.747', W111° 04.850' for starting trailhead

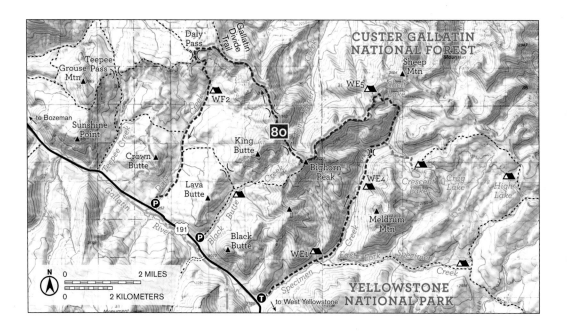

Getting there: From Bozeman, drive 61 miles south on US 191 to the Daly Creek Trailhead (the exit point) exactly 0.8 mile past where that highway enters Yellowstone National Park. For the starting point, drive another 4 miles south on US 191, then turn left at the short Specimen Creek Trailhead spur road.

Although the majority of Yellowstone National Park lies in Wyoming, Montana proudly claims a narrow portion of this world famous preserve. And while the Montana section has no geysers, it offers backpackers the park's finest mountain scenery and plenty of Yellowstone's famous wildlife. The highlight is the magnificent Sky Rim, a high-elevation ridge with tremendous views of mountains and valleys near and far. The route is dry and rugged with many steep ups and downs, but the scenery is hard to beat.

Yellowstone National Park has a few important rules for hikers. Dogs are prohibited. You are not allowed to approach within 100 yards of wolves and bears and 25 yards of any other large mammal. Finally, overnight permits are required (pick them up at the West Yellowstone backcountry office) and cost $3 per person in your party per night in the park. You should also consider reserving a permit to ensure you get one of the few available sites at the most convenient locations. As of 2017 a reservation costs $25 and can be made by snail mail or fax any time after January 1.

Starting at the Specimen Creek Trailhead, hike gently uphill through an open lodgepole pine forest with grasses, wildflowers, and some willows along Specimen Creek. Near 1 mile you pass an interesting rock formation, then travel through pretty meadows where moose are often seen, to a junction at 2 miles in a burn area. Bear left, pass Camp WE1, and then gradually ascend past the looming cliff-edged mass of Meldrum Mountain. Splash across North Fork Specimen Creek at a meadow near 3.9 miles, then just past 5 miles reach very comfortable Camp WE4. The pace of your climb picks up as you cross the creek on a wooden bridge then reach a junction at 6 miles.

Side trip: For an excellent side trip, turn right, hop over the creek, and climb two sets of well-graded switchbacks for 1.4 miles to Crescent Lake. This green-tinged lake sits in a very scenic cirque beneath craggy 700-foot-high cliffs and is quite photogenic.

Back at North Fork Specimen Creek, head upstream and climb, sometimes steeply, through forest and grassy meadows for 2.1 miles to the signed turnoff to Camp WE5 and Shelf Lake. This very attractive meadow-rimmed pool sits on a small shelf and is backed by grassy slopes and low cliffs. More importantly, the lake has designated campsites and is the last readily available water for many miles.

The trail goes southwest from Shelf Lake, soon ascending to the top of a broad, partly forested ridge forming the boundary of Yellowstone National Park and which hosts the route for the next several miles. The ridge is a wildflower bonanza in midsummer and a favorite late-summer haunt for grizzly bears that feed on the nuts of whitebark pines. The up-and-down route is constantly dropping into saddles and steeply climbing over high points, so expect a lot of elevation gain along the way. Also beware of thunderstorms, as this ridge is dangerously exposed to lightning.

The trail heads southwest toward the towering cliffs of Bighorn Peak, while also offering grand views to the north of Ramshorn Peak and the Gallatin Range and northwest to Lone Mountain and the Madison Range. After 2.8 very scenic miles you top the open, cliff-edged summit of Bighorn Peak.

The trail cuts across the very steep south side of Bighorn Peak, traveling above an array of cliffs and pinnacles before reaching a junction on a grassy plateau. Go straight on a faint trail across the open plateau toward the first of several cairns marking the route. Look for bighorn sheep in this area, with herds up to 40 animals being common. The trail temporarily disappears as you descend 800 feet down a super steep, partly forested slope to a saddle where the narrow, rocky trail reappears following the up-and-down, northwest-trending ridge. The scenery is outstanding, but the trail is almost never level, which makes for a slow and tiring hike.

The tread disappears again where you climb over a large grassy knoll north of King Butte, but becomes obvious on the other side as you follow the narrow ridgeline down to a saddle and then over the next cliff-edged high point. After 4 tiring and relentlessly steep up-and-down miles from Bighorn Peak, you reach a trail fork where the Gallatin Divide Trail goes right.

View north to Ramshorn Peak from Bighorn Peak

Bear left on Daly (sometimes incorrectly spelled "Dailey") Creek Trail and descend eight switchbacks past a large rock outcropping to Daly Pass and a four-way junction. Turn sharply left and descend through a beautiful rolling meadowland that is carpeted with wildflowers in July. At 1.3 miles from Daly Pass a short side trail leads to Camp WF2, a nice spot to rest your tired bones after a long day on Sky Rim. *Note:* By late summer the small creek at this camp may run dry. Ask about current conditions when you get your permit.

The main trail descends gradually through lovely grassy meadows to a hop-over crossing of Daly Creek then continues to a junction with the faint Teepee Creek Trail, which goes right. Keep straight and walk through meadows, increasingly dotted with sagebrush and yellow-blooming cinquefoil bushes. After 0.8 mile go straight at a junction, descend past the photogenic cliffs of Crown Butte, then make your way down a wide valley to a log crossing of Daly Creek and the trailhead. Without a car shuttle, it's an easy 4-mile walk along the highway back to your starting point.

81 *Elephanthead Mountain*

Distance: 7.6 miles roundtrip
Difficulty: very strenuous
Hiking time: day hike
Elevation gain: 3450 feet
Season: mid-July to mid-October
Best time: late July to mid-August

Contact: Custer Gallatin NF, Yellowstone Ranger District
Map: USFS Absaroka-Beartooth Wilderness
GPS coordinates: N45° 35.762', W110° 24.451'

Getting there: Take exit 333 off Interstate 90 and go north and east through the town of Livingston. About 1.5 miles east of town turn right (south) on Swingley Road, drive 7.2 miles, then turn right on Bruffey Lane. Go 1.7 miles, then turn right into the signed driveway for 63 Ranch, where a Forest Service easement allows public access. After 0.6 mile, bear left at a fork, following signs for national forest access, and drive 1 mile on this rough and narrow road to the trailhead.

Elephanthead Mountain guards the northern reaches of the Absaroka Range and offers a dramatic introduction to this scenic mountain mass. The distinctive mountain rises impressively from the plains just to the north and its summit is nearly encircled by enormous walls of limestone that tower above flower-filled alpine meadows. Reaching this scenic wonderland

Elephanthead Mountain over the wildflower meadow to the east

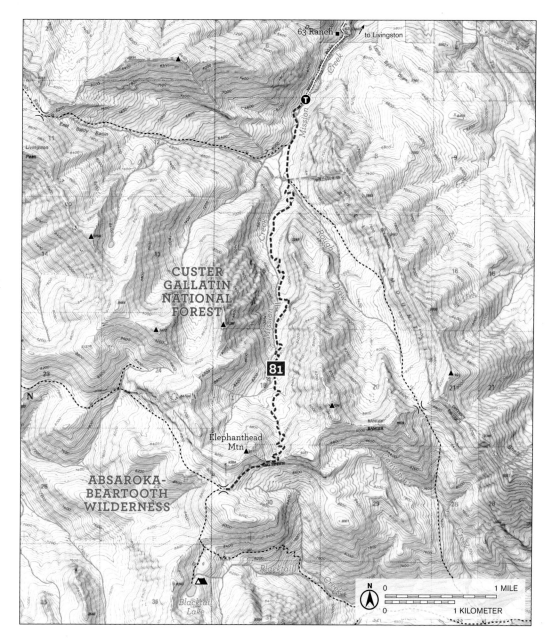

involves a long climb up a deep canyon, but the payoff is worth the sweat.

The trail heads up the forested canyon of Mission Creek, reaching an easy crossing of the rock-bound stream at about 0.25 mile. Just beyond, go left at a fork and steadily climb for 0.3 mile to the Absaroka-Beartooth Wilderness boundary. A few paces later, keep right at a junction with the little-used Rough Draw Trail and cross an unnamed side creek.

You now climb five switchbacks through an old burn area, then make a long, winding traverse where you'll enjoy frequent neck-craning views of the tall rock walls lining the canyon. Near 2 miles another set of switchbacks takes you past a series of cascading waterfalls after which you climb a series of twists and turns on rocky slopes, through forested areas, and over rolling wild-flower-covered meadows. The long climb ends at a cliff-edged overlook at the eastern base of the towering rock walls of Elephanthead Mountain.

Views to the south—of countless deep valleys, forested ridges, and tall peaks—are superb.

The trail cuts to the west, going up and down along the base of Elephanthead Mountain's dramatic cliffs to an alpine pass with good views looking west to the Gallatin Range. Day hikers should turn around here, but backpackers can continue to the campsites at Blacktail Lake, a forest-rimmed gem about 0.7 mile to the south.

82 *Pine Creek Lake*

Distance: 10.2 miles
Difficulty: strenuous
Hiking time: day hike or overnight
Elevation gain: 3500 feet
Season: mid-July through mid-October
Best time: late July through September

Contact: Custer Gallatin NF, Yellowstone Ranger District
Map: USFS Absaroka-Beartooth Wilderness
GPS coordinates: N45° 29.848', W110° 31.125'

Getting there: From Livingston, drive 9.5 miles south on US 89, then turn left on Pine Creek Road. Go 2.3 miles, turn right on East River Road, proceed 0.7 mile, and then turn left on Luccock Park Road toward Pine Creek Campground. Follow this narrow paved road for 2.7 miles to the campground, then follow signs to the trailhead.

Pine Creek Falls

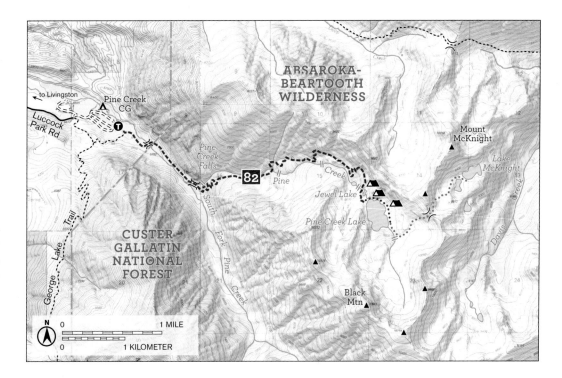

Tucked neatly into a dramatic cirque at the northern base of stunning Black Mountain, Pine Creek Lake is a popular but strenuous hike in the northern Absaroka Mountains. Although most folks turn around after an easy stroll to Pine Creek Falls, the long climb to the lake is well worth the effort. A night at this mountain lake is often rewarded with one of the best displays of alpenglow in Montana.

The heavily used trail passes a side trail to George Lake after 0.2 mile, then goes gradually uphill through forest to a bridge over substantial Pine Creek. From here enter the Absaroka-Beartooth Wilderness and continue upstream to tall and impressive Pine Creek Falls at 1.1 miles.

A log bridge takes you over the creek below the falls after which the real work begins as you switchback up the hillside at a steady, moderate grade. Cool mornings are the best time to tackle this long ascent. After the first two dozen zigzagging turns, the forest opens up in an old burn area with nice views of the tall canyon walls.

Cross the creek on a logjam below a sliding waterfall, then another set of switchbacks climbs past two more cascading waterfalls and up to a lovely basin with a small unnamed lake. A final set of ten switchbacks takes you to the top of a particularly tall falls and into the spectacular upper basin.

Your first taste of this paradise is the appropriately named Jewel Lake, which has one small campsite. You then cross this lake's outlet creek and climb a bit more to the main attraction, Pine Creek Lake. This deep lake fills a basin of incredible beauty at the base of snow-streaked Black Mountain. It's quite a sight and well worth the long climb. If you plan to spend the night, the most scenic sites are across the outlet along the north shore.

Extend your hike: If you are up for some exploring, follow the inlet creek to the small basin east-southeast of Pine Creek Lake (with very photogenic views of Black Mountain) or scramble over the divide and carefully descend a steep goat trail to isolated Lake McKnight.

83 *Silver Lake*

Distance: 16.6 miles roundtrip
Difficulty: strenuous
Hiking time: overnight
Elevation gain: 3100 feet
Season: July to mid-October
Best time: mid-July to mid-August

Contact: Custer Gallatin NF,
Yellowstone Ranger District
Map: USFS Absaroka-Beartooth
Wilderness
GPS coordinates: N45° 20.522',
W110° 13.904'

Getting there: From downtown Big Timber, go south on McLeod Street (State Route 298), and drive 26 miles to the end of pavement at the national forest boundary. Continue another 16 miles to the Fourmile Trailhead.

Secreted away in a high basin and surrounded by scenic white-granite peaks, Silver Lake is a hidden gem that makes an ideal one- or two-night backpacking trip in the impressive Absaroka Range. In addition to fine scenery, the lake offers decent fishing and is a fine place to set up a base camp while exploring off-trail to other nearby attractions.

Go through a gate, then walk up the short access road to the log Fourmile Cabin, which is available for nightly rentals. From here a foot-and-horse trail climbs through a fairly dense forest ascending several widely spaced switchbacks for 0.9 mile to a fork. Bear right and less than 0.1

mile later go left at a confusing and unsigned fork with an unofficial horse trail.

While crossing a series of muddy spots and small side creeks, the trail goes intermittently uphill through forest and small meadows to a junction at 3.4 miles. Keep straight and begin a long, very gradual ascent through forest.

At 5.8 miles, go right on Silver Lake Trail and after 0.5 mile of moderate uphill make a rock-hop crossing of a small creek. More uphill, in a series of turns and switchbacks, brings you to a junction with colorfully named Hi Ho Silver Trail, which offers a shortcut route to Silver Pass.

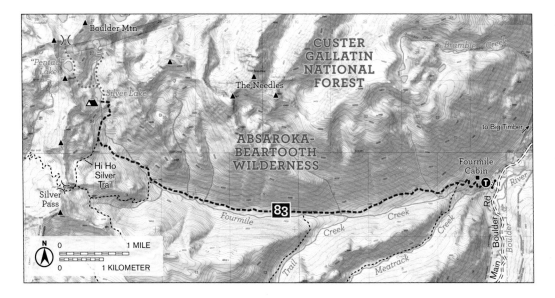

Silver Lake and the jagged ridge to the northwest

To reach Silver Lake, bear right and cross a series of pretty little meadows with good views of the nearby white granite peaks and ridges. A final switchbacking ascent leads to Silver Lake at 8.3 miles.

This small rock-lined lake occupies a spectacular basin surrounded by rugged granite peaks and pinnacles and is very photogenic. Boulder Mountain fills the sky to the north. There are excellent campsites beside the lake's outlet as well as near the inlet. You won't regret spending a night or two at this wilderness gem, which is worthwhile on its own but also makes a good base for further exploring.

Extend your hike: With an extra day or two, hike over to view-filled Silver Pass or explore the two dramatic off-trail lakes filling the very scenic basins above Silver Lake. Especially recommended is the lake northwest of Silver Lake, unofficially known as Pentad Lake, which sits directly beneath a sawtooth ridge of granite spires.

84 *Bridge Lake*

Distance: 16.5 miles roundtrip
Difficulty: very strenuous
Hiking time: overnight
Elevation gain: 3200 feet
Season: July to mid-October
Best time: mid-July to mid-August

Contact: Custer Gallatin NF,
Yellowstone Ranger District
Map: USFS Absaroka-Beartooth
Wilderness
GPS coordinates: N45° 17.251',
W110° 14.576'

Getting there: From downtown Big Timber, go south on McLeod Street (State Route 298), and drive 26 miles to the end of pavement at the national forest boundary. Continue 20.4 miles to the Bridge Creek Trailhead. The last few miles are a festival of rocks and potholes. Passenger cars can make it, but take it slow.

A shimmering alpine jewel beneath the cliffs of Crow Mountain, Bridge Lake is a surprisingly little-visited wilderness gem that makes an excellent overnight destination. For unknown reasons the trail ends in a meadow below the lake, leaving the last 0.8 mile to those willing to make a steep but nontechnical scramble up a rocky headwall. It's well worth the effort, however, and the off-trail section helps ensure solitude for those who make the trek.

A moderately graded climb leads to a bridge over Bridge Creek, then three long switchbacks ascend a rather brushy slope. At 1.2 miles, near the top of the climb, a short spur trail goes left to a nice viewpoint of Bridge Creek's canyon. The grade eases off as you make an up-and-down traverse of a forested hillside, eventually coming to creek level and a gradual upstream walk through forest and a few small meadows where elk and deer can often be seen.

Near 4.6 miles you bear left at a junction and hike 0.8 mile to a little meadow with a nice creekside campsite on your left. After rock-hopping what's left of Bridge Creek, the climb resumes as two dozen mostly short switchbacks lead past a lacy waterfall and up to a meadow at 7.5 miles. The trail ends here beneath a dramatic craggy peak.

To reach Bridge Lake, hike west up the meadow, then very steeply climb a headwall. At the top of this climb, cut to the right toward Bridge Creek then make a rocky scramble beside a little defile holding a cascading stream to the lake basin.

Bridge Lake is a meadow-rimmed gem with bulky Crow Mountain and rows of very rugged red-tinged peaks and ridges all around. There are a few possible campsites with subalpine firs providing protection from the wind. You'll likely enjoy complete solitude at this lake, which offers chilly swimming and fishing for skittish cutthroat trout.

Bridge Lake

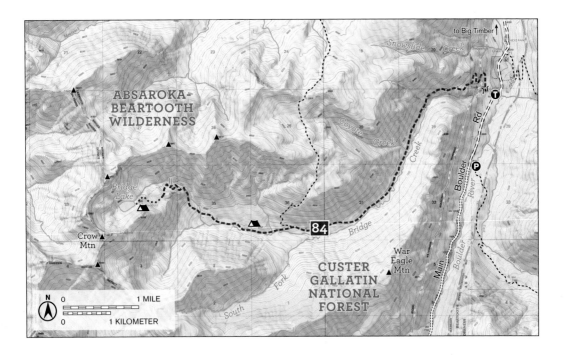

85 Lake Plateau

Distance: 34 miles roundtrip
Difficulty: strenuous
Hiking time: multiday
Elevation gain: 2700 feet
Season: mid-July to early October
Best time: late July to mid-August

Contact: Custer Gallatin NF, Beartooth Ranger District
Map: USFS Absaroka-Beartooth Wilderness and USGS Mount Douglas, Pinnacle Mountain, and Tumble Mountain
GPS coordinates: N45° 23.872', W109° 58.152'

Getting there: From Absarokee, go 3 miles south on State Route 78, then turn right on SR 419, following signs to the town of Nye. Drive 25 miles to a junction just past the Stillwater Mine and turn right onto West Stillwater Road (Forest Road 2846). Stay on the main public road at several intersections with private mine roads and drive 8.5 miles on this increasingly rough and rocky route (take it slow) to the road-end trailhead. A high clearance vehicle would be helpful, but if you are careful a passenger car can usually make it.

The Lake Plateau, a popular and delightful high-elevation realm with dozens of beautiful lakes, is perhaps the best destination in Montana for backpackers who like to hike into a base camp and spend several days exploring. The usual approach is from the Boulder River to the west, but the northern approach via the West Fork Stillwater River is arguably superior. Although a few miles longer, it is much less steep (and thus easier on the body), at least as scenic, and is a lot less crowded.

Heading upstream in a forest dominated by Douglas firs, Engelmann spruces, and a few lodgepole pines, the well-maintained and gently

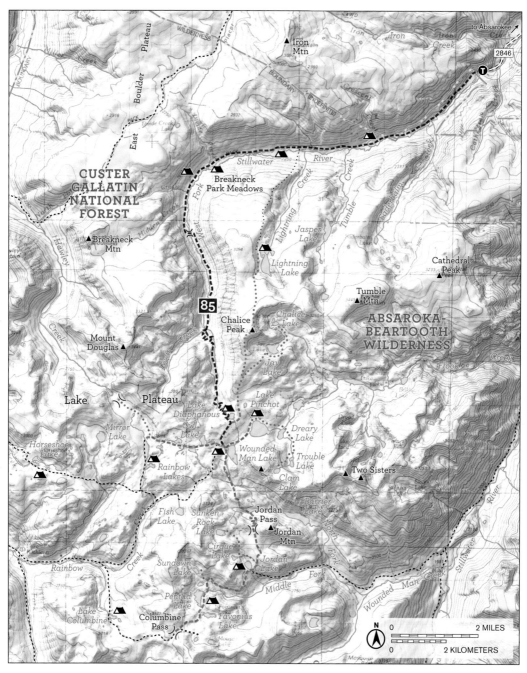

graded trail allows you to tick off miles rapidly with pleasant and easy hiking. With a nice mix of forests, meadows, and rocky areas, the scenery is consistently good and keeps you happily moving along. You pass potential campsites at small meadows near 3.2 and 6 miles before reaching spacious Breakneck Park Meadows at 7.9 miles with its numerous fine overnight options. This

Sunrise at Lake Pinchot

meadow is backed by tall Breakneck Mountain to the southwest and is very scenic.

The trail curves to the south at Breakneck Park Meadows, traveling through forest for 1.5 miles to a bridge over what's left of West Fork Stillwater River. The climbing now becomes more noticeable, although it remains no more than a moderate grade, as you head up the east side of the stream into progressively more attractive country. After rock-hopping a creek, you ascend eight quick switchbacks to reach higher-elevation forests and meadows set beneath ruggedly photogenic ridges. The trail winds its way uphill, with three crossings of the diminishing creek and a dozen well-graded switchbacks on an increasingly open and view-packed slope.

At the top of this climb is beautiful Lake Diaphanous (16 miles). This meadow-rimmed gem features a photogenic island, excellent views, and a couple of good campsites along the north shore.

The trail skirts the west side of Lake Diaphanous, then descends through tree islands and gorgeous meadows to a junction with Rainbow Lakes Trail, where the countless exploring options begin. Excellent and well-located base camp possibilities are at Wounded Man Lake, which lies 0.3 mile to the left (east) from this junction.

How long you stay and where you explore is limited only by the time available. It's best to use the USGS maps for exploring rather than the Forest Service's less detailed wilderness map. There are days of potential side trips, but I particularly recommend the following:

- Lake Pinchot: reached by a good trail from the north end of Wounded Man Lake
- Dreary, Trouble, and Clam Lakes: set in dramatic off-trail basins southeast of Lake Pinchot
- Jordan Lake, Pentad Lake, and Columbine Pass: reached along a long, up-and-down trail south of Wounded Man Lake

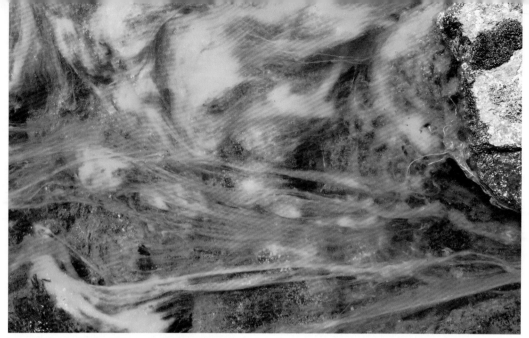

Green algae drifts in a mountain stream, Beartooth Mountains.

- Sundown, Cirque, and Sunken Rock Lakes: scrambles of varying difficulty off the trail to Columbine Pass
- Owl Lake: a short and easy trail to the west of Wounded Man Lake
- Unnamed ponds and pass north-north-west of the main Rainbow Lakes: easy off-trail wanderings over tundra
- Jay and Chalice Lakes: strictly for those comfortable with very steep bouldering,

set in dramatic basins northeast of Lake Diaphanous
- Chalice Peak: a straightforward and fairly easy climb (except for the wind and thin air) north of Lake Diaphanous
- Lightning Lake: reached by going over Chalice Peak, then very steeply dropping into this gorgeous lake basin. This is a particularly long outing, probably best done as an overnight.

86 *Lake Mary*

Distance: 11.8 miles roundtrip
Difficulty: strenuous
Hiking time: day hike or overnight
Elevation gain: 1950 feet
Season: mid-July to mid-October
Best time: late July to mid-August

Contact: Custer Gallatin NF, Beartooth Ranger District
Map: USFS Absaroka-Beartooth Wilderness
GPS coordinates: N45° 10.122', W109° 29.755'

Getting there: From Red Lodge, go 0.7 mile south on US 212, then turn right on West Fork Road, following signs to the ski area. Drive 2.8 miles, turn left at a fork onto Forest Road 2071, and continue 10.1 miles to the road-end trailhead.

Located just a short drive from Red Lodge, this extremely scenic hike offers interesting wildlife (especially moose), two nice waterfalls, a gorgeous mountain meadow, and a high-elevation lake set beneath towering peaks. It's a fine day hike or one-night sampler of the Beartooth Mountains. With off-trail travel experience you can complete a rugged loop via Crow Lake, but novice hikers can happily turn around at Lake Mary.

Starting from the north side of the spacious parking lot, the trail sets out through the huge burn zone of a 2008 fire. After 80 yards you reach a junction with the re-aligned Senia Creek Trail and the start of the possible loop.

Go left and head gradually upstream along loudly cascading West Fork Rock Creek. Moose are common here, so keep an eye out for these large mammals. At 1.3 miles an unmarked spur trail goes left to a viewpoint for roaring Calamity Falls. Just 0.5 mile later another unsigned

spur leads to photogenic Sentinel Falls. From here two quick switchbacks take you past a viewpoint of the upper part of Sentinel Falls before you enter unburned forest and meadows. You pass beneath towering spires high on the ridge to your right, then come to a junction at the lower end of very scenic Quinnebaugh Meadows at 4.9 miles. There are numerous good campsites around this sprawling mountain meadow.

Turn right on the Lake Mary Trail and immediately begin climbing. More than a dozen switchbacks keep the grade from being horrible, but it's still a steep climb until you finally level out at Lake Mary at 5.9 miles. Good camps can be found near the outlet of this very scenic high-elevation lake.

Extend your hike: The trail ends at Lake Mary. Experienced off-trail hikers, however, can turn this into a fun and incredibly scenic loop. To do so, follow an angler's path around the east side of the lake, and then climb steep, grassy slopes to a large cairn at a rounded low point about 0.1 mile to the right of an obvious (and lower) but harder-to-reach rocky pass. From here you angle to the right (don't go straight down to an obvious lower basin), steeply descending to a flat area with a very shallow, sometimes dry pond. After crossing this flat, follow cairns as you descend a relatively gentle rocky slope beneath a row of stupendous cliffs and crags on Grass Mountain.

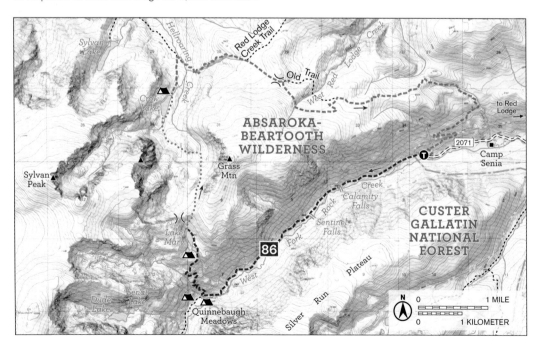

Crow Lake's dramatic setting is worth going the extra distance.

Before reaching the next basin, go over a little ridge on the left and steeply descend into increasingly forested and rough terrain, then pick your way downstream past a string of dramatically scenic meadows and ponds set beneath the towering ramparts of an unnamed peak to long and narrow Crow Lake. Follow rough angler's paths down either side of this incredibly scenic lake to reach the good camps and maintained trail on the west side of the outlet creek.

Back on good trail, head downhill for 0.4 mile, then turn sharply right at a junction and soon make an easy crossing of Hellroaring Creek. A long and tiring climb leads to a rolling above-timberline meadow and a junction with the faint Red Lodge Creek Trail.

Go straight and climb to an obvious alpine pass with 360-degree views that will make any mountain lover's heart sing. From this pass, ignore the old trail that goes straight. Instead, follow a newly constructed trail to the right (marked by cairns), which gradually ascends across view-packed slopes before looping back around to the plateau where it intersects the old trail.

From here the trail crosses a high tundra-covered expanse with great views to the northeast of the Yellowstone River plains around Billings. A few lazy downhill switchbacks lead back down to the land of scraggly trees and then the bleak landscape of the 2008 fire. Unlike what the wilderness map indicates, the new trail alignment eventually cuts across the scorched hillside well above the road, then descends eight switchbacks to deposit you back at the junction just above the West Fork Rock Creek Trailhead, finishing a 16.5-mile loop.

87 *Black Canyon Lake and Sundance Pass*

Distance: 13.6 miles roundtrip to Black Canyon Lake; 23 miles roundtrip to Sundance Pass
Difficulty: strenuous
Hiking time: day hike or overnight for Black Canyon Lake; multiday for Sundance Pass
Elevation gain: 2100 feet for Black Canyon Lake; 3900 feet for Sundance Pass

Season: mid-July through early October
Best time: late July to mid-August
Contact: Custer Gallatin NF, Beartooth Ranger District
Map: USFS Absaroka-Beartooth Wilderness
GPS coordinates: N45° 04.745', W109° 24.688'

Getting there: From Red Lodge, drive 9.8 miles southwest on US 212, turn right onto paved Lake Fork Road (Forest Road 2346), and then proceed 1.8 miles to the road-end trailhead.

Some of the best scenery in the Beartooth Mountains (and that's quite a recommendation) is in the upper reaches of Lake Fork around Sundance Pass. The lakes are stunning, the views are outstanding, and the hiking is a joy. The drainage is understandably popular, however, so don't expect solitude. Still, this is definitely a must-see area for any Montana backpacker.

Traveling through dense coniferous forest (look for moose), the trail immediately crosses a bridge over rushing Lake Fork and goes right at an unsigned junction. From there the route parallels the creek upstream, maintaining a gentle grade for the first several miles. There are frequent nice views of the craggy ridges to the north and south as well as a few good campsites along the way. At 4.9 miles a signed trail goes left and climbs 0.2 mile to two excellent but overused campsites next to beautiful Lost Lake, featuring views across the water to a high craggy cliff and pinnacles on the ridge bordering the Hellroaring Plateau to the south.

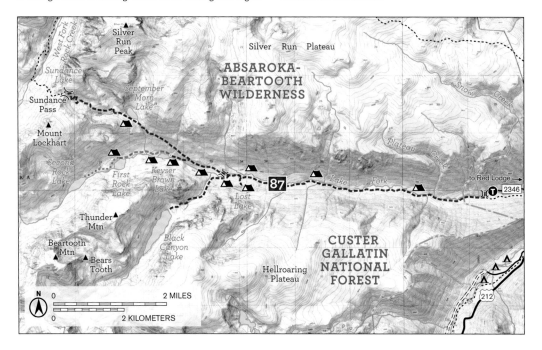

Thunder Mountain over Lake Fork near Lost Lake

At 5.1 miles, excluding the side trip to Lost Lake, and immediately before a bridge over Lake Fork, is an unsigned junction.

To visit Black Canyon Lake, turn left, passing a campsite, and follow this rough and sometimes sketchy unofficial trail for 1.7 miles. The last part of the route goes steeply over loose rocks, so step carefully and watch for landmarks to navigate on the return. The reward comes at large and starkly beautiful Black Canyon Lake. Because this lake is surrounded by rocks, there are no good campsites here, but anglers will delight in a healthy population of Yellowstone cutthroat trout and everyone can enjoy tremendous views of blocky Summit, Beartooth, and Thunder Mountains. Fires are prohibited in the Black Canyon drainage.

The main trail to Sundance Pass crosses the bridge over Lake Fork, passes a nice campsite, and then climbs to a signed fork. The trail to the left contours for about 0.4 mile to tranquil and very pretty Keyser Brown Lake, which has many good campsites at both its lower and upper ends. A rough and brushy intermittent route continues upstream from there to the two Rock Lakes.

The main trail goes right at the Keyser Brown turnoff and makes a steady, moderately steep ascent passing some excellent viewpoints of Keyser Brown Lake and the surrounding peaks and valleys. After 1.9 miles you reach September Morn Lake, with its good campsites and wonderful views up to a rugged spur of Silver Run Peak.

The crowning glory of Sundance Pass, however, is still ahead, so keep plodding uphill into increasingly alpine terrain with superb scenery. A traverse into above-timberline terrain followed by a set of fifteen switchbacks up a rocky slope brings you to the 11,007-foot pass. The reward is world-class views, especially the glacier-draped summits of Bowback and Sundance Mountains to the west and the beautiful basin of Shadow Lake far below.

The usual backpacker's itinerary from here is to descend dozens of switchbacks to the valley of tiny Shadow Lake then to exit via West Fork Rock Creek. This is a great trip if you can arrange the necessary car shuttle.

88 *Line Creek Plateau*

Distance: 6 to 10-plus miles roundtrip
Difficulty: easy to moderate
Hiking time: day hike
Elevation gain: 1100 to 1300 feet
Season: late July through September
Best time: late July to mid-August

Contact: Custer Gallatin NF, Beartooth Ranger District
Map: USGS Black Pyramid Mountain, Mount Maurice
GPS coordinates: N45° 0.408', W109° 24.341'

Getting there: From Red Lodge, drive southwest on US 212 for a little over 23 miles to the top of the Beartooth Plateau and an unsigned junction about 0.2 mile before the Wyoming state line. Turn left onto this gravel road and proceed 0.2 mile to the road-end parking area.

If you're a fan of wide open alpine hiking, then Line Creek Plateau is for you. At the eastern extremity of the largest alpine area in the continental United States, this unique and breathtaking landscape offers views across vast stretches of two states and such unusual flora it has been designated a research natural area (RNA) by the Forest Service. In fact, at over 22,000 acres, this is the largest RNA in the entire national forest system. Access is absurdly easy from US 212, making it a mystery why so few people hike this fun trail.

The unsigned but obvious trail heads east, descending across often-windy tundra barrens toward a small lake. *Note:* The first part of the trail has been rerouted and is shown incorrectly on many maps.

For a brief time in midsummer, alpine flowers thrive in this harsh environment. Look for alpine gentian, willow, yarrow, alpine lupine, aster, and harebells. Prairie falcons, golden eagles, common ravens, and northern harriers often soar overhead.

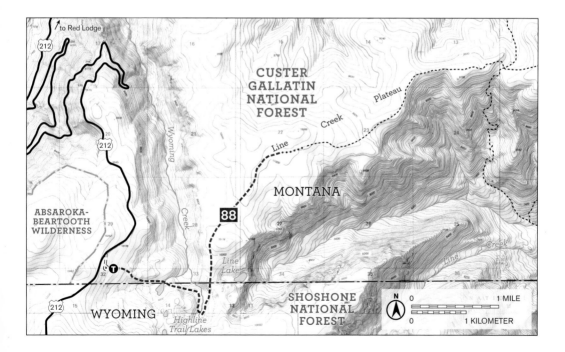

Looking northwest from near Wyoming Creek crossing

The path rapidly descends to the shallow unnamed lake, crosses the outlet, and then descends just below timberline into the scenic basin at the head of Wyoming Creek. Follow that nascent creek steeply upstream, soon returning to above-timberline meadowlands where you cross the flow. From here you gain about 200 feet to reach the vast rolling expanse of Line Creek Plateau.

How far you go depends on your whim and energy levels, as well as the potential need to head for cover if thunderstorms are in the area. The trail goes for miles and there is no real destination. It's all easy and grandly open high-elevation hiking with endless views. The tread fades away at around 3.5 miles (as good a place to turn around as any) but the open country is perfect for exploring.

Opposite, top: Evening primrose, Sand Arroyo Badlands

Opposite, bottom: Layout Creek Canyon where it meets Bighorn Canyon

Eastern Montana

Mineral-encrusted rocks below The Wall

When outdoor enthusiasts think of Montana, the first thing that comes to mind is the state's famous mountains. But a look at the map reveals a different story. It turns out that the majority of Montana isn't mountainous at all, but rather consists of vast expanses of rolling prairies. This open terrain offers a subtle beauty that is all too often overlooked by hikers heading for the more "dramatic" mountain landscapes. In May and June the endless grasslands are particularly lovely because that is when the prairie wildflowers bloom. As an added bonus, not all of eastern Montana is prairies. Hidden amid these flat expanses are wonderful treasures of natural beauty including deep canyons, wildly eroded badlands, isolated buttes, wildlife-rich marshes, and even a few low mountains featuring ponderosa pine forests.

Although most of the land is private property, eastern Montana possesses the best remaining publicly owned and intact prairie landscapes in North America. Efforts are currently underway to protect and restore these last vestiges of the wild Great Plains. Visionary souls are working to change grazing patterns to improve prairie health, buy key tracts of land, and set aside some of the best remaining prairies as wilderness areas and parks. Together with the adjoining Grasslands National Park in Canada, these efforts would protect a vast area of this critically endangered ecosystem. There are even efforts to reestablish free-ranging American bison and to turn the Montana prairie into a safari destination similar to the Serengeti Plains of east Africa.

Like any hiking area, the prairies have their own unique appeal and difficulties. Those who feel constricted in forest environments will love the wide open spaces, but not necessarily the strong winds that are not blocked by trees. Grizzly bears aren't found here, but prairie rattlesnakes are common, so be careful where you step and sit down. The region's dirt roads have no scary drop-offs, but when it rains they turn into a completely impassable "gumbo" of sticky and slippery mud that will thwart even four-wheel-drive vehicles. But those who come prepared for the rigors of this landscape will greatly enjoy its many subtle charms.

89 Bull Creek

Distance: 7-plus miles roundtrip
Difficulty: moderate to strenuous
Hiking time: day hike
Elevation gain: 800 feet
Season: year-round (if the road is dry)
Best time: May to June, September to October

Contact: Upper Missouri River Breaks National Monument
Maps: USGS Cow Island, Shetland Divide
GPS coordinates: N47° 46.613', W108° 50.425'

Getting there: From the junction of US 191 and State Route 66, 56 miles southwest of Malta, go 1.5 miles north on SR 66, then turn west on gravel Powerplant Ferry Road. Drive 1.8 miles, then keep straight where the good road veers right. The condition of this dirt road varies depending on moisture. If the road is wet, you should probably forget it; the mud will stop practically all vehicles. If conditions are dry, however, most cars with decent ground clearance will be fine. **Warning:** If rain clouds roll in while you're hiking, head back quickly to avoid getting stranded by the mud. At 10.8 miles from SR 66, park at the top of a small hill next to a wooden post and just before the road makes a significant downhill. You should see irregularly shaped Twin Snag Reservoir about 0.8 mile ahead of you. A jeep road angles off to the right (west).

The Missouri River above Fort Peck Lake flows through some of the wildest terrain in Montana. Protected in the Upper Missouri River Breaks National Monument, this region includes several large roadless areas that offer outstanding scenic and wildlife values as well as tremendous hiking. The easiest way to reach this area is by floating the river because overland access usually involves negotiating terrible roads and crossing private land. The exceptional, partly off-trail hike recommended here, however, can be reached by reasonably good (*if* they are dry) public roads. The payoff is a dramatic, 4-mile long sandstone escarpment along Bull and Winter Creeks in the impressive Cow Creek Wilderness Study Area.

Head west on the grassy jeep track, staying atop a wide ridge that is covered with sagebrush, wildflowers, grasses, and short ponderosa pines and junipers. Views across the area's numerous rugged gullies and ridges are inspiring and seem to extend to eternity. May wildflowers sprinkling

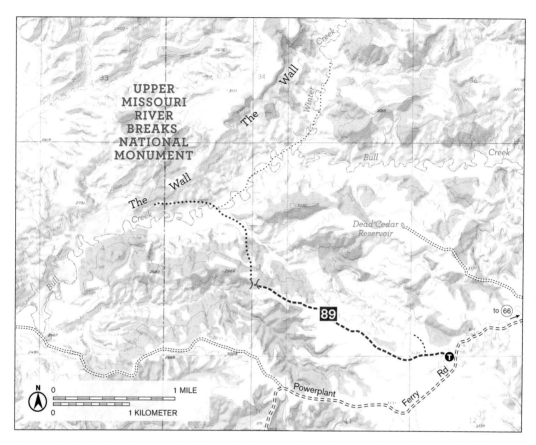

these uplands include locoweed, white and yellow daisies, vetch, golden pea, and desert parsley. To the northwest you can see the long sandstone escarpment that is your goal.

After a little over 0.2 mile, go left where a lesser jeep road veers right, then wander along the wide ridge gradually losing elevation. At about 1.6 miles the road ends at a brown wilderness study area sign. Keep walking on a faint continuation of the jeep track for about 0.25 mile to a saddle, then leave the route and head off trail going steeply down the north side of the ridge. Try to angle northwest following faint game trails that stay on the tops of little ridges rather than fighting through the dense vegetation in the gullies. The plant life includes an unusual mix of moisture-loving Douglas firs on shadier slopes living right beside small cactuses growing in sunnier spots.

At the bottom of the drainage the hiking is once again easy as you cross an eroded gully then head downstream on a game trail. Soon you reach the wide canyon of Bull Creek, a stream that usually has some pools of water into May. High on the ridge on the opposite side of the canyon rises the towering sandstone barrier known, rather unimaginatively, as "The Wall." The tan and yellow cliffs have some breaks in them, but generally continue for almost 3 miles upstream and into the side canyon of Winter Creek. They also go downstream along Bull Creek for about 1 mile. Explore either direction, but I especially recommend the downstream jaunt as the cliffs are taller and more impressive. A game trail simplifies the task of hiking through the area's sometimes thick stands of sagebrush and rabbitbrush, but it frequently crosses the meandering creek where mud should be expected.

90 *Mickey Butte*

Distance: 6.5 miles roundtrip
Difficulty: moderate to strenuous
Hiking time: day hike
Elevation gain: 650 feet
Season: March through November
Best time: May and June

Contact: Charles M. Russell National
Wildlife Refuge
Map: USGS Mickey Butte
GPS coordinates: N47° 37.152',
W107° 47.982'

Getting there: From downtown Malta, go 1 mile south on US 191 to a poorly signed junction directly across from the National Guard armory. Turn left and follow this paved road for 4.1 miles to a fork where the pavement ends. Keep right on Regina Road, drive 31 miles to a T intersection, turn left, and proceed 7.6 miles to a junction where you go straight, following signs to the Charles M. Russell Refuge. You enter the refuge after another 7.4 miles where the road gets progressively worse. If conditions are dry, an ordinary passenger car with good ground clearance can make it, but if conditions are wet, even four-wheel-drive is probably useless.

Now on NWR 201, go 7.5 miles, then turn left onto signed NWR 416, a grassy dirt track. Slowly drive 1.4 miles, then veer left onto NWR 417, which only deserves the title of "road" if you're being very generous. Another tortuous 2.4 miles takes you to road's end at a fenceline.

Although flat-topped Mickey Butte is rather unimpressive when viewed from a distance, the hike to the top is actually highly rewarding. Situated in the UL Bend National Wildlife Refuge, which, in turn, is nearly surrounded by the larger Charles M. Russell Refuge, Mickey Butte offers terrific views of the wild and deeply dissected semi-desert terrain north of Fort Peck Lake. The butte is also home to abundant wildlife, fascinating and very scenic sandstone formations, ponderosa pine forests, and plenty of spring wildflowers. The off-trail summit hike is simple and relatively easy.

Hop over the fence and head southeast following faint traces of an abandoned two-track that gradually ascends rolling sagebrush-dotted grasslands with lots of small cactus. Ahead of you is the rounded hump of Brandon Butte on the left and mesa-like Mickey Butte on the right. At about 0.8 mile the track crosses the dam forming Eva May Reservoir, really just a moderate-sized stock pond. Water birds are

Castle-like sandstone tower on the south side of Mickey Butte

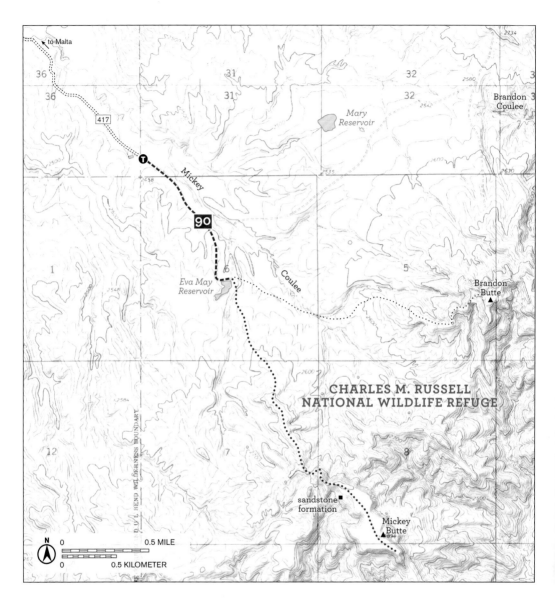

common here, including various ducks, Wilson's phalaropes, and sandpipers.

After crossing the dam, turn south-southeast, cross a deep gully, and then head across open terrain toward Mickey Butte. The simplest route follows the top of a wide, grassy ridge a little to the right of a direct line to the summit. The gradual uphill is easy and unobstructed and offers endless vistas of rolling prairies and buttes. As you gain elevation, the sagebrush peters out and is replaced by increasing numbers of junipers and ponderosa pines. The ridge reaches the northwest base of Mickey Butte at about 2.5 miles. A photogenic cluster of sandstone and shale turrets and other rock formations litter the ridge above you.

To reach the top, go around the left side of the rocky area and make a short, steep 100-foot climb. Once on top, explore this grassy tableland to your heart's content. There are fine views in all directions, especially south to the waters of Fort Peck Lake. Game trails offer easy walking and there is plenty to see. Of particular interest is a small castle-like sandstone formation on the south side of the butte. Also look for bighorn sheep, which are common here. It's about 0.6 mile across the narrow tableland to your turn-around at the southeast edge of the butte. Eva May Reservoir makes a convenient landmark on the return hike.

91 *Frenchman Creek Breaks*

Distance: 3-mile loop
Difficulty: moderate
Hiking time: day hike
Elevation gain: 400 feet
Season: year-round
Best time: May and June

Contact: Bureau of Land Management, Glasgow Field Office
Map: USGS Thoeny Hills East
GPS coordinates: N48° 59.424', W107° 21.002'

Getting there: From Malta, drive 23 miles north on US 191, turn right on State Route 208, and then go 9.2 miles to Whitewater, where both the pavement and all road signs

Looking west across Steelman Coulee

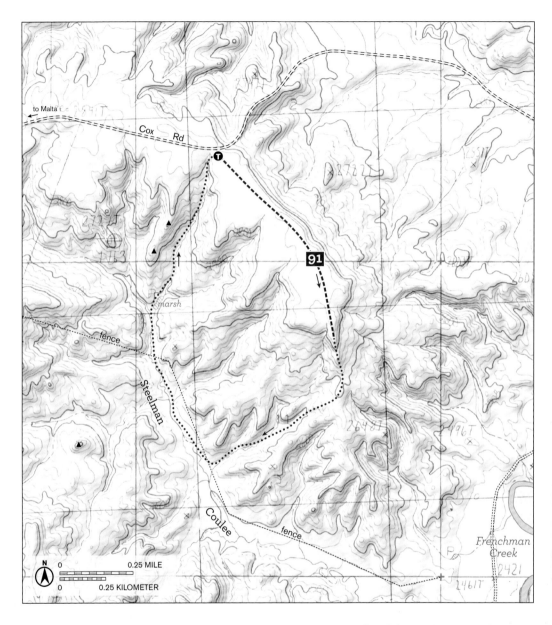

end. After 1.5 miles, go right at a fork, then right at a second fork 5.6 miles later. Drive 3.5 miles, go left at a T intersection, and proceed 7.6 miles to another junction where you go right. Drive 8.1 miles, (now on Cox Road, although no sign tells you this) then park just before the road begins a prominent downhill.

With exceptional grasslands scenery and good gravel road access, the Frenchman Creek Breaks offer a superb introduction to hiking on the Montana prairies. The waving grasslands here are broken by deeply eroded coulees adding variety to the landscape. Prairie wildflowers and wildlife are both abundant. There is no official trail, but an old jeep track and livestock trails offer relatively easy hiking.

Go south-southeast across a wide grassy plateau following a faint jeep trail from which the views seem to extend forever. The jeep trail offers an obvious course of travel, but feel free to explore the open terrain, checking out wildflowers and the inspiring views of Frenchman Creek Canyon to the east and Steelman Coulee to the west. With luck you may discover teepee rings and other evidence of Native American use of the region. Wildlife is common, including mule deer, pronghorns, and white-tailed jackrabbits.

It's easy and fun to explore this grassy mesa, but for a longer and more varied trip make a more challenging off-trail loop back to your car. To do so, where the jeep track fades away at the southeast tip of the mesa, follow a cow track downhill past a tiny outcropping of badlands, and then head southwest through an area with scattered boulders covered with colorful lichens. Your goal is the bottom of Steelman Coulee about 300 feet below the mesa. Look for small but potentially dangerous prairie rattlesnakes as you descend. From the bottom you'll enjoy a different perspective on this enchanting landscape as you look *up* at the relatively rugged and eroded walls of the coulee.

You cross a fence just before reaching the bottom of Steelman Coulee, where you should turn right (upstream). Hike on intermittent livestock trails for about 0.5 mile, then continue

Badlands outcropping in Frenchman Creek Breaks

going north when the fence makes a jog to the west-northwest across your route. You'll soon see a prominent cluster of four tall pyramid-shaped buttes that serve as a good landmark and hiking goal. Pass an old cattle pond, now just a shallow marsh, then walk up a livestock trail in the gradually steepening coulee immediately south of the buttes. At the top of the coulee you'll find yourself back at your car.

92 *Bitter Creek*

Distance: 6.5-plus-mile loop
Difficulty: easy to moderate
Hiking time: day hike or overnight
Elevation gain: 350-plus feet
Season: year-round
Best time: May through mid-June

Contact: Bureau of Land Management, Glasgow Field Office
Map: USGS Gay Dam
GPS coordinates: N48° 37.932', W106° 45.475'

Getting there: From milepost 521.4 on US 2, about 16 miles northwest of Glasgow, turn north on Britsch Road, following signs to Bitter Creek Wildlife Viewing Area. The road is

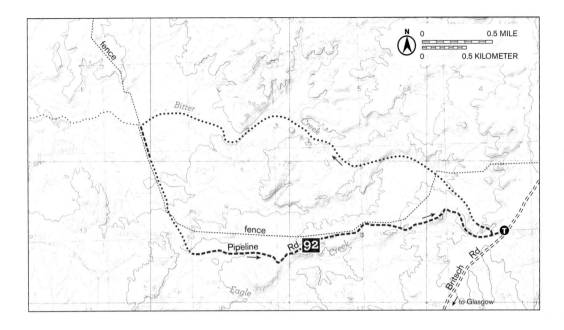

good gravel for the first 9.7 miles to where a ranch access road goes right. Keep straight on a reasonably good two-track that becomes difficult or even impossible when conditions are wet. Continue 10.9 miles, then park at a junction with a pipeline road marked as Route 7.

Montana is home to the best remaining wild prairies in the United States and Bitter Creek is the best of that best. This area is a vast rolling land of gullies, low buttes, and seemingly endless grasslands, much like what most of the central United States looked like 200 years ago, except that those moving black dots are now domestic cattle rather than bison (close enough). The area is a precious refuge for rapidly declining grasslands species of plants and animals, and despite a complete lack of trails, it offers wonderful and relatively easy hiking. Conservation groups are calling for wilderness protection for this unique place, so visiting here will give you both a fun outdoor experience and an opportunity to see what's at stake.

This landscape has a certain grand sameness to it, so it really doesn't matter where you start or where you go, as there is no particular destination. It's easy to lose your bearings, however, so anyone striking off on their own should bring a GPS to help find their way back.

Go 100 yards west-southwest on the pipeline road, then pick up a game and livestock trail that goes right, drops down a wide gully, and enters the drainage of Bitter Creek. In May and early June this broken landscape of hills, gullies, and rolling terrain is sprinkled with prairie wildflowers such as locoweed, long-plumed avens, vetch, desert parsley, and golden pea.

Work your way generally northwest down the drainage, climbing low hills on either side when the fancy strikes. Intermittent animal trails are available or you can just wander along in whatever direction you care to, generally following the usually dry drainage. You'll hop over a fence at about 0.7 mile, then keep going gradually downhill enjoying the surprisingly easy and scenic ramble. Keep an eye out for prairie rattlesnakes and expect strong winds, but those are about the only hazards to worry about. In the spring or after summer thunderstorms the drainage may have occasional muddy areas or small pools of water.

Typical prairie scenery in the Bitter Creek area

For a change in perspective, somewhere between 1 and 1.5 miles (the exact distance is irrelevant) saunter over the low hills on your right then cross the vast prairies of the main drainage of Bitter Creek. This "creek" has somewhat more water than the one you were following and may even have a meager flow in wetter years.

Near 2.5 miles Bitter Creek passes a prominent pyramid-shaped butte after which you continue downstream following a well-trod animal trail on the south side of the drainage that offers an obvious course of travel.

At a little over 3 miles another fence crosses the route. Although you can continue exploring for many miles, this fence makes a good landmark to start the return leg of your loop. So go left (south) following an animal trail along the fence that heads up a wide gully. Stay with the fence as it jogs to the left then climbs to a higher prairie plateau. Cross the fence here and head southeast for about 300 yards to intersect the pipeline road. Turn left and follow this primitive road for about 2.5 miles back to your starting point.

Note: Spending a night under the prairie sky is a memorable experience, but backpackers must carry all the water they'll need as natural sources are unreliable.

93 Sand Arroyo Badlands Loop

Distance: 4- to 8-mile loop
(depending on your route)
Difficulty: moderate
Hiking time: day hike
Elevation gain: 500-plus feet
Season: year-round

Best time: mid-April to June,
September and October
Contact: Bureau of Land Management,
Miles City Field Office
Map: USGS Sand Arroyo
GPS coordinates: N47° 50.893',
W106° 09.432'

Getting there: From Fort Peck, drive about 25 miles south on State Route 24 to milepost 36.4 and park in a large, unsigned lot on the east side of the highway.

With fascinating geologic features and all-weather access off a paved highway, the Sand Arroyo Badlands could be a major tourist attraction in eastern Montana. Instead, they are virtually unknown and almost never visited. But rest assured, the colorfully striated hills and otherworldly formations of this wonderland will keep your camera busy and provide lasting memories despite the lack of publicity. There are no trails, but the landscape is relatively easy to navigate, with the only major concern making sure you remain on public Bureau of Land Management (BLM) land and not trespass on private inholdings. There are few if any fences or signs marking where the private land begins, so watch the map carefully.

Pyramid-shaped butte in the Sand Arroyo Badlands

Cross the highway, then hike west-southwest, remaining in a strip of BLM land. Go over a pair of fences, then cross a flat covered with grasses and sagebrush. Your goal is an obvious break in a line of colorfully striated buttes that you reach at about 0.3 mile.

This notch in the badlands is at the head of a westward-flowing coulee and contains many photogenic geologic features including toadstool rocks, small caves, seams of reddish and black soils, and scattered boulders. All around are low buttes with several colorful layers of soil, including black, tan, orange, and creamy white.

Follow an animal trail down the winding coulee as it descends toward the main drainage of Sand Arroyo. The drainage hosts many interesting features, including thickets of junipers, small caves, colorful rock formations, and scenically eroded hillsides. At about 0.7 mile you enter the huge open basin of Sand Arroyo. Here you should leave the gully and climb to the top of the lip on the south side of the wash to gather nice views of the wide basin and rounded Goat Mountain to the west. From this point on the described route is merely a suggestion and only one of many possible explorations of this scenic region.

For a relatively short but rewarding loop, travel south-southwest, crossing a series of tiny drainages and never straying too far from the colorful and deeply eroded badlands on your left. This leads to a rugged up-and-down crossing of a large side drainage. At the south end of this crossing you go around the west (right) side of a highly scenic, pyramid-shaped butte, then climb

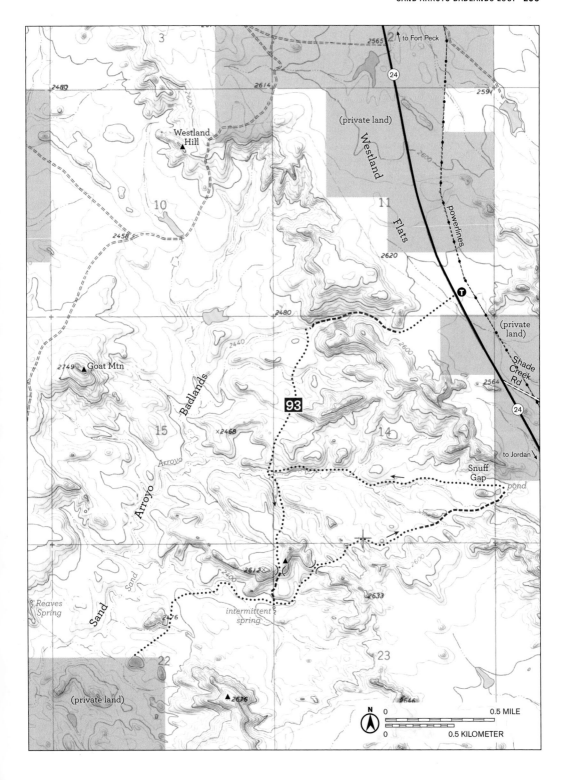

One of countless odd rock formations in the Sand Arroyo Badlands

through a little notch and follow a steep animal trail that descends into the next wide drainage.

You bottom out near an intermittent muddy spring. You could spend hours in this basin exploring all the gullies and colorful badlands around the perimeter, or hike downstream to the main wash of Sand Arroyo to a cluster of interestingly eroded buttes in that area.

Having exhausted the exploring opportunities, make your way up through a prominent gap in the northeast corner of the basin that leads you back into a higher portion of the wide drainage you crossed earlier in the hike. Turn east and follow the edge of a line of bizarrely eroded buttes and through a colorful and highly scenic Dr. Seuss-type landscape full of strange mushroom rocks, fins, columns, and other contorted landforms.

Eventually you'll pick up a good animal trail that goes left at a fork in the drainage and passes an intermittent muddy pond. The trail then takes you through a wide opening whimsically named Snuff Gap, from which you can see the powerlines and SR 24 a short distance ahead of you. Going directly there, however, would involve crossing private property, so without landowner permission, you should turn around and walk west through the very scenic wide drainage until you intersect the route you came in on, then turn right and return the way you came.

94 *Weatherman Draw*

Distance: 7.5-mile loop
Difficulty: moderate to strenuous
Hiking time: day hike
Elevation gain: 1050 feet
Season: year-round (if the road is dry)
Best time: May and June, September and October

Contact: Bureau of Land Management, Billings Field Office
Map: USGS Hunters Creek
GPS coordinates: N45° 05.815', W108° 49.492'

Getting there: From Bridger, drive 1.3 miles south on US 310, then turn right on State Route 72. Go 4.8 miles, turn left on gravel Golden Lane, and go 1.4 miles to a fork. Bear right on Cottonwood Road, a dirt-and-gravel road that becomes impassable when wet. Proceed 10.5 miles to the trailhead parking lot on the left.

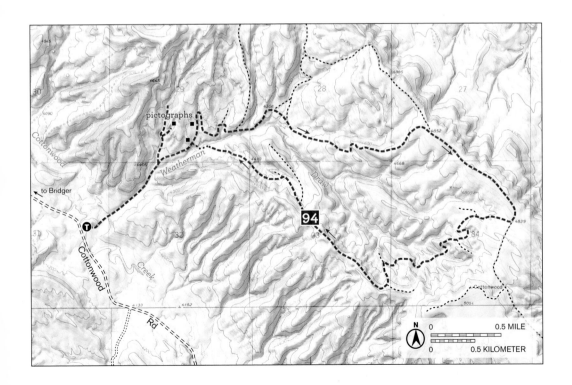

Weatherman Draw is a scenic destination in the semi-desert country south of Billings. Centuries ago this land was wetter than today, with a permanent creek that provided water for Native Americans. These people left behind numerous rock art sites on the canyon's sandstone walls. In fact, Weatherman Draw has the largest collection of polychrome pictographs in the northern Great Plains. You'll have to search around to find the art, but that adds to your sense of discovery, and even if you fail, the canyon scenery is reward enough for your trip.

Travel east on a wide hiking trail that crosses a broken landscape of sandstone-lined coulees and bluffs, juniper-dotted ridges, and sage- and cactus-covered flats. Expect to be startled by desert cottontail rabbits bounding away at your approach. Just past a small corral, you hop over the dry flow of Cottonwood Creek, ignoring several confusing cattle trails that branch off to either side. Your dusty path then heads northeast up the wide defile of

Shield-like pictographs in Weatherman Draw

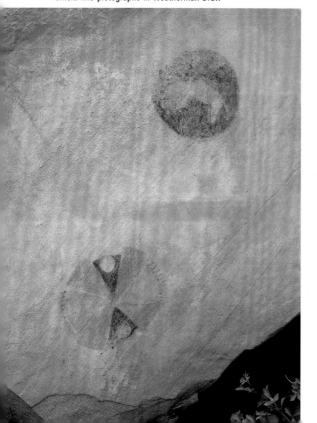

Weatherman Draw, beginning on the left side of the drainage, but soon dropping to the dry creekbed. To avoid muddy spots, the trail detours back up onto the left bank, taking you to an unsigned junction at 0.7 mile on a little ridge between Weatherman Draw and a side drainage from the left.

For a scenic and interesting side trip, go left at the junction and after almost 0.2 mile look for a faint grassy track to the right. This path leads to a rocky alcove where you'll find a pictograph site with depictions of spears and a round shield-like design. The artwork has survived for almost 900 years, but modern visitors are a much greater hazard than centuries of weather, so PLEASE do not disturb, deface, or even touch any of the art as even the oils on human skin can be damaging. For a short hike, this coulee makes a good destination.

For the longer loop, return to the main trail and soon pass a second scenic alcove with a rock art site. From here you make detours around the heads of two deep gullies, ignoring a confusing path that goes straight up the second coulee, instead looping back to the right and continuing up Weatherman Draw. That main drainage soon widens out and forks.

Stick with the path going straight (east), which loops past a series of small side gullies and faint trails before beginning an extended ascent up a rounded ridge. The path is sometimes indistinct, so decent map-reading and navigation skills come in handy. At the top of the climb is a junction on a wide, northwest-southeast trending ridge. The view looking east to the Pryor Mountains is excellent.

Keep right, following the undulating ridgeline for almost 1 mile, then turn right and begin a gradual, winding downhill past unmarked side trails that lead to fine viewpoints. After about 1.5 miles, the trail turns northwest along a narrow ridge, which you follow for 0.8 mile before the path descends to the right. This uneven descent takes you to just above the bottom of Weatherman Draw where the faint tread disappears. To close the loop, scramble across the draw, then climb up the opposite bank to the trail you came in on.

Cairn atop Big Pryor Mountain

95 *Big Pryor Mountain*

Distance: 3.4 miles roundtrip
Difficulty: moderate
Hiking time: day hike
Elevation gain: 1700 feet
Season: June through early November
Best time: mid-June to mid-July

Contact: Custer Gallatin NF, Beartooth Ranger District
Map: USGS Big Ice Cave
GPS coordinates: N45° 10.204', W108° 27.187'

Getting there: From Bridger, drive 2.5 miles south on US 310 to a junction near milepost 23.3. Turn left on Pryor Mountain Road and go 2.1 miles to the end of pavement. After another 10.3 miles, go left at a T intersection and proceed 2.8 miles to where the road enters the Crow Indian Reservation. The next 7 miles are badly rutted and often impassable when wet. At 23 miles from US 310 you enter national forest land where the road improves, becomes Forest Road 2308, and climbs 7.7 miles to sagebrush-covered Tie Flat and a junction with Tie Flat Road. Turn right on this rough and rutted road (you may prefer to walk) and park after 0.1 mile where an abandoned two-track angles right.

With dozens of limestone caves, abundant wildflowers, dramatic scenery, unique flora, Montana's only herd of wild horses, unusual geology, and numerous historic and cultural features, the Pryor Mountains are special. Elevations approach 9000 feet, so they also tower over the surrounding deserts and plains providing a cool, forested retreat for both humans and wildlife. This

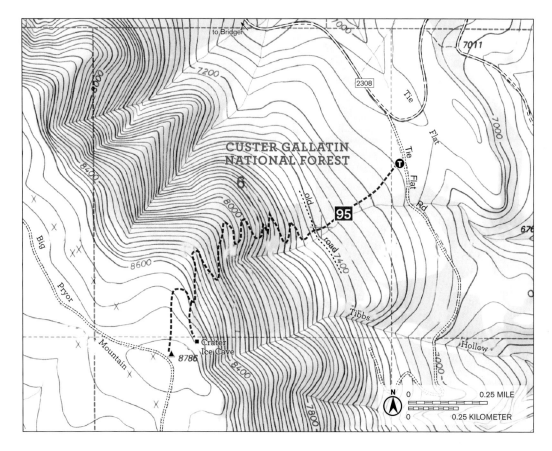

hike accesses the highest point in the range with superb views, dense forests, alpine meadows, and even an ice cave along the way.

Walk southwest on the abandoned two-track, initially across grass- and sagebrush-covered Tie Flat, then in a shady forest of Douglas firs. From here, ascend a moderately steep incline to an old road at 0.4 mile. Turn left and 80 yards later veer right where a sign identifies Crater Ice Cave Trail.

Now on a narrow hiker's trail, begin a series of fourteen switchbacks of variable length that climb the steep face of Big Pryor Mountain. After ten switchbacks, small forest openings offer just enough sunshine for a host of colorful wildflowers to flourish. In late June and early July look for clematis, larkspur, balsamroot, shooting star, bistort, forget-me-not, lomatium, aster, wallflower, monument plant, arnica, phlox,

paintbrush, pasqueflower, buttercup, and several other species.

At the thirteenth switchback, and just as you enter the huge alpine meadows atop Big Pryor Mountain, a post marks an obscure fork. The left branch goes less than 100 yards to Crater Ice Cave, whose entrance is usually blocked by snow until early July. The right branch follows marker posts up to the open summit plateau. Wildflowers are everywhere and the views extend across huge areas of two states. On clear days you can see the Beartooth Mountains to the west, the Bighorn Mountains to the southeast, and even the distant peaks of Wyoming's Wind River Range to the southwest. You may share this view with motorized users as machines are able to reach this spot by primitive roads from the west, but on weekdays you'll probably have the scenery all to yourself.

96 *Bighorn Canyon*

Distance: 1 mile roundtrip for Stateline Trail; 3.4 miles roundtrip for Lower Layout Creek
Difficulty: moderate
Hiking time: half-day hike
Elevation gain: 150 feet for Stateline Trail; 350 feet for Lower Layout Creek
Season: year-round

Best time: April to early June, October to November
Contact: Bighorn Canyon National Recreation Area
Maps: USGS Hillsboro, Mystery Cave
GPS coordinates: N45° 0.024', W108° 15.923' for Stateline Trail; N45° 01.441', W108° 15.582' for Lower Layout Creek

Getting there: From Laurel, go 11.6 miles south on US 212/310 to a junction at Rockvale. Go left on US 310 and drive 64 miles to a junction at the east end of Lovell, Wyoming. Turn left (north) on US 14 Alt and go 2.5 miles to the turnoff for State Route 37 and the Bighorn Canyon National Recreation Area. Go left and drive 13.6 miles to the Montana border. The Stateline Trailhead is on the right about 50 yards after you cross into Montana.

For Lower Layout Creek, drive another 6.4 miles to a cattle guard and park on the side of the road. If you reach the Ewing-Snell Ranch turnoff, you've driven 0.2 mile too far.

Montana's most colorful, steeply walled, and dramatically scenic canyon has been carved by the Bighorn River into the ancient rocks of south-central Montana. In addition to outstanding scenery, wildlife is common, with a particular abundance of birds of prey (eagles, hawks, and falcons), bighorn sheep, and the Pryor Mountain herd of wild horses, which are

Looking west toward Sykes Ridge from lower Layout Creek Trail

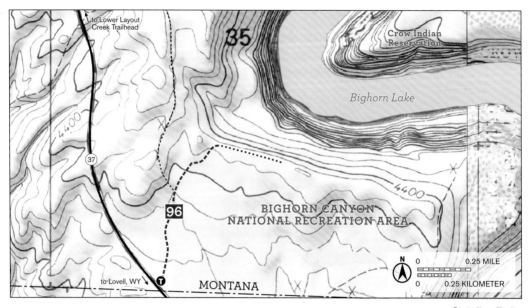

Stateline Trail

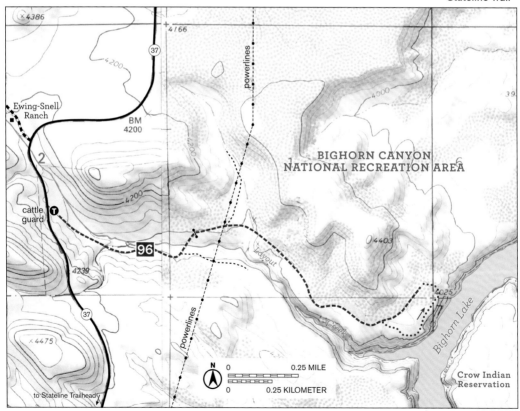

Lower Layout Creek Trail

usually easy to spot. Although the canyon is accessible all year it gets very hot in midsummer and can be bitterly cold in winter, so shoulder season hiking is better. The two best short trails to explore the canyon are combined here into a fun day of hiking.

Stateline Trail: The well-worn route follows brown signposts heading north-northeast across a mostly flat plain populated by juniper, sagebrush, and cactus. In May, a few death camas and other wildflowers provide spots of color.

At 0.25 mile a connecting path to the Ranger Delight Trail veers left, but you bear right, still on the Stateline Trail. The often-rocky path climbs a couple of moderately steep pitches, then curves to the right just before reaching the top of a colorful little knoll. At just shy of 0.5 mile the trail abruptly ends atop a rimrock cliff with a dramatic view down into Bighorn Canyon. Spend some time here watching the impressive aerial show put on by white-throated swifts that swoop and dive near the rim.

To get even better views of the canyon, go southeast along the rim enjoying the oranges, yellows, whites, and grays of the nearby rocks and the reds, tans, and browns of the cliffs lining the canyon below.

Lower Layout Creek: From the south side of the cattle guard, descend a jeep road to a hiker's V access through a wooden fence. From there simply follow the jeep road down the gully of small but reliably flowing Layout Creek. The views are very good, especially looking west to the long, high escarpment of Sykes Ridge. The top of this ridge sports a dramatic assortment of limestone towers and cliffs. The desert landscape surrounding your route is also quite beautiful with relatively lush vegetation featuring dense stands of sagebrush and junipers amid the grasses, wildflowers, and cactuses. Look for wild horses, bighorn sheep, desert cottontail rabbits, rattlesnakes, and other wildlife as you hike.

At 0.4 mile, go left at a fork, hop over Layout Creek, and then go through a gate and come to a set of powerlines. Here the main road goes straight, staying with the powerlines, but you turn right on an older jeep track that goes down

the canyon of Layout Creek. As it heads downstream, the trail stays on a rolling plateau above the creek while that waterway rapidly drops into a deep and steep-walled defile. There are frequent opportunities to walk over and look down into this narrow chasm. In addition, the views back to the Pryor Mountains are a constant dramatic backdrop to your travels.

At 1.3 miles, just as the deep gash of Bighorn Canyon comes into view, you reach a large flat area that is dotted with cactus and sagebrush plants. The faint jeep track curves left here, but the better views can be found to the right. Walk off trail across the flat for about 0.1 mile to an

Bighorn Canyon from the end of the Stateline Trail

incredibly dramatic rocky viewpoint directly above the confluence of Bighorn Canyon and the canyon of Layout Creek. The bright red walls of the smaller canyon offer terrific photo opportunities.

It's fun to walk around the outer edge of the flat past several dizzying viewpoints atop the cliffs above Bighorn Lake. Once you've had your fill, loop back to the left to find the old jeep track and return the way you came.

97 *Tongue River Breaks*

Distance: 3–8 miles roundtrip (depending on your route)
Difficulty: easy to moderate
Hiking time: day hike
Elevation gain: 300–600 feet
Season: March to November
Best time: May to June, October

Contact: Custer Gallatin NF, Ashland Ranger District
Maps: USGS Birney Day School, Green Creek
GPS coordinates: N45° 24.462', W106° 25.217'

Getting there: From the east end of Ashland along US 212, turn south on gravel Ashland-Birney Road (Tongue River Road). Drive 17.2 miles, then turn left at an unsigned junction with a jeep road (Forest Road 45152). There are no good landmarks for this

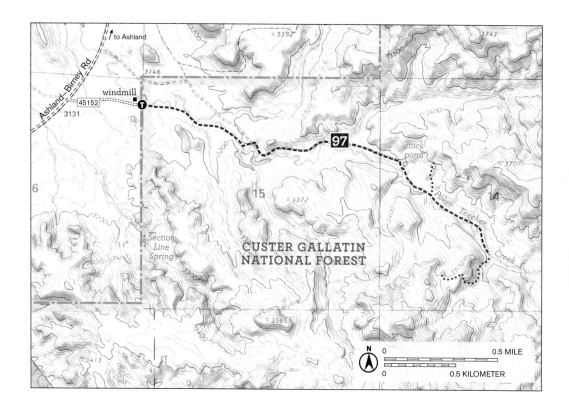

Colorful hillside in lower Tongue River Breaks

junction, so it might be easier to continue until you reach a major junction with a road going right to a bridge over the river. From there, backtrack 1.3 miles to find the jeep road. If the jeep road is dry, most cars can drive 0.6 mile to its end at a fenceline and windmill.

The Tongue River flows through a scenic region of badlands, farmlands, and rolling hills in south-central Montana. The stream, especially its rugged "breaks" region, makes a fine destination for those looking to get away from it all and enjoy some excellent eastern Montana scenery. There are no official trails, but the hiking is relatively easy and the rewards for your efforts include dun-colored sandstone cliffs and buttes, multi-colored hillsides and badlands, sagebrush meadows alive with spring wildflowers, and rolling hills dotted with ponderosa pines.

Go through the gate in the fence and pick up a livestock and hiking trail that heads up the wide defile of intermittent Poker Teechee Creek. The dominant features of this area are sage- and grass-covered flats punctuated by buttes of a reddish or orange hue. In the spring, abundant greens add to the soil colors for an enchanting and scenic mix of prairie grasslands and open forest.

There is no official trail and many livestock paths branch off in several directions. Try to stay on what looks like the main route, heading east-southeast. As you gradually gain elevation, Rocky Mountain junipers and a few ponderosa pines become increasingly common and the scenery improves with colorful hills and badlands topography.

At 1.2 miles, pass a muddy stock pond followed by a cluster of dun-colored cliffs on your left. It is well worth the short scramble up the hillside to investigate this area. With a little searching you'll discover sandstone formations and several brightly colored hillsides and gullies.

Continuing up Poker Teechee Creek, you gradually ascend into a wetter landscape where ponderosa pines start to dominate. About 0.5 mile from the pond you reach a point where the trail curves to the right and enters a sloping meadow lined on its right side by photogenic sandstone cliffs, pockmarked with miniature caves. In May and June wildflowers such as blazing star, larkspur, and vetch are common in the grassy meadows at the base of these cliffs.

For a change in perspective, scramble up a steep gully to the top of the cliffs, where you'll enjoy sweeping views of the forested hills and ridges to the east and the valley of Tongue River

to the west. Watch for swooping white-throated swifts and violet-green swallows, which often nest on these cliffs.

This cliff-top viewpoint, about 2.2 miles from your car, makes an excellent turnaround point. More ambitious hikers can explore farther up the ridges and canyons. The soil and rocks become more strikingly red as you ascend, although thicker ponderosa pine woodlands often block the view. There are no established hiking routes, so let the explorer in you take over and just wander.

98 *Terry Badlands Natural Bridges*

Distance: 2.4 miles roundtrip
Difficulty: moderate
Hiking time: half-day hike
Elevation gain: 400 feet
Season: year-round (if the road is dry)
Best time: May to June, September to early November

Contact: Bureau of Land Management, Miles City Field Office
Map: USGS McClure Reservoir
GPS coordinates: N46° 48.829', W105° 32.508'

Getting there: From Terry, take exit 176 off Interstate 94, go 0.5 mile north, then turn left on Spring Street (Old Highway 10), following signs for the business district.

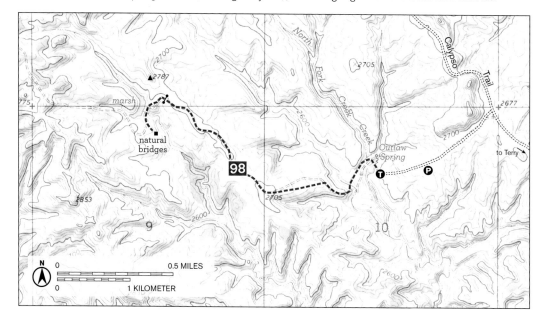

Two of the remarkable natural bridges in Terry Badlands

Drive 2.9 miles, through the town of Terry, to a junction with gravel Milwaukee Road. Go right, drive 3 miles, and then cross an old one-lane railroad bridge over the Yellowstone River. Exactly 0.2 mile past the bridge turn right at a tiny sign saying CALYPSO and drive past a series of information boards. From here you follow the Calypso Trail (actually a primitive road) across a large flat area with a prairie dog town, then through the rugged Terry Badlands. The road is subject to washouts, has many deep ruts, turns into muddy gumbo when it rains, and has several very steep sections. In other words, it's miserable to drive when it's dry and completely impassable when it's wet. Even when dry, you'll need a vehicle with good ground clearance. After 8.1 miles, go left at a fork, drive 0.4 mile, and park at the top of a hill just before the road makes a sharp downhill.

Of the many surprises hidden in the prairies of eastern Montana, the Terry Badlands are near the top of the list in both scenic appeal and interest for hikers. This rugged landscape hides colorful buttes, steep coulees, towering pinnacles, wide views, and interesting wildlife. The most unusual attraction, however, is an otherwise nondescript little gully that houses a fantastic collection of natural bridges. In addition to the scenery and geologic interest, one of the best things about hiking here is the sense of discovery that arises as you stand beside this unexpected and little-visited marvel. In addition to deserving your attention, this dramatic and fragile region deserves some kind of permanent protection before ATVs become rampant or someone discovers a mineral that they can

profitably turn into kitty litter (or some other marketable material).

From the hilltop parking spot, walk down the continuation of the steep and rugged road enjoying wide views over the grassy benches, deeply cut gullies, and oddly shaped hills of this badlands region. After 0.1 mile the road ends at Outlaw Spring, which has a wooden fence around it and a developed watering trough.

Carefully walk through the boggy area below the spring to a brown BLM sign that says TRAIL. Take this faint up-and-down route, which is regularly marked with more brown signs, as it crosses a gully holding the intermittent flow of North Fork Crooked Creek at 0.25 mile and then climbs up to and across a sloping, grassy plateau. Along the way you'll pass a small grove of limber pines, demonstrating that this region holds the easternmost examples of this species. At about 0.6 mile, just after starting a short downhill, you curve to the right at a potentially confusing signpost.

After a bit more up and down, go through a gate and immediately reach another confusing spot at the base of an eroded butte. Bear left, go around the butte, and then drop to cross a gully before reaching an old marshy area, whose small dam is now breached, robbing the marsh of most of its water.

Cross below the dam, then follow a signpost telling you to make a hard left turn. Less than 0.1 mile later the trail ends at a gully holding a remarkable surprise: directly below you are two large, flat-topped natural bridges. The first and largest bridge, which is right in front of you, is about 8 feet wide and you can easily walk across its top to the other side of the gully. If you explore a bit you'll find remains of other bridges that have collapsed, a couple of smaller bridges upstream, bridges in the process of being formed, and a few caves.

99 *Makoshika State Park*

Distance: 0.6-mile loop for Cap Rock Trail; 1.6-mile loop for Kinney Coulee
Difficulty: easy for Cap Rock; moderate for Kinney Coulee
Hiking time: half-day hike
Elevation gain: 240 feet for Cap Rock; 500 feet for Kinney Coulee
Season: year-round

Best time: April to early June, October and November
Contact: Makoshika State Park
Map: USGS Glendive
GPS coordinates: N47° 03.288', W104° 40.847' for Cap Rock; N47° 03.090', W104° 40.338' for Kinney Coulee

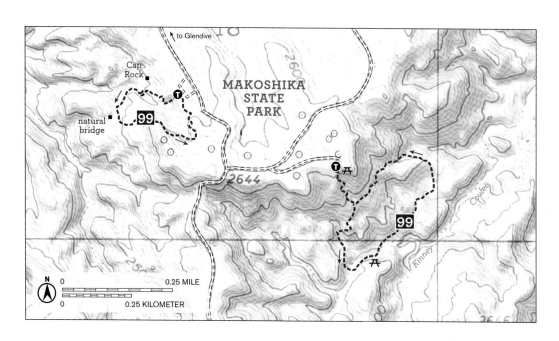

Badlands near the Kinney Coulee Trailhead

Getting there: Drive to Glendive, then follow signs to Makoshika State Park, which lead you to Snyder Avenue, the park's entrance road, and the visitor center.

To find the Cap Rock Trail, follow the main park road as it climbs a steep hill and turns to gravel. At 3.3 miles from the visitor center turn right onto the short loop that passes the parking area for the Cap Rock Trail.

For Kinney Coulee, continue on the park road another 0.3 mile, turn left at a junction near several radio towers, drive 0.1 mile, and then veer right at a poorly marked junction. Follow this road 0.2 mile to its end at a hilltop picnic table next to a small sign for the Kinney Coulee Trail.

In Lakota, the language of the Sioux People who once inhabited this region, *makoshika* means "bad earth." But that hardly does justice to the harshly beautiful landscape of this badlands region. Here, in Montana's largest state park, you'll wander past intricately eroded hillsides, see interesting hoodoos and natural bridges, enjoy the many colors found in the rocks, and marvel at the infinite array of contours that wind and water have carved into the land. Numerous dinosaur fossils have been retrieved from the park's soft sandstones and mudstones—the visitor center offers numerous examples for you to inspect. But if you're more interested in scenery, there is more than enough to keep you enthralled for hours. The park has three major trails; the two best are described here.

Cap Rock Nature Trail: This short trail provides a lot of excellent scenery and geologic interest in a relatively compact package. Interpretive signs and numbered posts corresponding to an information brochure offer interesting facts about the geology and fossil history of this unique area.

The trail begins next to a large interpretive sign and drops in a series of wood-lined steps into the wildly eroded landscape below. The up-and-down route then travels through a wonderland of unusual and colorfully scenic geologic features including cap rocks, eroded pinnacles and buttes, and even one large natural bridge. The loop ends with a short, stiff climb back to the trailhead.

Kinney Coulee Trail: Starting from a ponderosa pine-studded hilltop, the little-used path makes a moderately steep descent in a series of irregularly spaced switchbacks that offer views of the colorful and oddly eroded landscape of Kinney Coulee.

At just over 0.2 mile a post marks an easy-to-miss junction at the start of the loop. The trail signage is designed for a counterclockwise tour, so go straight and follow an up-and-down route that takes you past a remarkable array of eroded hillsides, pinnacles, mushroom rocks, and oddly contorted badlands. At the bottom of the coulee, and near the midway point of the trail, a picnic table set beneath a grove of pines makes a nice lunch stop. More up-and-down rambling, and a few steep uphills, takes you back to the junction at the close of the loop. **Warning:** The Kinney Coulee Trail is prone to washouts. Inquire at the visitor center about current conditions.

100 Chalk Buttes

Distance: 1.5 miles roundtrip for north butte; 5-plus miles roundtrip for the largest Chalk Butte
Difficulty: moderate to strenuous
Hiking time: day hike
Elevation gain: 350 feet for north butte; 650 feet for largest Chalk Butte
Season: April to November

Best time: May to June, September to October
Contact: Custer Gallatin NF, Sioux Ranger District
Map: USGS Chalk Buttes
GPS coordinates: N45° 43.776', W104° 40.955'

Getting there: First, make your way to Ekalaka—no easy feat for most Montanans, because this isolated burg is a *really* long way from just about anywhere else in the state. Approaching from the north on State Route 7, there is a junction with SR 323, which goes left. Curve to the right, go 75 yards, and then bear right onto Main Street. Two blocks later you've reached the end of "downtown," where you angle right onto Speelmon Street. Drive one block, then turn left onto gravel Central Avenue, which eventually becomes Chalk Buttes Road. At a little over 2 miles from town is a junction with Ekalaka Dump Road, where you turn left. Proceed 13.5 miles, then turn right on Trenk Pass Road, following a small sign to Chalk Buttes. Drive 0.8 mile, go through a gate (be sure to close it behind you), then drive 1 mile to where you enter Forest Service land and the road abruptly deteriorates. Most people should park here rather than continuing on rough, four-wheel-drive Forest Road 3816. Those with four-wheel-drive vehicles can continue 0.25 mile up FR 3816 to Trenk Pass, where a fenceline crosses the road.

Rising abruptly from the rolling plains of southeastern Montana, the Chalk Buttes resemble a misplaced segment of England's famous White Cliffs of Dover. Here, in the middle of the plains, a cluster of flat-topped, pine-covered hills are surrounded by chalk-colored cliffs hundreds of feet high. They draw your attention not only because they seem so anomalous,

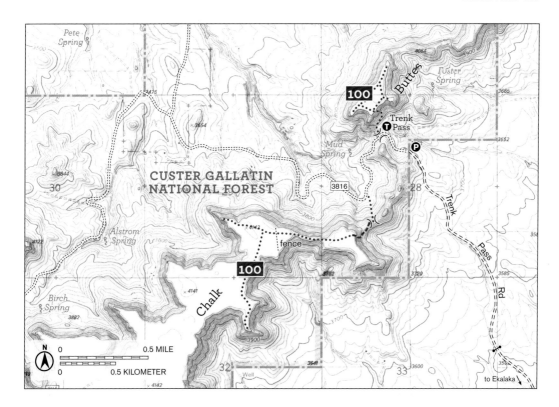

but because they are very scenic. Although no official trails explore the Chalk Buttes, access is fairly reasonable and the off-trail hiking is within the capabilities of most fit pedestrians.

Walk 0.25 mile up Forest Road 3816 to Trenk Pass, where a fenceline crosses the road. Trees limit the views, but you'll catch enticing glimpses of nearby buttes and cliffs, especially to the northwest. There are two excellent hiking goals from Trenk Pass.

North Butte: The shorter option is the cliff-edged butte to the north. To reach it, leave the road and walk uphill through lovely ponderosa pine woodlands, staying to the right of a fence-line. A tall and photogenic yellowish-white cliff on your left gives striking evidence of why this place is called the Chalk Buttes.

The ascent gets much steeper, but does not turn technical or dangerous for hikers. Intermittent game trails offer somewhat easier hiking, so follow them whenever possible. In general, make your way slightly to the right of a straight uphill

course until you reach the base of some low cliffs where you can pull yourself up the last 8 feet to the top of the butte. Carefully note this location so you can find it on the return.

The top of the cliff-edged butte is remarkably flat and covered with forest. Views from the rim are outstanding. You can look out across the seemingly endless plains and view the nearby forested hills punctuated by scenic towers and cliffs. Turkey vultures and golden eagles soar on the thermals and swallows find great sport zipping back and forth. It takes about thirty minutes to explore the rim of this small butte, before you carefully return down the steep slopes to Trenk Pass.

Largest Chalk Butte: For a longer hike, visit the largest of the Chalk Buttes. To reach it, walk down Forest Road 3816 as it gradually descends the west side of Trenk Pass. After 0.25 mile you'll pass the small water tank at Mud Spring on your right, then go less than 0.2 mile to where the road makes a sweeping right turn. Leave the road just before this turn and walk southeast up

Chalk cliffs northeast of Trenk Pass

a grassy hillside with scattered pines. The forest gets thicker as you follow a steep game trail that leads to a notch in the top of the ridge about 0.2 mile from the road. There are good views across the vast plains to the southeast.

Turn right and make a brief but steep climb up the wooded ridge to a small flat area. You then resume climbing, following a game trail on the left side of the ridge that neatly bypasses a cluster of short, rocky cliffs. You'll top out after 0.2 mile on the flat, grassy summit of a butte with lots of May and June wildflowers, especially golden pea and field chickweed. Walk directly across the meadow atop this butte, pick up the narrow ridge that extends to the west, and follow this remarkably level ridge for 0.25 mile until it opens up at a fenceline atop the largest of the Chalk Buttes.

Step over the fence and explore off trail to your heart's content. The enormous flat-topped butte is almost 2 miles long so there is plenty to see. The top of the butte features beautiful meadows dotted with ponderosa pines and the surrounding cliffs, especially those on the northwest side, are very impressive. Views from the rim are unsurpassed.

There is no water, so if you want to spend the night—a great idea with particularly superb sunrises and sunsets to enjoy—you'll have to pack plenty to drink.

Recommended Resources

NATIONAL FORESTS

Beaverhead-Deerlodge National Forest
www.fs.usda.gov/bdnf

Butte-Jefferson Ranger District
1820 Meadowlark
Butte, MT 59701
(406) 494-2147

Dillon Ranger District
420 Barrett Street
Dillon, MT 59725
(406) 683-3900

Madison Ranger District
5 Forest Service Road
Ennis, MT 59729
(406) 682-4253

Pintler Ranger District
88 Business Loop
Philipsburg, MT 59858
(406) 859-3211

Wisdom Ranger District
P.O. Box 238
Wisdom, MT 59761
(406) 689-3243

Wise River Ranger District
P.O. Box 100
Wise River, MT 59762
(406) 832-3178

Bitterroot National Forest
www.fs.usda.gov/bitterroot

Stevensville Ranger District
88 Main Street
Stevensville, MT 59870
(406) 777-5461

West Fork Ranger District
6735 West Fork Road
Darby, MT 59829
(406) 821-3269

Custer Gallatin National Forest
www.fs.usda.gov/custergallatin

Ashland Ranger District
P.O. Box 168
2378 Hwy 212
Ashland, MT 59003
(406) 784-2344

Beartooth Ranger District
6811 Hwy 212
Red Lodge, MT 59068
(406) 446-2103

Bozeman Ranger District
3710 Fallon Street, Suite C
Bozeman, MT 59718
(406) 522-2520

Hebgen Lake Ranger District
P.O. Box 520
330 Gallatin Road
West Yellowstone, MT 59758
(406) 823-6961

Sioux Ranger District
P.O. Box 37
101 SE First Street
Camp Crook, SD 57724
(605) 797-4432

Yellowstone Ranger District
5242 Highway 89 South
Livingston, MT 59047
(406) 222-1892

Flathead National Forest
www.fs.usda.gov/flathead

Glacier View Ranger District
10 Hungry Horse Drive
Hungry Horse, MT 59919
(406) 387-3800

Spotted Bear Ranger District
Spotted Bear, MT
(406) 758-5376

Swan Lake Ranger District
200 Ranger Station Road
Bigfork, MT 59911
(406) 837-7500

Helena–Lewis and Clark National Forest
www.fs.usda.gov/lcnf

Belt Creek Ranger District
4234 US Highway 89 North
Neihart, MT 59465
(406) 236-5100

Helena Ranger District
2880 Skyway Drive
Helena, MT 59601
(406) 449-5201

Judith Ranger District
109 Central Avenue
Stanford, MT 59479
(406) 566-2292

Lincoln Ranger District
1569 Highway 200
Lincoln, MT 59639
(406) 362-7000

Rocky Mountain Ranger District
1102 Main Avenue NW
Choteau, MT 59422
(406) 466-5341

Townsend Ranger District
415 S. Front
Townsend, MT 59644
(406) 266-3425

Kootenai National Forest
www.fs.usda.gov/kootenai

Cabinet Ranger District
2693 MT Hwy 200
Trout Creek, MT 59874
(406) 827-3533

Eureka Ranger Station
949 US Hwy 93 N
Eureka, MT 59917-9550
(406) 296-2536

Libby Ranger District
12557 MT Hwy 37
Libby, MT 59923
(406) 293-7773

Three Rivers Ranger District
12858 US Hwy 2
Troy, MT 59935
(406) 295-4693

Lolo National Forest
www.fs.usda.gov/lolo

Ninemile Ranger District
20325 Remount Road
Huson, MT 59846
(406) 626-5201

Plains/Thompson Falls Ranger District
P.O. Box 429
408 Clayton
Plains, MT 59859
(406) 826-3821

Seeley Lake Ranger District
3583 Highway 83
Seeley Lake, MT 59868
(406) 677-2233

Superior Ranger District
P.O. Box 460
209 West Riverside
Superior, MT 59872
(406) 822-4233

NATIONAL PARKS, MONUMENTS, WILDLIFE REFUGES, AND RECREATION AREAS

Bighorn Canyon National Recreation Area
P.O. Box 7458
Fort Smith, MT 59035
(307) 548-5406
www.nps.gov/bica

Charles M. Russell National Wildlife Refuge
P.O. Box 110
Airport Road
Lewistown, MT 59457
(406) 538-8706
www.fws.gov/refuge/charles_m_russell

Glacier National Park
P.O. Box 128
West Glacier, MT 59936
(406) 888-7800
www.nps.gov/glac

Upper Missouri River Breaks National Monument
920 Northeast Main
Lewistown, MT 59457
(406) 538-1900
www.blm.gov/publish/content/mt/en/prog
/nlcs_new/UMRB_NM.html

Yellowstone National Park
P.O. Box 168
Yellowstone National Park, WY 82190
(307) 344-7381
backcountry office (307) 344-2160
www.nps.gov/yell

INDIAN RESERVATION
Blackfeet Nation, Fish and Wildlife
P.O. Box 850
Browning, MT 59417
(406) 338-7207
http://blackfeetfishandwildlife.net

BUREAU OF LAND MANAGEMENT
Billings Field Office
5001 Southgate Drive
Billings, MT 59101
(406) 896-5013
www.blm.gov/mt/st/en/fo/billings_field
_office.html

Glasgow Field Office
5 Lasar Drive
Glasgow, MT 59230
(406) 228-3750
www.blm.gov/mt/st/en/fo/glasgow_field
_office.html

Havre Field Office
3990 Highway 2 West
Havre, MT 59501
(406) 262-2820
www.blm.gov/mt/st/en/fo/havre_field_office
.html

Lewistown Field Office
920 NE Main Street
Lewistown, MT 59457
(406) 538-1900
www.blm.gov/mt/st/en/fo/lewistown_field
_office.html

Miles City Field Office
111 Garryowen Road
Miles City, MT 59301
(406) 233-2800
www.blm.gov/mt/st/en/fo/miles_city_field
_office.html

STATE PARKS
Lewis & Clark Caverns State Park
P.O. Box 489
25 Lewis and Clark Caverns Road
Whitehall, MT 59759
(406) 287-3541
http://stateparks.mt.gov/lewis-and-clark
-caverns

Makoshika State Park
P.O. Box 1242
1301 Snyder Avenue
Glendive, MT 59330
(406) 377-6256
http://stateparks.mt.gov/makoshika

OTHER AGENCIES
Montana Fish, Wildlife & Parks
http://fwp.mt.gov/recreation/permits

Natural Resources Conservation Service
www.nrcs.usda.gov/wps/portal/nrcs/main
/mt/snow

OUTFITTERS AND LODGING

Gates of the Mountains Boat Tours
3131 Gates of the Mountains Road
Helena, MT 59601
(406) 458-5241
www.gatesofthemountains.com

Granite Park Chalet
(888) 345-2649
www.graniteparkchalet.com

Sperry Chalet
(burned in 2017)
(888) 345-2649
www.sperrychalet.com

Waterton Shoreline Cruise Company
www.watertoncruise.com
(403) 859-2362

MONTANA HIKING, OUTDOOR, AND CONSERVATION ORGANIZATIONS

Absaroka–Beartooth Wilderness Foundation
P.O. Box 392
Red Lodge, MT 59068
(406) 425-1944
www.abwilderness.org

Alliance for the Wild Rockies
P.O. Box 505
Helena, MT 59624
(406) 459-5936
https://allianceforthewildrockies.org

Bob Marshall Wilderness Foundation
P.O. Box 190688
Hungry Horse, MT 59901
(406) 387-3822
www.bmwf.org

Continental Divide Trail Coalition
P.O. Box 552
Pine, CO 80470
(303) 996-2759
http://continentaldividetrail.org/

Continental Divide Trail Society
3704 North Charles Street, #601
Baltimore, MD 21218
(410) 235-9610
www.cdtsociety.org

Friends of the Missouri Breaks Monument
324 Fuller, Suite C-4
Helena, MT 59601
(406) 502-1334
www.missouribreaks.org

Friends of Scotchman Peaks Wilderness
P.O. Box 2061
Sandpoint, ID 83864
www.scotchmanpeaks.org

The Great Burn Study Group
1434 Jackson Street
Missoula, MT 59802
(406) 240-9901
www.greatburnstudygroup.org

Greater Yellowstone Coalition
215 South Wallace Avenue
Bozeman, MT 59715
(800) 775-1834
www.greateryellowstone.org

Helena Outdoor Club
www.helenaoutdoorclub.org

Montana Wilderness Association
80 South Warren Street
Helena, MT 59601
(406) 443-7350
www.wildmontana.org

Montana Wildlife Federation
P.O. Box 1175
Helena, MT 59601
(406) 458-0227
www.montanawildlife.org

Northern Plains Resource Council
220 South 27th Street, Suite A
Billings, MT 59101
(406) 248-1154
www.northernplains.org

The Pryors Coalition
www.pryormountains.org

Rocky Mountaineers Outdoor Club
P.O. Box 4262
Missoula, MT 59806
www.rockymountaineers.com

Selway-Bitterroot Frank Church Foundation
120 Hickory Street, Suite A
Missoula, MT 59801
(208) 871-1906
www.selwaybitterroot.org

Sierra Club, Montana Chapter
P.O. Box 7201
Missoula, MT 59807
(406) 549-1142
www.montana.sierraclub.org

The Wilderness Society
Crown of the Continent Regional Office
503 West Mendenhall Street
Bozeman, MT 59715
(406) 586-1600
www.wilderness.org

Wilderness Watch
P.O. Box 9175
Missoula, MT 59807
(406) 542-2048
www.wildernesswatch.org

Yaak Valley Forest Council
265 Riverview Drive
Troy, MT 59935
(406) 295-9736
www.yaakvalley.org

Yellowstone to Yukon Conservation Initiative
(United States Office)
P.O. Box 157
Bozeman, MT 59771
(403) 609-2666
www.Y2Y.net

A mountain goat strolls with hikers near Gunsight Pass in Glacier National Park.

Acknowledgments

Although the author happily hiked all of this book's trails, took all the pictures, drew all the maps, and thus bears full responsibility for all errors and stupid mistakes, this guidebook would not have been possible without the assistance of a few stellar individuals.

Most importantly, my wife, Becky Lovejoy, provided her love and time in taking care of the home and dog while my booted feet hit the trails. Some debts cannot be repaid, and a simple thank you is ridiculously inadequate, but it is sincerely offered nonetheless.

I also want to thank the dedicated people at the Montana Wilderness Association, who in addition to their work on behalf of the state's wildlands, offered me specific advice on great little-known places to explore and possibly include in this volume. So my sincere appreciation to Mark Good, Amy Robinson, Cameron Sapp, John Todd, and most especially Zack Porter.

Leslie Nyce, the Montana fisheries biologist in the Hamilton office, went out of her way to help this non-angler track down what species of fish could be found and caught in what bodies of Montana water.

Finally, thanks to the talented people at Mountaineers Books, for publishing this book in the first place and turning my initial manuscript and efforts into the polished tome you hold in your hands today. Specific mention must go to Kate Rogers, Laura Shauger, Sarah Gorecki, and cartographer Bart Wright of Lohnes+Wright.

A bighorn sheep ram in the southern Cabinet Mountains

Index

About the Author

Douglas Lorain's family moved to the Northwest in 1969, and he has been obsessively hitting the trails of his home region ever since. With the good fortune to grow up in an outdoor-oriented family, he has vivid memories of countless camping, hiking, birdwatching, and other trips in every corner of this spectacular region. Over the years he calculates that he has logged well over 32,000 trail miles in this corner of the continent, and despite a history that includes being bitten by a rattlesnake, shot at by a hunter, stuck in quicksand, charged by grizzly bears (twice!), and donating countless gallons of blood to "invertebrate vampires," he happily sees no end in sight.

Lorain is a photographer and recipient of the National Outdoor Book Award. His books cover only the best trips from the thousands of hikes and backpacking trips he has taken throughout Montana, Washington, Oregon, Idaho, Wyoming, and beyond. His photographs have been featured in numerous magazines, calendars, and books. He has written or co-written more than a dozen guidebooks, including *100 Classic Hikes in Oregon, Backpacking Idaho, Backpacking Washington, Top Trails: Olympic National Park and Vicinity*, and *One Best Hike: Mount Rainier's Wonderland Trail*.

For several years he has been lucky enough to live in Hamilton, Montana, with his wife, Becky Lovejoy, and their yellow lab, Seabrook.

recreation · lifestyle · conservation

MOUNTAINEERS BOOKS is a leading publisher of mountaineering literature and guides—including our flagship title, *Mountaineering: The Freedom of the Hills*—as well as adventure narratives, natural history, and general outdoor recreation. Through our two imprints, Skipstone and Braided River, we also publish titles on sustainability and conservation. We are committed to supporting the environmental and educational goals of our organization by providing expert information on human-powered adventure, sustainable practices at home and on the trail, and preservation of wilderness.

The Mountaineers, founded in 1906, is a 501(c)(3) nonprofit outdoor recreation and conservation organization whose mission is to enrich lives and communities by helping people "explore, conserve, learn about, and enjoy the lands and waters of the Pacific Northwest and beyond." One of the largest such organizations in the United States, it sponsors classes and year-round outdoor activities throughout the Pacific Northwest, including climbing, hiking, backcountry skiing, snowshoeing, camping, kayaking, sailing, and more. The Mountaineers also supports its mission through its publishing division, Mountaineers Books, and promotes environmental education and citizen engagement. For more information, visit The Mountaineers Program Center, 7700 Sand Point Way NE, Seattle, WA 98115-3996; phone 206-521-6001; www.mountaineers.org; or email info@mountaineers.org.

Our publications are made possible through the generosity of donors and through sales of more than 800 titles on outdoor recreation, sustainable lifestyle, and conservation. To donate, purchase books, or learn more, visit us online:

MOUNTAINEERS BOOKS
1001 SW Klickitat Way, Suite 201 • Seattle, WA 98134
800-553-4453 • mbooks@mountaineersbooks.org • www.mountaineersbooks.org

Mountaineers Books is proud to be a corporate sponsor of the Leave No Trace Center for Outdoor Ethics, whose mission is to promote and inspire responsible outdoor recreation through education, research, and partnerships. • The Leave No Trace program is focused specifically on human-powered (nonmotorized) recreation. • Leave No Trace strives to educate visitors about the nature of their recreational impacts and offers techniques to prevent and minimize such impacts. • Leave No Trace is best understood as an educational and ethical program, not as a set of rules and regulations. • For more information, visit www.lnt.org or call 800-332-4100.

OTHER TITLES YOU MIGHT ENJOY FROM MOUNTAINEERS BOOKS

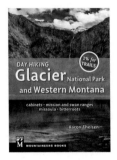

Day Hiking Glacier National Park
Aaron Theisen
125 awe-inspiring hikes in
a compact format

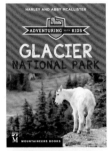

**Glacier National Park:
Adventuring with Kids**
Harley and Abby McAllister
Fun for all ages in one of America's
most stunning parks

**Yellowstone National Park:
Adventuring with Kids**
Harley and Abby McAllister
Kid-tested hikes and adventures
in this iconic park

**Cycling the Great Divide:
From Canada to Mexico on North America's
Premier Long-Distance Mountain Bike Route,
2nd Edition**
Michael McCoy and the
Adventure Cycling Association
2774 miles of wilderness biking on
the backbone of the Rockies

**Prophets and Moguls, Rangers and
Rogues, Bison and Bears:
100 Years of the National Park Service**
Heather Hansen
An engaging, accessible tale of the history
and characters of the NPS

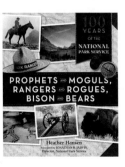

www.mountaineersbooks.org